CONTENTS

FOREWORD

By Gary Lineker

MY ALL-TIME FOOTBALLER OF THE YEAR XI

Banks

Wright   Moore

Keane   Mackay

Charlton

Best   Dalglish   Henry   Ronaldo

Shearer

WHEN I was asked to introduce this collection of articles by leading football writers, I accepted with pleasure. For one thing, there was its association with the work of Great Ormond Street Hospital, which is a cause close, I think, to all of our hearts. It was also irresistibly tempting to be invited by my old Observer and Sunday Telegraph colleague Patrick Barclay to pick a team from all the great players who have been honoured by the Football Writers' Association as the Footballer Of The Year.

Patrick told me only one winner of the award was ruled out – Gary Lineker. But he'd have struggled to get in anyway.

First, though, I'd like a word about the book itself. Congratulations to Christopher Davies on an excellent idea, which his fellow writers have done proud. The relationship between players and football writers is bound to be difficult at times, because form is fickle and so are the moods of the game's chroniclers. But we do respect the tradition behind the Footballer Of The Year award and, because it goes back so far – the Sir Stanley Matthews Trophy is named after the first winner – it has an unrivalled gravitas.

That football writers have an enduring affection, indeed a passion, for the game is obvious from these articles. I hope you enjoy them as much as I did and that you will not be too upset if any of your favourites have been left out of my all-time XI. For all the enthusiasm with which I approached the task, I found it incredibly difficult to make the choices. Which just goes to prove that management, even if you have some of the best players in the game's history at your command is, as someone once said, an impossible job.

Picking a goalkeeper was relatively easy. Even Neville Southall, with whom I played at Everton, could not keep out Gordon Banks. Not only did he play for Leicester – which was always going to be an advantage in my book – he helped to win England the World Cup. I saw Banks towards the end of his career, when he was still managing to keep goal well with one eye.

There are some other gritty characters in my team and one, Roy Keane, is having to operate just in front of my two defenders. Yes, two defenders. This is because full-backs, quite rightly, have seldom won the award and, anyway, with the array of creative talent at my disposal I believe we can out-score anyone. So at the back we have Bobby Moore, our 1966 skipper, who would be in any all-time British side, and one of his predecessors as captain, Billy Wright, who, although I never saw him, must have been special to win more than a century of caps.

Dave Mackay, with Keane, will make sure no-one messes with our midfield. But these two are in for their footballing ability as well. Keane is arguably the best player to have appeared in the Premier League.

Bobby Charlton, who will operate in front of him, is probably England's greatest ever footballer – to have scored so many international goals while not playing as an out-and-out striker is incredible. Yet in the Manchester United hall of fame there is a growing challenge from Cristiano Ronaldo, who cannot be left out of the side. He will drive down the right, allowing Thierry Henry, on the opposite flank, to cut inside on his favoured right foot. I so enjoyed watching Henry in the Premier League.

But in my time as a player the pick of them all was Kenny Dalglish. In a previous era, George Best had the lot. He, too, must start.

According to my granddad, the greatest player ever was Tom Finney – yet I have decided to leave him on the bench, along with Matthews, because they were so long before my time. There are other painful omissions too. Dennis Bergkamp I simply cannot fit in if it means omitting Dalglish.

Which leaves one place – at the front. We need a proper centre-forward to lead the line and score lots of goals for us. I do have one in mind. In every respect he fits the bill. So do others, it is true, but Alan Shearer gets the last spot in the team because I have to work with him on Match Of The Day and, if I left him out, life wouldn't be worth living. Seriously, he wasn't a bad striker – after all, he learned from the master!

Gary Lineker OBE has been involved with Great Ormond Street Hospital and Leukaemia Research since his son George had leukaemia as a baby. George defeated the disease and Lineker said: "I will be forever grateful to everyone at Great Ormond Street Hospital for saving the life of my son." Lineker is Patron of The Tick Tock Club, established to help Great Ormond Street Hospital make significant progress in the treatment of heart and lung disease. He said: "It is easy to take our health for granted, but when a child's life is at risk you realise just how precious health is. If it is your child whose life is in danger, you do everything humanly possible to save them."

INTRODUCTION

THE IDEA was straightforward enough. Around 70 leading football writers in England would contribute an original article for a book with proceeds going to the Great Ormond Street Hospital for Sick Children's charity. A unique collection of modern football writing by members of the Football Writers' Association, who cover the beautiful game, often in less than beautiful surroundings. There would, literally, never have been a book like it.

Thanks to Simon Lowe of Know The Score Books, the idea became reality. But what to call it? Headlines and intros – even when they have to be changed after a stoppage time winner – are easier to think of than book titles so the good and great of the FWA's national committee put their collective heads together – half an hour later the blank sheet of paper was ... still blank.

Then someone remembered the late Frank McGhee's proposed title for the autobiography he never wrote (and what a book that would have been). For 30 years Frank, who died in 2000, was the Voice of Sport for the Daily Mirror and for most of those years he told anyone and everyone that his book would be called Forgive Us Our Press Passes.

We're sure Frank won't mind the FWA giving this football book, for such a good cause, "his" title.

Special thanks, also, to FWA national committee colleagues Patrick Barclay and Mike Collett for their help in putting the book together, Andrew Cowie of Colorsport, who supplied the photographs, Gary Lineker ... plus all who contributed.

The response was overwhelming and despite the demands of those who have the best job in the world –apart from playing football (and that is not even open to debate) – extra hours were found with the contributors delighted to be part of a unique book ... the first time so many outstanding football writers have combined to be part of Team FWA and helping such a good cause.

Having said that, I can exclusively reveal that I used up three sets of worry-beads when, with four days to the deadline, I was still waiting for half of the articles.

Football writers. Bloody hell.

As usual, cometh the deadline, cometh the copy.

Thanks to everyone for their support of Great Ormond Street Hospital Sick Children's Charity.

Enjoy.

Christopher Davies
Editor

THERE IS NO DOUBTING THOMAS

Geoff's wit masks the pain but he always comes back stronger

By Neil Ashton

ARY O'SULLIVAN was Paul Gascoigne. Chris Rawes would jink down the wing every lunchbreak believing he was John Barnes. And Graham Wooster marshalled the midfield like David 'Rocky' Rocastle.

Me? It was Geoff Thomas every time. How my schoolfriends laughed at the only Crystal Palace supporter they knew. They loved Monday mornings, when they would tease me about another defeat to Shrewsbury Town and shake their heads in sympathy at our attendances of six and seven thousand.

In May 1979 they peaked at 51,482, but no-one at my school was listening. The Team of the Eighties? Some team that turned out to be. Things were stirring again in south London, though, towards the end of that barren decade. Steve Coppell was the king-maker and Thomas was the king-pin. My playground pals knew nothing of the spiky haired number eight who arrived at Selhurst Park from Crewe in the summer of 1987 for £50,000 and on £275 a week. I did. I idolised him. I didn't know it then, but it was the beginning of a journey that led to a long-lasting friendship, brought on by his courageous battle with chronic myeloid leukaemia and then on to the Tour de France.

Rookie Ian Wright was the star of the Palace roadshow, terrorising Second Division defences and scoring the goals that took them into the top flight in 1989, but Thomas was the heartbeat of a team who were on the up and up under Coppell. Thomas scored against Portsmouth in the FA Cup third round in January 1990 and four months later he was leading Palace out at Wembley in their first FA Cup final against Manchester United. They drew 3-3 and the following Thursday they were back at the old stadium for the replay, wearing a one off kit in the colours of Littleborough United, his schoolboy club just outside Manchester.

Bryan Robson went on to lift the Cup, but Palace were an emerging team. They went on to finish third in the First Division the following season, squeezed out of a place in Europe when UEFA lifted the ban on Liverpool. Wright made it into the England team and Thomas soon followed him. He deserved it. No-one worked harder than Thomas in the centre of Palace's midfield and he was up there with the best players in the country. He had his critics, not least because of a wayward chip against France at Wembley in 1992, but there was always a comeback. He won nine caps for his country and he never lost a game. Have some of that.

Then it emerged that George Graham wanted him at Arsenal and Thomas told him he thought Palace were just as big a club. Brilliant. I couldn't wait to tell Amersham's legions of Arsenal supporters that one.

I never expected to meet Geoff Thomas. Never meet your heroes and all that. Or at least that is what they say. Before the summer of 2003, there never had been cause to call him. That soon changed. My career had taken me to the Sunday People, once the biggest selling Sunday newspaper in the country, and Thomas had recently retired after spells with Wolves, Nottingham Forest, Barnsley, Notts County and Crewe. It had been a long time since Thomas had been on the back pages of the newspapers, but he returned to them in the most traumatic of circumstances. He had been diagnosed with chronic myeloid leukaemia, a blood cancer that gave him a 30 per cent chance of living beyond the age of 40. That was less than three years away. The football world was stunned and so was I.

All those conversations with my friends, when I would argue that he was a better bet in England's midfield than Gascoigne or David Platt, seemed fairly insignificant now. Picking up the phone to him from the People's offices on the 23rd floor of London's Canary Wharf tower in July 2003 was undoubtedly the hardest professional call I've ever had to make. He was reluctant to be interviewed at first. Understandably he wanted privacy at a distressing time, but a nostalgic trip down memory lane, including his Palace debut at Huddersfield in August 1987, a looping last minute header against Nottingham Forest that preserved their unbeaten start in 1990 and his celebrations in front of the Palace fans when he scored on his return for Wolves (the bastard), did the trick. He approached his battle with leukaemia in the same way as his football career: head on. He was incredibly positive, telling the specialists who advised him to have a bone marrow transplant to 'Bring It On'. That is bravery on a different scale. Mixing it with Dennis Wise is one thing. Waking up to a course of chemotherapy every morning is another. Still, he was up for the fight in the same way as he was during 550 appearances for seven different clubs during his 20-year professional playing career.

Thomas always had a point to prove when he was playing for Palace and this was no different. He would get through it, he was sure of that. "I'm ready for whatever they throw at me," he would tell me during our frequent telephone conversations and doubtless he would say the same to his friends and family. He had his detractors as a player – Norwich striker Lee Power once told him he was "the most hated man in football" – and there was no doubt he could be a nasty piece of work on the pitch. I loved him for that. Who wants to make friends on a football field? Save that for a beer in the bar after the game.

He loved telling me those stories during his various treatments, giving me from the gossip from inside the Palace dressing room nearly 20 years too late. I lapped it up though, like the time when Liverpool midfielder Ronnie Whelan sidled up to him during Liverpool's 9-0 annihilation of Palace in September 1989 and said: "What do you lads do in the week then – have you not got a ball to train with?"

Those nuggets would send me away smiling for another couple of weeks, eager for more insight, but aware that he was often in agony.

His dry wit masked the real pain. Chemotherapy tested his resolve, so did the radiotherapy treatment to destroy the cancerous cells and then came the bone marrow transplant in January 2004 that was Kill or Cure. Geoff knew that when he entered the Queen Elizabeth Hospital in Birmingham, where he spent four weeks in an isolation unit after the bone marrow from his brave sister Kay was grafted into his system. No-one could say for sure whether he would survive, not even his consultant Professor Charlie Craddock. Thomas never gave up and no-one who has ever come across him would expect him to. He is a fighter, for sure. He spent the next six months convalescing at home, punctuated by various trips to hospital to combat the various side affects of his transplant and as he was wiling away the hours his mind incredibly began to turn to what his next challenge would be. As if he hadn't had enough already.

Thomas fancied riding the Tour de France route in the same 21 day time frame as the professionals, a firm nod in the direction of Lance Armstrong's inspirational account of his own cancer ordeal in his book It's Not About The Bike. It seemed unthinkable, impossible even. Geoff went through 27 operations on his knees during his playing career, but the legacy of his leukaemia treatment appeared insurmountable. "Normally at this stage of their recovery people ask me if they can go swimming," was Professor Craddock's response. That settled it then.

In July 2005, along with Daily Mail football correspondent Matt Lawton, football reporter Ian Whittell, cycle shop owner Robbie Duncan and myself, Geoff set out to ride the 3,500 kilometre route, taking in the legendary climbs of the Alps, the Pyrenees and the Massif Centrale, in 21 days. He applied himself to his training schedule in the same way he did when he was a player. With courage, conviction and a clear sense of purpose. It is impossible not to admire him. On some days during the Tour, his eyes were red raw, a result of the treatments that have burned his tear ducts and sweat would be dripping into them. Drip, drip, drip. On others, he battled against the elements, taking in the incredible climbs to the heliport at the top of the ski resort in Courcheval, reaching out to touch the jagged edges at the top of the Galibier, or the slog in total darkness to the summit of the Col de Val-Louron-Azet at the end of a 15 hour day in the saddle.

Watching professional athletes punish their bodies and put them on the line is inspiring, but riding side by side with someone so determined is different again. The members of our team were eye-witnesses to sporting excellence, part of something unique, but we were a long way removed from such a remarkable show of strength. He rode the Tour for unselfish reasons, pushing down on every pedal stroke with the thoughts of those who have not been so fortunate. He met many of them during his treatment and they were with him throughout the 2005 Tour.

Geoff's efforts helped raise more than £200,000 for charity and he has dedicated the next five years – the expected period of remission – to the Geoff Thomas Foundation. In 2007 he retraced his footsteps, riding the Tour route again alongside Ian Wright and five other cancer survivors. His remarkable efforts will continue until his Foundation has helped pay for leukaemia research centres in Birmingham, Nottingham, Manchester, Oxford and London.

No-one who knows Geoff Thomas ever doubts him. When they do, he comes back even stronger.

Neil Ashton has been a football reporter with the Daily Mail since November 1, 2004. Prior to that, he spent four years with the People.

__Favourite player:__ Was fortunate enough to be in Montpellier to watch Zinedine Zidane's comeback for France against Ivory Coast in Aug 2005. He scored. Inevitably. A beautiful player.

__Most memorable match:__ Personally, Crystal Palace 4 Liverpool 3. FA Cup semi-final at Villa Park, April 1990. Nothing compares for drama.

Professionally, Argentina 0 England 1, World Cup Group F, Sapporo Dome, June 2002. Beckham. Penalty. Argentina. Revenge. Enough said.

JE T'AIME

I remember emerging from Arsenal station for my first evening game as vividly as I remember my first falling in love

By Philippe Auclair

I LOVED music, I loved football, I had no choice – I had to look across the water; England was tantalisingly close for a very young boy born in Normandy, an hour's drive away from Dieppe's ferry harbour.

There, on the other side, were the grounds where George Best was playing every weekend, the theatres in which the most beautiful girls in the world danced to the music of the Small Faces. In very short skirts.

"England," people said "is 20 years behind everybody else – florins and half-crowns! Bowler hats! Pubs closed on Sunday afternoons! And ten years ahead at the same time."

That England, of course, has vanished, and would seem even more incomprehensible to a modern-day London teenager than it did to me, to us, in the late Sixties. But its attractions were not faux-semblant; they were real enough, and potent. My voice hadn't broken yet, my hair had to be cut short enough to satisfy the kapos who haunted my boarding-school dormitories.

France had been rocked by events which took place in May 1968 – nothing to do with Manchester United beating Benfica at Wembley, a victory virtually unnoticed in the chaos. What free time I had was spent feeding the same 7" singles in my 'record-eater' and playing elaborate games of something very much like Fantasy Football with Ludovic, the only one of my friends who truly understood why Arsenal had to be a far greater club than Inter Milan.

They were English. Better – they played in London (these 10-year-olds were well-informed). We'd write down the names of the 22 teams then comprising the First Division on slips of paper, put the lot in a bag, draw one of these slips, each in turn, then roll a dice to find out how many goals our team had scored.

Teams scored a lot of goals then, but maybe not quite as many as the numbers we came up with. On one occasion, Stoke City (my team on that evening) beat Manchester City 6-1. Neither Ludovic nor I could believe it. We knew our stuff, you see; when we bought our weekly copies of *France-Football* or its (whisper it) communist rival, *Le Miroir du football*, we went straight for the last few pages, where three or four columns of text had been put aside for *le match du week-end en Angleterre*.

The English might have ignored us. And forgotten, or never bothered about a couple of facts: until 1966, the French had a superior record in the World Cup; and better results in the European Cup too, until 1968. We took this as another proof of the English's innate superiority: when you have the FA Cup to compete for, why bother about the fancy cosmopolitan stuff?

When *France-Football* chose its first *Ballon d'Or* in 1956 it had to be an Englishman – Stanley Matthews. Honouring Puskas, Di Stefano or Kopa would've made more sense, if performance alone had mattered; but matter it did not; at this point in time. What *did* matter was to imbue the trophy with the legitimacy which could only be conferred by England, the mother of all footballing nations.

Thirty years later, the young Normandy boy lives in London, has become a musician himself, watches 100 games a season, and isn't that sure he will ever grow up. A bespectacled owl, whose eyes-filled face looks very much like Philip Larkin's, is perched on my shoulder and whispers: "I have started to say/ 'A quarter of a century'/Or 'thirty years back'/About my own life/It makes me breathless/It's like falling and recovering/In huge gesturing loops/Through an empty sky."

I have started to say myself: "all these seasons ago", but the owl flies away, for what I feel is not fear; gratitude, rather, for the sense of lightness aiming for a ground still fills me with, despite the appalling transport, the disappointments and the deadlines.

I remember emerging from Arsenal station for my very first evening game as vividly as I remember my first falling in love. An appalling confession from a middle-aged man, surely; and one which is easier to forgive if what should be forgiven is that that man has managed to remain a child, like many of the thousands of unknowns who flowed like so many drops of rain to Highbury on that night, each of them an infinite difference, each of them an irreplaceable part of a whole.

Caught as we are in the ugly nothings which we turn into news, it is easy (not to say convenient) to leave aside what makes sport, football, English football, great; it is that this greatness is entirely consumed in the present. That, unlike ballet to which it is compared too often, football's beauty cannot be replicated. A manager is not a choreographer; the chalk lines Herbert Chapman drew on the dressing room board were just empty staves on which Drake and Bastin could write their own notes.

It's just that (Chapman becoming Duke Ellington for a moment), some footballers are born to be Freddy Guy, indispensable but hidden in the mix, whilst other soloists like Johnny Hodges. And some of the tunes they come up with hit me like Bechet's clarinet hit Larkin ("on me your voice falls as they say love should/Like an enormous yes").

Maybe every single club strip is like the white tuxes the Duke's men wore on stage, part of a ritual devoid of transcendence, an artless artifice, the robes you don to play in the present, out of time; for football involves a suspension of time akin to that experienced in music. I've always wondered – why do the most violent shots always seem to take forever before they hit the net?

To me, the particular poignancy of English football, on the pitch as in the stands, lies in its instinctive understanding of the primacy of the here and now, from which is born its unique attachment to memory; the faith invested in a club, the reverence towards its past, the urge to find intimations of legend in the humdrum of a season, all this partakes of a refusal to age.

Should it lose this (unarticulated, and often inarticulate) understanding, it would lose its memory, it would lose itself. We French instead possess a confused sense of absence, and a bewildering need to define it. How could we fail to feel such an overwhelming attraction?

The English are not the best at self-analysis, whereas, since Montaigne and Chateaubriand, the French have done little else but exploring the cosmic folds of their belly-buttons. You are what we cannot be.

Here's another memory – I was talking to Robert Pires at the end of a European night. Robert told me: "Sometimes, during the game, despite myself, I stop and listen to the crowd. I can't believe what I hear. My flesh crawls. And I'd give anything for them."

What Robert said, dozens of others have felt, from Eric Cantona to Franck Queudrue, from Nicolas Anelka to Antoine Sibierski. To them, as it has been to me, coming here was coming home, a home they dreamt about when they were children.

Philippe Auclair has been France-Football's *England correspondent since the 1997/98 season. A philosophy teacher by training, he had stumbled into sports writing by chance 10 years before that. He also has a parallel career in music under the name of Louis Philippe.*

***Favourite player:** Dennis Bergkamp, the footballer-artist par excellence, who could make time stand still with a flick of his boot.*

***Most memorable match:** France v West Germany, 1982 World Cup. When they replay that game in heaven, we always end up winning it.*

CHINA CRISIS

Can the biggest ever be the best?

By Tony Banks

CHINA is a vibrant, rapidly growing nation of more than one billion people, where football is one of the most popular sports. It is played by millions of people and followed avidly by many millions more. Yet China is an infant on the world soccer scene. Its national team's performances in the World Cup have been abysmal, with only one finals tournament so far reached, despite the hiring of expensive foreign coaches and players, such as Paul Gascoigne and millions of yuan being invested in the sport by governments and companies. Attendances for top Jia A club games hover feebly at around the 10,000 mark, struggling sides attract fewer than 4,000 and teams at the bottom struggle to get 1,000 in. Many fans have given up on the domestic game altogether and prefer to watch Manchester United or Chelsea on the television.

But with the rising status of China as a political and economic power on the global stage, there is now a growing frustration inside the country at its lack of ability, or indeed in many eyes for too long even a desire, to make its mark on the biggest sport in the world. During the summer of 2008 Chelsea toured China, playing games in Gouangzhou and Macao. The previous year it was David Beckham's Los Angeles Galaxy. Manchester United have visited, as have Real Madrid and Barcelona.

Without exception they are met by fanatical, enthusiastic but polite crowds who flock to the stadia to watch their games in their thousands, the matches also watched by millions on state and regional television. These clubs don't just visit China by accident. They do it because there is a massive market there, identified some years ago as the next big – make that huge – growth area for soccer, for big European clubs that are as much marketing organisations these days as football teams.

But look below the surface and you find a country still groping to find its feet in football. More than any other country in the world, China has seen the social and political upheavals over its turbulent history this last 150 years, its wars and bitter civil wars, disrupt its social organisation and therefore its sport. Sometimes stopping it happening altogether.

Look around the world and you will generally find that football in many countries started the same way. Often it was visiting British ex-pats or sailors who started playing the game that was catching on back home and it took off in whatever country they were visiting at the time. It happened in Argentina, France, Germany, Italy and Brazil. With varying degrees of rapidity in the late 19th century in those countries, the game, so simple to organise and play, caught on and spread.

It looked like it was going to happen that way in China. It was downtown Shanghai were it all started – although, in fact, a version of the game was played and many believe it started in the country as far back as 3000BC – as British sailors on shore leave started kickabouts. The first documented football match in China played under Football Association laws was when the Shanghai Athletic Club played the Engineers in 1879. Eight years later the Shanghai Football Club was formed and in 1907 the first league started, in the city. It was dominated mainly by British ex-pats, though other nationalities, particularly the Portuguese, soon began to join in. Three years later the Shanghai FA was formed, and the game quickly began to spread to Tientsin, Guangzhou, Singapore and Canton. We are off and running, you may think.

But hold on. This is China. Nothing is that simple. Creaking along, it was only in 1924 that the Nationalist government included the Chinese FA in the newly formed China National Amateur Athletic Federation. And only in 1936 did a team enter the Olympic Games for the first time. The problem was that, at that time, the game was limited to universities and colleges and the wealthier classes in the foreign-controlled ports. Then came the first big disaster to even that fragile set up – the Japanese invasion of 1937 and civil war. Any chance the game had of establishing roots among the masses was shattered. After the war, when Mao Zedung's communists seized power in 1949, once again much of China's top sporting talent (what was left of it) scattered across the globe.

Effectively football started all over again, but once again it was selective and government-controlled – you played if you were in army garrisons, universities, or, for instance the railways. Otherwise, no chance. The top players were creamed off into the Olympic and national teams which played loads of games, mainly against other communist countries. Everyone else played in the workers' unions – under which amateur football did start to grow. The first national league was eventually started in 1954.

Then another disaster. In 1958 China withdrew from FIFA due to the acceptance by that body of Taiwan. China were outcasts in world football. The national team still played games, but mainly in Africa and against other Communist countries. Football limped along under rigid state control. But Mao's

Great Leap Forward in the late 1950s dealt a near mortal blow to the sport. Teams and players were dispersed. Football simply disappeared.

League football eventually reappeared in 1964 but then came the Cultural Revolution and as millions were sent back to the countryside for 're-education', we were back to square one again.

It took nine years for any kind of structured football to begin again. In 1974 China was allowed to enter the Asian Games and in 1980 came full acceptance from FIFA again. Post-Mao the new Chinese leadership began to realise the worth of football as a tool for building relations with the rest of the world. The New York Cosmos came to visit, with Pele and Franz Beckenbauer – and then West Bromwich. Soccer was at last spreading though to schools, even though the emphasis was still very much on finding the best and creaming them off for the glory of the national side, through selected regional academies (or as some called them, talent factories).

Gradually though, as China began to open up, the big industrial enterprises realised the value of having football teams. Clubs and sponsorship began to emerge, in teams such as Baiyunshan Pharmaceuticals of Guangzhou. The first club to be established as a self-governing entity was, fittingly, Shanghai Shenua FC. The Chinese Professional Soccer League was founded in 1994. Divided into Divisions 1 and 2 – Jia A and Jia B – decades after most countries had got that far. For a while it went well but these were not clubs founded in towns, in communities. They were formed by companies and plonked down into big, mostly empty, concrete stadiums. There was no fan base, no loyalty. It foundered eventually in a welter of corruption, illegal betting scams and quite simply, lack of interest.

Underneath the supposedly new shiny clubs and leagues, there was, unlike in most other countries, little or no amateur or semi-professional game. The Chinese tried again in 2004 as the Super League kicked off. Crowds, though, are still low, the standard of football poor and corruption rife.

Ask a Chinese youngster if he follows his own league and he will most likely tell you it is not worth it. With teams switching sponsors and often names, connections with their communities are minimal. He would rather watch United on the television. Fans end up switching loyalty on a regular basis and so clubs can grow little or no regular, long term following.

On the face of it the flaws in Chinese football are immense. The answer to the conundrum to the outsider may seem obvious. Encourage more people outside of the commercial game to play football, especially the kids. And for once in Chinese history, take it out of the state's dead hand to stop the whole process just being an excuse to look for the gifted and the exceptional, and then taking them away to form a supposed 'elite' to represent the system. Money is flooding into China right now and money will and is flooding into Chinese football where quite often, as many companies and clubs have found over the years, it disappears in a fog of bureaucracy and indecision.

But money is only partly the answer. The reason why China is not a world power in football is quite simple. Over the years, thanks to a variety of reasons, mostly political but also cultural – not enough people have been playing the game. What China has is a top downwards football structure, thanks to decades of government control. What it needs is a base. The simple concept of a football club, any kind of club, is still a new one in a country where at one time gatherings of more than 10 people was illegal.

But with the growth of a new and increasingly wealthy and increasingly independent middle class, looking for ways to spend that wealth, there is hope. People are starting to play.

Is China ready to become a world power in football? Not yet, not by some distance. Not until the country taps into the vast reserves of talent it has never begun to reach into; into those millions of people in that still mysterious interior. It is not about money in China. It is about culture. And that is a very tough nut to crack indeed.

Tony Banks has been a football writer for the Daily Express for ten years, covering mostly London football but also branching out into tennis and motor racing on occasions. Before that he worked for the Sun, Today and the Press Association, after moving on from local newspapers.

__Favourite player__: Pat Jennings: Quite simply the best goalkeeper I have ever seen play – a man who, relatively rarely for a player in his position, could win matches for his team. He served Tottenham with distinction, and then Arsenal, and alongside George Best, is probably the only genuinely world-class player Northern Ireland have ever had.

__Most memorable match__: The 1972 UEFA Cup semi-final between Tottenham and AC Milan at a packed and seething White Hart Lane. Steve Perryman scored twice, the brilliant Gianni Rivera replying for the Italians as Bill Nicholson's side took a vital lead to Milan. There, a 1-1 draw saw them through to a final with Wolves, which they won 3-2 on aggregate, with Martin Chivers rampant.

FOOTBALL HAS OUTGROWN FANS

The game's love of money means supporters have to pay more

By Patrick Barclay

WHO would have thought that the Bible, which some of us invoke mainly as a sobriquet for the annual tome formerly known as Rothman's (now the Sky Sports Football Yearbook), would contain such an insight into the game's ills?

But it does: the love of money truly is the root of all evil in football. Well, almost all. The more money dilutes the sporting values on which the people's game was built, the less there is for the people's children to inherit, as became all too clear during the ostensibly prosperous English season of 2007/08, when a group of leading Premier League clubs jousted among each other to be champions of not only their country but Europe – yet manifested the long-term uncertainty that is an inevitable consequence of international ownership.

Take the acute case of Liverpool. Shortly before they embarked on a Champions League semi-final against Chelsea – the clubs' third such meeting in four seasons – their former chairman, David Moores, observed that a once-respected institution had become a laughing stock. By which he meant that the feud between the two Americans to whom Moores had sold ownership of Liverpool was inviting a ridicule that diverted attention from the achievements of Rafa Benitez's team.

He was right, and brave to say it in the sense that Moores himself bore some responsibility for the situation, a point to which he alluded in remarking that, upon encountering Tom Hicks and George Gillett Jr, he had taken them to be decent fellows with the best interests of the club at heart. Far more significant, though, was the response to Liverpool's off-the-field unrest of some of their most thoughtful and concerned supporters.

Led by Rogan Taylor, a lifelong fan and football academic, they devised a plan through which those people with the club in their hearts could buy it from Hicks and Gillett and thus be in a position to ensure that never again could it be a commodity to be traded in by Americans (or Thai politicians such as Thaksin Shinawatra, who had switched his attentions to Manchester City after being rebuffed at Anfield, or indeed the Maktoum family from Dubai, who were poised to make their move for Liverpool after years of taking a close interest in the club).

The theory Taylor outlined was that, if 100,000 fans chipped in £5,000 each, they could buy out Hicks and Gillett and have enough left over to build a new stadium. If ever there was a case of figures speaking for themselves, this was it. Though some fans rallied round with pledges, the silence from the vast majority was deafening. At a time when one of the great political issues was the level of indebtedness of the British public, asking members of it for a £5,000 investment that would probably never be repaid took optimism to a new high.

The truth was that football had outgrown its audience. The fans could no more buy Liverpool, and therefore have a say in its running like the *socios* of Barcelona or Real Madrid, than the housewife with a trolley full of baked beans and breakfast cereal could buy Tesco.

The origins of football's indecent growth could be traced back to May 1985, when riots involving Liverpool followers led to the deaths of 39 Juventus fans before the European Cup final at the Heysel Stadium in Brussels. It was a distressing era. There were other football-related tragedies, including the fire at Bradford that killed 56, and the game became so unloved that the highest bid for television rights was a mere £1 million – for an entire season, to be split among all the clubs.

Four years later came the deaths of 96 innocent Liverpool supporters attending an FA Cup semi-final against Nottingham Forest at Hillsborough, after which the report of Lord Justice Taylor ordered the all-seat stadiums that were to provide such a theatrical backdrop for the next stage of the revolution.

This was the Premier League. It was such a success that by 2005 – just 20 years after Heysel – the clubs were sharing hundreds of millions of pounds a year. Yet it wasn't enough. It never is while rivalry between the clubs feeds the roots of evil, swelling the game's economy so the players are given more and more money that can be raised only through increased admission prices and television subscriptions (the latter being such a clever stealth tax that many fans now pay considerably more for their digital boxes than their season tickets).

Most alarmingly, debt started to grow after the arrival of Roman Abramovich. There were some who portrayed him as almost cuddly, a Russian version of 'Uncle' Jack Walker, the Blackburn fan who bankrolled his beloved club's rise to Premier League supremacy in 1995, but Abramovich with his billions made things worse as well as better. True, into what had become an annual race for the title between Manchester United and Arsenal came a third horse, Chelsea winning in consecutive years under Jose Mourinho, and England became the talk of every dressing-room in Europe as players queued to secure lucrative transfers here.

But United were sold to heavy borrowers from America, as were Liverpool, and the fans' role in this business was to pay off their interest. Arsenal promised to hold out for the foreseeable future, but the cost of a sparkling new stadium was more debt. Chelsea's debt was 'internal' – in other words, to Abramovich – but it was difficult to see what could happen should the Russian find another hobby, and ask for his money back, other than their going bust. For all the money that had flowed into the game, it was as vulnerable as ever and the fans could do nothing about it but watch, wait and, having read the sports pages, turn to the business section. Football had outgrown them.

The paradox was that supporter ownership was enjoying its own boom below Premier level. But the dream factor had become Premier League history. Maybe in the FA Cup romance lived – Cardiff City's arrival in the final in 2008, exactly 20 years after Wimbledon, having risen from the semi-professional ranks, won one against the mighty Liverpool, reminded us of that. But seldom could any club break into the English game's elite top four now, let alone be promoted and win the championship in their first season as did, for example, Brian Clough's Nottingham Forest in 1977/78.

The Champions League had created a class of its own into which only temporary membership was ever granted to strangers such as Everton and, before them, Leeds United. And the criterion for admission (though no-one liked to say it) was not any notion of true distinction, but money, whether it came from an owner who had obscenely benefited from Russia's mad and bad politics in the last days of Boris Yeltsin, or one who had borrowed from an American bank on the basis of future profits.

Research confirmed that the spirit of true competition was being diluted at a steady and perturbing rate, but, although the Premier League's chief executive Richard Scudamore paid lip service to it in vainly trying to explain why a 39th fixture overseas for all clubs would actually help to combat inequality, no-one read his lips. So much, then, for the people's game.

The essential sin of money as a driving-force, however, is that it achieves nothing, for all that increasingly figure-obsessed headlines daily trumpet its power. Research into football became fashionable during the 1990s and one study revealed that every section of the game thought elite players overpaid. Every section, that is. Not only the fans and club executives who, in their different ways, dole out the wages – but the players themselves.

I doubt if there is a single footballer regularly playing in the Premier League who, if you told him his wages were being cut in half, would quit the game and choose another profession. The beauty of football is that a club requires only 11 employees, each of whom would swear a willingness to do the job for next to nothing. The game has become swollen and over-priced because of myopic administration and, of late, often cynical profiteering by everyone from owners to agents, not the supposed greed of players, which is, in fact, practically forced upon them by the modern system.

Footballers expect the game to set them and their families up for life only because they can. For three quarters of a century after the game became professional, such a luxury was not on offer, and never was there any shortage of aspirants to a shirt. Now the game searches overseas for talent.

The solution to all its institutional difficulties is simple. Debt in football should be restricted to projects that will be of future benefit, such as stadiums and other facilities. A line can easily be drawn, incorporating sporting values into the structure of every club or (if we must) company in a league: it already happens in the matter of, for instance, player bonuses, which have to be agreed at the start of a season (an admirable attempt to fend off the advance of the footballing jungle).

Once the accounts have been reformed, sanctions can be imposed on debtors like they now are on those who go into administration. Clubs who balance the books can keep all their points; those who attempt to cheat by spending money they have not earned are docked points depending on the degree of the transgression.

It would, of course, have to be done internationally and that involves the politicians. This is indeed being considered by UEFA whose chief executive from 2003 to 2007, Lars-Christer Olsson, put football's essential administrative problem in a nutshell. "Debt," he asserted, "is financial doping."

If only UEFA could push through the measures Olsson envisaged. If only debt could be identified for the cheating it is. If only the people could have their game back. But I fear it has been sold over their heads.

Patrick Barclay has been football columnist of the Sunday Telegraph since 1996. Before that he was with the Observer, the Independent, Today and the Guardian. A member of the FWA national committee, Barclay supports Dundee FC.

__Favourite player__: Diego Maradona. Although my hero was Rodney Marsh – glamorous and puckishly gifted, he represented everything to which I vainly aspired – even Rodney could not have cleaned the boots of Maradona. I was but one of 70,000 Scots whose hearts he won on his first UK appearance at Hampden Park in 1979 – and to see him so dazzlingly win the World Cup in Mexico seven years later was a privilege.

__Most memorable match__: It has to involve Brazil and thus it has to be the 1970 World Cup final. The Italians were tired and the greatest of all Brazilian sides had such fun at their expense. The long, lingering build-up to the fourth goal; Pele's layoff; Carlos Alberto's shot. Heaven.

BIG RON FORGAVE MY BIG WRONG

One wedding and thankfully no funeral

By Steve Bates

FOR A sports journalist timing can be everything. Any journo will tell you there's no feeling like scooping the opposition with an exclusive and for jobbing hacks at the sharp end it's the lifeblood of the job. But the bizarre vagaries of our noble profession mean sometimes the rule book has to go out of the window – and there are occasions when a so-called 'exclusive' story, far from bringing joy and satisfaction leads to ... well, plain embarrassment.

One such moment with Ron Atkinson, Manchester United manager in the 1980s, left me a little red-faced, ever-so slightly contrite – but with the certain knowledge that it's always best to face tricky moments head-on rather than run for cover. And as Big Ron preceded the formidable Old Trafford reign of Sir Alex Ferguson, three decades and still counting, it was perhaps the soundest career advice I've ever heeded.

For those who didn't know him in his heydey, Bojangles, as Ron was affectionately known, held court on the red side of Manchester while John Bond, another larger than life character, presided over the Blue half in a cloud of fine cigar smoke and popping champagne corks – and that was before a match. As a young journalist in my mid-20s to have close quarters access to two ebullient managers with a penchant for talking in headlines, in between grabbing them, was a pleasure. Bondy's Friday penchant for announcing his team for the next day at Maine Road with a glass of bubbly in one hand and an expensive Havana in the other was slightly at odds with Big Ron's contentment at having a large pot of tea on the go while imparting his wisdom. The public perception of Flash Ron wasn't always quite the same as the reality, especially behind the scenes at the training ground as he sipped Tetley instead of Tattinger – but why let facts get in the way of a good story?

The existence of the sun-bed in a small annexe off Ron's office at the old Cliffe Training Ground was true, however. But although Big Ron might well have been the first manager to have unknowingly realised image rights could play a part in the modern game, that shouldn't disguise the fact that football was closer to his heart than anything. The charge across Manchester in those heady days from Maine Road to The Cliffe in Salford on a Friday lunchtime was affectionately labelled 'Whacky Races' by reporters who dared not miss the likely back page tale you'd pull from one of them. Arriving in Big Ron's office, as the youngest amongst the press pack, I'd be appointed tea boy. As a good friend of Ron's daughter Sue and her soon to be hubby Ross Sellors, son of former Manchester City finance director Fred, the United boss was happy to keep me in my place as tea monitor. When Sue and Ross decided to tie the knot in 1987 Big Ron's reign at Old Trafford had ended under the pressure of failure to deliver United's first league title since 1967. As the fingers were pointed and the accusations begin to fly fate reared its ugly head. Bumping into Terry Gibson one day, a United player who had tempted Big Ron to buy him after a productive spell at Coventry, the wee striker told me that he'd like to tell the story of how and why his career stalled at Old Trafford. Clearly upset, annoyed and frustrated by his spell at United which produced only one League goal in 23 appearances, Terry had been shown the door by new boss Fergie and was ready to pour his heart out. For a front line tabloid it made good copy and the office were delighted by Gibbo's honesty – and his spikiness at refusing to completely carry the can for his failure to make an impact at United. I could see a tiny problem looming on the horizon in that the story was being fast-tracked into the next edition of the Sunday People – the day of Sue Atkinson's wedding at which I was a guest of the family. Whether my brain went into denial I'll never really know, but somehow I didn't think it would present much of a problem if the feature appeared that same day. That notion was exploded early Sunday morning when Terry Gibson called to thank me for the story but questioned whether the headline needed to be so strong. "What headline?" I asked Gibbo, having not yet seen my paper.

"Big Ron Made Me Weep," he replied.

My silence probably said it all as the full impact dawned. Knowing Ron was an avid Sunday People reader the realization dawned that there was no escape. Arriving at the Mottram Hall Hotel for the wedding reception that morning was like heading to the headmaster's office – a real sweaty palm moment.

It didn't get much better when all the guests were lined up to be ushered in to the function room to meet the happy bride and groom – and their parents. Big Ron spotted me first as the queue snaked towards the wedding party. My first instinct was to find another way into the room but fronting up was the only way. Having charmingly greeted my wife Joanna, Ron gripped my hand tightly and I waited for the ping. "Ah Batesy, saw the paper this morning. 'Big Ron made me weep?' Are you sure about that?"

Before I had time to mumble anything, the line had moved and the worst was over. Ron was big enough not to bear a grudge, we had a great time at the wedding – and I'm still a family friend. I can laugh now, but it certainly wasn't funny at the time and it was one of the few moments when, for a while at least, I'd wished my name wasn't on the story.

Laughs go hand in hand with the serious side of covering football but, believe me, managers and players often get their own back on journalists – sometimes in the most bizarre of ways.

Playing in a press game against Italian journalists the day before Manchester United's European Cup Winners' Cup game with Juventus in April 1984, it was agreed the match would take place at The Cliffe. Glancing up at the end of the game at the laughing faces of United stars like Bryan Robson, Frank Stapleton, Arthur Albiston, Lou Macari and Kevin Moran – watching from the players' canteen overlooking the pitch – we could only assume their mirth centred on the game being played in slow motion and with little finesse. Wrong.

Sat in the dressing room in muddy boots and kit the industrial-sized tea pot dispensed a much needed cuppa for Brits and Italians alike. Showers were taken but while changing it soon became clear a practical joke had been played on the hacks. The ends of the journalists socks had been snipped off! The Italian media men were less than happy and suffered a humour by-pass, while their English counterparts knew a certain revenge had been extracted by sniggering United stars who couldn't miss a chance to score a direct hit on the journos.

But much worse was to come. The Italians went apoplectic when the sock ends were located after an anonymous tip off – in the tea pot. A diplomatic incident was only just averted by some hastily arranged gifts of badges and pennants for the Italian press lads. The culprit was ultimately unmasked as Lou Macari – the club's practical joker who couldn't resist this parting farewell to the press in his last few weeks at the club.

Steve Bates has been with the People since 1987 and was chief northern football reporter for many years, before becoming chief football writer in 2007. He started his career with the Rochdale Observer in 1978 before joining the renowned Hayters Sports Agency in 1981. After a spell freelancing in Manchester with the Lancaster and Crowther Agency he joined the People and is the current Football Writers' Association national chairman.

__Favourite player:__ Eric Cantona. The Frenchman triggered Manchester United's dominance of the Premier League and even today is still hailed as The King by Old Trafford fans. His kung-fu kick at Crystal Palace may have brought him notoriety, but he was touched by genius and in his pomp was a joy to behold.

__Most memorable match:__ Champions League final 1999. For sheer dramatic impact Manchester United's Nou Camp win over Bayern Munich takes some beating. The Germans, leading 1-0 with moments left, were such certainties UEFA officials were even tying their colours to the trophy when Teddy Sheringham and Ole Gunnar Solskjaer struck.

THE ROM THAT GOT AWAY

A hard day's niet every day since Abramovich bought Chelsea

By Rob Beasley

IT WAS one of those shopping expeditions with the wife that will stay with me forever. For once we weren't scouring Knightsbridge looking for the latest designer handbag that all the Wags and celebs were parading. We'd just pulled up outside a kitchen tiles showroom on an industrial estate near Birmingham International Airport when my mobile phone rang. A good friend and top contact called to say they had a hell of a story. It was a Monday morning – Monday June 30, 2003 to be precise. As a Sunday newspaper journalist it should have been my day off. But in this game there's no such thing as a day off when there's a story to be had. And this sounded like a real humdinger.

So while Mrs Beasley frowned and frothed away alongside me I grabbed for a pen and paper.

And the story? Ken Bates had sold Chelsea for £60m. Wow, what a bombshell.

"Who to?" I spluttered.

"A Russian billionaire," came the reply.

"What's his name?" I pleaded.

"Roman Abramovich."

It sounds daft now but I answered: "Roman who? How the hell do you spell Abromavich(sic)?" And that was the moment I first learned the name of a man destined to become one of the most famous figures in world football.

What a phone call. What a tip-off. Even Michelle, my missus, was impressed all of a sudden.

Because although I've had a good few yarns in my time (how else do you get and keep the chief football writer's post on the News of the World?) this was without a doubt the biggest story of my career.

Naturally I was elated. However I was equally frustrated. There were still six long days left before I could 'sensationally reveal' this blockbuster. What a nightmare. Five more days in which this 'secret' deal had to STAY secret.

Nevertheless I acted fast. I immediately rang my sports editor Mike Dunn and told him the news. He was stunned. I then rang the reference library at the News of the World and asked them to compile a complete biography of a Russian businessman called Roman Abramovich and e-mail it to me. However, and call me paranoid if you like, I was very careful never to venture why I wanted such a dossier of information.

And then I went off and bought some tiles for our new kitchen. Well what else could I do? I just had to sit, hope and pray.

You won't be surprised to know that I tuned into as many radio and TV bulletins as I could that day. Or that I was up early next day to anxiously scour the day's papers. What joy. Not a word. They hadn't got a clue that one of the most amazing deals in English football history had been done and dusted.

So I spoke to Mike Dunn again and we began to dare to believe this could be our biggest scoop. Andy Coulson, the editor, was told and there was a real buzz about the place. This was huge and we were all going to be covered in glory. But just as I was cockily considering what I'd say in my acceptance speech for my 'Journalist of the Century' award the phone rang again.

It was my contact. And this time it was news I didn't want to hear.

"Chelsea are going to make an announcement to the City tomorrow morning."

I was crushed.

"Are you sure it's tomorrow?" I asked despairingly.

"Afraid so," came the reply. "They're putting the statement together right now."

I kept hoping that there might be a delay to the announcement. A snag in the deal, an unexpected last minute hitch but deep down I realised it was futile. Late in the afternoon Mike Dunn rang to say he feared the Abramovich story was breaking. The word was that our sister paper, the Sun, was splashing on the front page with a big Chelsea story.

To put myself out of my misery I rang Shaun Custis, the Sun's chief football writer, and asked him if they had a big Chelsea takeover story. He said he'd check with his office and ring me back. When he did he only confirmed my worst fears. And sure enough the following morning the Currant Bun's splash was headlined 'Chelski. Russian tycoon buys Chelsea FC'.

It was written by a news reporter called John Kay. And that same John Kay later won the 'Story of the Year' award for his great scoop.

But I'm not bitter!!!!!!!!!!! I was just unlucky. Anyway I knew I had the story first. And my wife, my sports editor and my editor knew I'd had the story two days earlier. It was just the other 60 million who didn't have a clue. So what the hell – upwards and onwards.

I'd missed the big story but now I set myself the challenge of getting the first big interview, so off I headed for Stamford Bridge to stake out the place. And just as I was nosing around behind the West Stand I suddenly came face to face with the man himself. There, walking straight towards me was Chelsea's new owner. What a moment. What an opportunity. Here was my chance for a world exclusive after all – the first in-person piece with this mega-rich but media shy international man of mystery.

I strode forward purposefully and said: "Roman, welcome to Chelsea."

He nodded, smiled and we shook hands. But he didn't say a word even though I'm sure he was wondering who the hell I was to be welcoming him to a club that had cost him £140m – £60m to buy and another £80m to make solvent. My excuse is that I've been a mental Chelsea fan since they lost the 1967 FA Cup final against Tottenham and it seemed like the right thing to say at the time.

But then I got my hack's head into gear and announced: "I'm Rob Beasley from the News of the World – any chance of a couple of minutes?"

His response was instant and decisive.

In a quiet but firm voice he said: "Niet."

And he's been saying "Niet" ever since.

That's why the Russian oligarch remains almost as much of an unknown quantity today as he did when he first burst into the nation's consciousness back in that summer of 2003.

But in this job you do get a glimpse into his normally ultra-private world. I have seen him at his happiest, at his most relaxed, and also at his most uncomfortable. Never happier than on April 30, 2005 as Chelsea celebrated their first league title since 1955 – and in their centenary season. I was in the visitors' dressing room at Bolton's Reebok stadium that day as Abramovich partied with Blues boss Jose Mourinho and the champagne flowed.

But less than two years later I then witnessed how that love affair between owner and manager was heading for the rocks. For I was one of a small group of Chelsea fans who sat around the Russian in a five star hotel in Porto talking about the club's future, and particularly that of the manager. It was February 2007 and by then Abramovich could not bear to even mention Mourinho's name. It looked like the end, but there was a brief reconciliation.

I sat with Mourinho in the Beverly Hills Hotel on Chelsea's pre-season tour to California as he declared "peace in our time". A few nights later in the Hotel's Sky bar – in the midst of the Hollywood elite – I saw the confirmation as the pair hugged, laughed and joked together. Abramovich looked more relaxed than ever.

The famous Los Angeles hotel was brimming with stars like Al Pacino, Jennifer Aniston, Matthew Perry, Matthew McConaughey and a certain Paris Hilton. Gliding unnoticed amongst all these A-listers was the orphan boy from Saratov, a humble town that nestles near the banks of the Volga River in Southern Russia, a million miles away from the excesses of tinsel town.

The LA luvvies didn't even glance at the quiet, unassuming guy in the open-necked shirt and jeans, while he just wore a whimsical smile and his trademark designer stubble, safe in his anonymity and probably with the thought that he could buy them all for breakfast.

In fact Abramovich was so chilled with life in California that summer he even turned up for the much anticipated challenge match between Mourinho's Chelsea staff – Jose played in goal – and Her Majesty's Press XI at UCLA. He even brought his new squeeze, sexy ex-model Daria Zhukova with him, much to the amazement of Fleet Street's finest.

Roman laughed his socks off when I threw his Head of Security, Mark Skipp, to the ground as the minder unleashed a flurry of kicks at a stricken Matt Dickinson down on the deck. And I laughed my socks off when an infuriated and embarrassed Skipp jumped up and thought it was the Daily Mail's Neil Ashton who had sent him crashing to the turf.

I then gleefully played the role of peace maker as the two squared up, and all this in front of the guffawing Abramovich and the entire Chelsea first team squad and staff. The banter was amazing. A genuine good time occasion when the barriers were lifted and he was just one of the lads on tour. Maybe, just maybe, he misses all of that as he gazes out beyond his bodyguards and through the bullet-proof glass.

As my mum always tells me, money's not everything.

Rob Beasley is the chief football writer of the News of the World.

Favourite player: Peter Osgood. Not as good as George Best, Johan Cruyff or Cristiano Ronaldo, but Ossie was Chelsea and that puts him on another level. I was always 'Osgood' in the playground at school and my kids know all about the King of Stamford Bridge.

Most memorable match: Chelsea v Leeds at Wembley in the 1970 FA Cup final. I was only 10 years-old but Chelsea mad. My elder sister decided to support Leeds for the day and teased me mercilessly throughout. I cried both times Leeds went in front and both times we equalised.

BLATTER IS A MAN UNOPPOSED

FIFA president was like a medieval king accepting homage from his subjects

By Mihir Bose

SEPP BLATTER is the ultimate politician, except the field he operates in is not party politics but football.

Football has been his life and as president of FIFA he has made world football his fiefdom in a way no other sports official, not even Juan Antonio Samaranch, the former president of the International Olympic Committee did.

Like the ultimate politician, Blatter never takes a step without assessing how it will benefit him personally. The Goal project is the classic illustration of this. Launched to help develop football in the poorer countries, Blatter has used it as his personal weapon. While the money has poured into Asia, Africa and Eastern Europe, it has also always advanced the cause of Joseph S Blatter, the football politician, making sure his electoral base is strengthened. In these countries he is treated as a politician who makes sure that he keeps his constituents happy and provides them what they need. Indeed, over the years, talking to many of the people who run these national association there is no mistaking the support Blatter has. They react to him much as constituents of a politician might to a man fulfilling his election pledges.

He can inspire devotion that seems extraordinary. In 2002 when he was fighting a tough re-election campaign, one of his most prominent supporters proudly boasted how he had abandoned his sick child to go campaigning for Blatter. He could not, he said, leave Blatter's side for his child.

The result is he has now been re-elected twice, the second time unanimously. If his first term as FIFA president was a constant fight against his enemies on the executive, now there is nobody left to challenge his uncontested power over the world game and he could carry on as long he wanted.

Blatter's status is such that at times he seems the equal of elected world politicians. This was most evident in November 2007 at the World Cup draw in Durban. Blatter walked in with Thabo Mbeki, the South African president. The event was organised as if FIFA was a sovereign state no less equal than the Republic of South Africa. Indeed I am told as South Africa prepares for Africa's first ever World Cup, Blatter invariably addresses his communications directly to the South Africa president – the head of the football state, a sort of sporting Vatican, writing to the head of the nation. I am also told he is miffed if the reply comes not from Mbeki, but from some other South African official.

But then Blatter is used to presidents and prime ministers always courting him. He knows he has the ultimate prize of hosting the World Cup to award and makes the most of this. One of the first visitors Gordon Brown had when he arrived at No. 10 was Blatter, with Brown keen to try to canvass Blatter for supporting England's bid to host the 2018 World Cup.

It is easy to debunk sports administrators as men who were not good enough to play sports, people in blazers concerned solely with their plush seats in the stadium and their car parking spaces.

Most football administrators look uncomfortable next to real stars. Not Blatter. I well remember back in 2000 when England launched their ill-fated campaign for the 2006 World Cup. They took Michael Owen to FIFA headquarters in Zurich. Blatter put on an act on the terrace of FIFA's headquarters that according to some FA old-timers was like the music hall shows they had seen as children. Blatter's duet with Owen also ensured that he produced the sound bites that dominated the next day's media.

All this is part of Blatter revelling in being the unlikely Swiss. He could not be more different than the stereotypical Swiss pictured by Orson Wells, the country that only produced the cuckoo clock, and maybe some Chocolate, but nothing else.

As a child he loved being on stage and he told me once he looked back on his childhood days of performing with fond memories. He loves nothing more than putting on an act and football has provided him with the stage career he has missed.

Blatter became president after long years as FIFA general secretary. The one job of the secretary he most enjoyed was conducting the World Cup draw. Televised to a worldwide audience it provides a unique stage but which makes most football administrators look uncomfortable. Not Blatter, the role of pulling balls out of a bag while the world looks on is designed for him. On his elevation to the presidency he could no longer conduct the World Cup draw and misses it terribly.

It is this aspect of the showman, the man who loves the stage and is willing to grab it, that marks him out from the rest of the blazer brigade that run sports. This was most evident in Seoul just before the 2002 World Cup in Korea-Japan.

The first four years of the Blatter regime, starting in 1998 when he, to the surprise of some, defeated Lennart Johanssen, then president of UEFA, for football's top job, had produced many failures. He had to abandon his plan to hold the World Cup every two years, he had failed to win the 2006 World Cup for South Africa, and, under his leadership, FIFA had overspent by 1.248 billion Swiss francs and had to borrow against projected income to stay solvent.

The elections had been fought against serious allegations of mismanagement against Blatter. He stood accused of plunging FIFA into financial crisis.

As he faced re-election, a Swiss prosecutor was looking into a complaint made by five of his seven vice-presidents. They later withdrew the complaint but that was not until after the election and as the campaign went on it seemed a very serious barrier to Blatter's re-election.

His then general secretary, Michel Zen-Ruffinen, had prepared a devastating dossier on his reign. At the 2002 FIFA congress, Zen-Ruffinen had said: "FIFA is not working any more. We will have to start at the bottom and change FIFA completely."

Indeed, 24 hours before the election Blatter had been booed off the podium at the organisation's extraordinary congress and became involved in an ugly physical confrontation with his chief opponent for the presidency, Issa Hayatou.

These setbacks came amid chaotic scenes as Blatter refused to allow 15 countries to ask potentially damaging questions about FIFA's finances. At the end there was an encounter on the podium between Blatter and Hayatou. One senior executive member feared Blatter might be punched by Hayatou, who stormed out, shouting: "This is scandalous."

Never before in FIFA history had there been such a deep, public tear in the organisation.

All this should have made Hayatou a certain winner. He was the first African to stand for such a high office and therefore all 52 votes from Africa should have been his. With UEFA support adding another 52 votes that would have given him 104 out of a possible 204 votes and a great platform for victory.

Hayatou, though, could not match Blatter for charm and, as I discovered talking to delegates, Blatter had even eaten into Hayatou's African stronghold. Indeed that campaign showed how as a football politician he could teach full-time politicians lessons. He was facing a fight against a French-speaking African, so he wooed the English- and Portuguese-speaking Africans and they did not support Hayatou.

But perhaps the most memorable scene of the election and the one that summed up the Blatter effect came immediately after Blatter had won re-election. The scene in my experience of reporting such events was unique in sport.

As he accepted his triumph he could have been a US presidential candidate with tears in his eyes, saying: "I register your deep trust in FIFA and in me. You cannot imagine what it means for me, having during the last few months been accused by certain press of being a bad man."

After that he closed the congress by getting all the delegates to stand up and hold hands as though they were at a revivalist meeting. "Do it, do it," he urged.

It was then that the majority of delegates did something I had seen in political rallies but never before in a sports setting. Instead of heading for lunch, which had been delayed by several hours as the debate on finances rumbled on, they headed for the podium.

There they formed a long queue as a garlanded Blatter received them like a medieval king accepting homage from his subjects – except that in this case the homage offered was a football which an ecstatic Blatter happily signed.

Since then Blatter has reorganized FIFA finances and further consolidated his power. He has now taken the World Cup to Africa, made his FIFA headquarters something like a modern castle with a studio in the basement which would be the envy of some television stations and made himself the voice of football. Whenever an issue arises in football there is always Blatter ready to speak and, while he may often outrage his audience, he never fails to supply a compelling sound bite.

Blatter may be the butt of many a joke in the British media, with whom he has a love hate relationship not least for his ill-judged "slave" remark – but there can be no doubting the power of this football politician and showman.

Mihir Bose is the BBC sports editor. He was the chief sports news reporter for the Daily Telegraph from 1995-2007 and before that worked for the Sunday Times.

***Favourite player:** Pele, because he had everything, athleticism, power, balance, a wonderful ability to improvise and the ability to make believe the game was both simple and beautiful.*

***Most memorable match:** The World Cup final between Brazil and Italy in 1970. I do not believe I shall ever see such football perfection again.*

I'VE COVERED 14 WORLD CUPS

...and I can't wait for the next one

By Malcolm Brodie

THE WORLD CUP. Three words that spell magic to me. All other football tournaments pale into insignificance, even the fervour and passion of the European Champions League.

As one World Cup ends, I look forward to the next like a child on a countdown to the summer holidays. Who will next lift the trophy to the skies watched by countless millions around the globe? The anticipation lasts for four years, which is all part of the appeal.

What dramatic changes have been made since Switzerland 1954, the first of 14 World Cup finals which I covered – it could have been 15 had I not just been married before Brazil 1950 and home life was naturally the priority. This proved to be a decision which meant missing out on one of football's greatest shocks – USA 1 England 0 at Belo Horizonte. Now wouldn't that have been a wonderful story to tell the grandchildren: "I was there."

Switzerland, therefore, was my Jules Rimet trophy baptism. This was the era when football controlled the competition without starting time edicts from television, commercial enterprise or vested outside interests. The era when the media had virtually free access to the training camps and were not, as happens so often today, looked upon by the authorities as pariahs to be banished at all costs.

Stadiums did not have an overpowering security presence. Yes, there were the flare-ups on the pitches but primarily the World Cup meant football.

But Switzerland 1954, in an idyllic Alpine setting, was not without its ugly side, pinpointed by the infamous Battle of Berne, where the Brazilians invaded the Hungarian dressing room, went on the rampage, created havoc and tarnished their name – a scar which remains to this day despite their unquestioned supremacy in the competition. The Hungarians were by no means innocents. Allegations that Magyars captain Ferenc Puskas, who was injured and watched the match from the dug-out, had thrown a bottle at the Brazilian as he left the pitch could never be proved.

Only the professionalism of English referee Arthur Ellis, who sent-off three players, ensured the match finished, with the Hungarians winning 4-2. The mantle of 'Villain of the Piece' went to the Brazilians, but for the neutral it was a classic textbook example of professional refereeing. Underlining the freedom given to the press, I reached the corridors of the players' dressing rooms shortly after the mayhem ended. The Brazilians shouted and protested behind a closed door as Ellis, from Halifax, was escorted to safety through rows of irate Brazilian supporters by Scottish referee Charlie Faultless.

Can you imagine a newspaperman loitering near the dressing rooms of a World Cup finals today? No chance. The nearest we get is the so-called 'mixed zone' where journalists wait behind wire for players to emerge from the stadium and be interviewed in an undignified scramble. I find this somewhat embarrassing, like waiting for crumbs of bread to be thrown to the starving.

Hungary qualified to meet Uruguay at rain-lashed Lausanne. What a pity this game was not televised live as it proved to be one of the World Cup classics. The conditions were appalling, the standard awesome. "This is what I call football," commented Charlie Buchan, the former England and Sunderland defender, publisher of his monthly magazine and my companion in the Press tribune that night. "Who said these teams could not play in these conditions – they could perform anywhere. Yes, that is football."

Uruguay, inspired by Juan Schiaffino, one of the most accomplished inside-forwards of all time, lost 4-2 after extra-time but earlier they had destroyed a mediocre Scotland, managed by Andy Beattie, former left-back and manager of Huddersfield Town, in a nightmare occasion at Basel by seven goals to nil. Beattie resigned because of interference from officialdom, turmoil reigned in the camp and the Scots, who had helped give the game to the world, were given a douche of cold reality and a signal they were not the power many of their patriotic fans imagined them to be.

The media facilities were efficient if somewhat spartan. Calls had to be placed with a central desk in the media centres; it cost a fortune to have a telephone installed while there were interminable delays on calls, many of which never materialised. Most of us in the overspill for the Germany-Hungary final – arguably the biggest World Cup final upset as the underdog Germans won 3-2 in 'the miracle of Berne' – at the Wankdorf Stadium were soaked to the skin as rain fell incessantly. Many correspondents without early deadlines opted to return to hotels and file copy from there. Again it was a question of contacting the international operator, which was quite a daunting task, but sometimes Irish charm worked. Laptops and instant dialling were a world away. Still, it was fun.

Sweden '58 saw the explosion on to the scene of Pele – or to give him his correct name, Edson Arantes Do Nascimento – to become the world's greatest footballer and subsequently politician, international sporting ambassador and cultural icon. The Brazilians were crowned world champions for the first time and one of my lasting memories is of them running round the pitch, totally euphoric with Pele in tears, holding first their own flag and then that of the defeated Swedes. Brazil had established their football supremacy which, despite many personnel changes, has lasted until today.

Northern Ireland, one of the four Home teams to reach the finals, came of age in this series – the Cinderella nation who had arrived unsung and unheralded but emerged belles of the Swedish ball. Managed by Peter Doherty, former Manchester City and Derby County inside-forward, whose distinguished career was fragmented by the Second World Ward, and captained by the inimitable Danny Blanchflower they surprised everyone by reaching the quarter-finals only to be defeated by France. They had only 18 players in the party and by the end of the Group Stage most them were walking wounded; Newcastle United's Tommy Casey played throughout the 90 minutes with blood seeping from leg gashes, goalkeeper Norman Uprichard had a broken finger, while Rangers centre-forward Billy Simpson pulled a muscle in training and never participated in any of the matches. The Irish exemplified the spirit of sport with fans pitching a tent in the grounds of their hotel at holiday resort Tylosand, near Halmstad, whose residents took them to their hearts. They called Northern Ireland "Our Team" and a 12-year-old boy Bengt Jonasson, son of a local industrialist, followed the players everywhere acting as interpreter, guide and mascot.

When the Irish left for home he was a picture of sadness. "Why don't we bring him to Belfast for our next match in October?" suggested Blanchflower. They did just that and he was introduced as the guest of honour before the start of the British Championship game with England at Windsor Park. He was the little boy who won the hearts of men.

Northern Ireland goalkeeper Harry Gregg, hero of the Munich air crash in February of that year which had robbed the squad of Manchester United centre-half Jackie Blanchflower, was named Goalkeeper of the Tournament, his display in the 2-2 draw with Germany at Malmo being universally rated one of the most outstanding in the competition's history. He travelled to Sweden by ship accompanied by an Irish FA official but opted to return by plane, his first flight since that dreadful snowy day when a team died. To avoid publicity, however, he departed 24 hours earlier than the main party, which was fortuitous in the extreme as next day Northern Ireland's aircraft was forced to circle for almost two hours over Brommen Industrial Airport, Stockholm, consuming fuel as the undercarriage would not retract before an emergency landing could be made.

World Cup memories keep flooding back. Gordon Banks' wonder save from Pele at Guadalajara, England's quarter-final defeat by West Germany in Mexico and Sir Alf Ramsey stopping me at the entrance to his chalet at the Estancia Motel and offering me a drink. A broken man, he made some unguarded comments on the game which I've kept to this day from the public domain.

Spain 82 was, of course, another glory era for Northern Ireland, qualifying for the quarter-finals after defeating host nation Spain 1-0 thanks to Gerry Armstrong's goal – a team which included Manchester United's Norman Whiteside who surpassed Pele's record as the youngest player in the World Cup.

The World Cup can make many managers icons or send them into oblivion as it did for Scotland's Ally MacLeod in Argentina, 78. That is the cruel side of the World Cup, the apotheosis of the beautiful game.

Dr Malcolm Brodie MBE is former sports editor and football correspondent of the Belfast Telegraph and Ireland's Saturday Night and is currently Northern Ireland representative of a number of British national daily and Sunday newspapers.

Favourite player(s): *A trio – Pele, Best, Maradona. They possessed all the attributes of genius. It is impossible to separate them. Their names will live forever.*

Most memorable match: *England 3 Hungary 6, Wembley Stadium, November 1953. The wake-up call for British football. No longer were they masters of the game they founded. Here was a new conception by a Hungarian side with a bewildering mixture of skill, tactical innovation and, as late Geoffrey Green of the Times put it 'could shoot with the accuracy and speed of archers – Agincourt in reverse'.*

THE WEIRD AND WONDERFUL WORLD OF BARNET

Manager sacked and reinstated 20 times in a season

By Jon Brodkin

I N OUR Premier League-obsessed world it is often assumed that supporting a considerably less glamorous team must be dull. Not so if you happen to be a Barnet fan. The past two decades alone have witnessed three promotions, two relegations, a winning cup final, threats of expulsion from the Football League and an experience no top-flight follower can claim to have shared: standing next to the club's manager on the terraces at Halifax Town the weekend after he had been sacked.

That manager was Barry Fry. The chairman who sacked him was Stan Flashman – all part of the popular pantomime which ensured that watching Barnet in the early 1990s could never be described as boring. Even the Sun became sufficiently excited by internecine problems at a tiny bottom-division football club to launch a 'Ban Fat Stan' campaign, complete with stickers featuring a grotesque picture of Flashman's face and a huge poster mounted on the back of a van.

If standing with Fry on the terraces at Halifax on that December afternoon in 1992 was fun, it also demonstrated that Barnet had become something of a laughing stock. Photographers lapped up the bizarre scenes as Fry urged the team on to a 2-1 victory. Bust-ups between Fry and Flashman were nothing new. Fry once famously remarked that "Stan Flashman wouldn't know the difference between a goal line and a clothes line," and their clashes were often far fruitier than such jibes. In May 1992, after Barnet had beaten Blackpool 1-0 in a first-leg play-off game which they should have won more convincingly, Flashman entered the dressing room, slagged off the team and scrapped with an outraged Fry before sacking him. Typically, Fry was reinstated the following day and told by the chairman that he had a "job for life."

Fry also returned as manager after his sojourn on the Halifax terraces. The caretaker that day, Edwin Stein, revealed he himself had been sacked and reinstated 20 times that season. It was all part of the weird and wonderful world of Flashman, the ticket tout who on many afternoons would be found working from his sofa wearing little more than his underpants and whose determination to see Barnet beat Enfield, their traditional local rivals, would – according to Fry – see him put £2,000 in cash on the dressing room table as an incentive to his players prior to that derby match.

The national exposure the club were getting on the back of the Fry-Flashman furore had hardly seemed likely when I ventured to Barnet for the first time in 1987. The club were then going well in the Vauxhall Conference, pushing for promotion to the Football League, but the modest Underhill stadium was hardly the surrounds of which schoolboy football dreams are made. The attraction? It was a local, cheap and fun day out in the company of a few mates and there was certainly never a worry about getting a ticket. It was friendly, too. Home and away fans passed each other at half-time as they changed ends to take up a spot behind the goal their teams were attacking, and entertainment was rarely in short supply. Even the early memory of getting drenched at Underhill as rain gushed through the less than watertight roof on one of the stands failed to dampen my enthusiasm and the bug bit to the extent that I co-edited two club fanzines.

The fare served up by Fry's attack-minded sides was entertaining and the pain of two near misses when it came to promotion was forgotten when, in 1991, Barnet reached the Football League for the first time. The Surrey Docks Stadium, home of Fisher Athletic, may not be Wembley but it seemed every bit as alluring as the national stadium that afternoon as Barnet won 4-2 to go up. Fry and Flashman embraced, fans and players celebrated on the pitch and the usual fuss from earlier in the season during which Flashman had threatened to sell the club and sack Fry suddenly felt insignificant. At last Fry's wheeler-dealer style had reaped rewards.

His predilection for buying and selling became well known at Birmingham City, where Steve Claridge once likened the first day of pre-season training to "a scene from Zulu played out on the Dunstable Downs" as a bloated squad containing dozens of full-time professionals and numerous triallists went through its paces. But that was old hat for Barnet supporters. Players came and went, often at an astonishing rate (even the former Liverpool defender Mark Lawrenson played twice in 1989) and an equally astonishing profit. Andy Clarke, a mesmerising striker, was discovered by Fry playing Sunday football and sold to Wimbledon, then a top-flight team, for £350,000. Lee Payne, a young winger signed from Hitchen, joined Newcastle United for a reported £125,000 after only nine games for the club. Payne never established himself at Newcastle and it summed up his meteoric rise that he later talked of how he would go to St James' Park late at night, pull his hood over his head and run around the pitch, trying to take in the scale of the club he had joined and what could be achieved there.

For Barnet it felt just as exciting to be in the Football League, though when the opening game ended in an extraordinary 7-4 home defeat by Crewe it was difficult to know whether to laugh or cry. "It was a carnival occasion and Barnet were the clowns," Fry reflected. "My defenders must have thought tackle is what they go fishing with."

To prove lessons had been learned, the following match ended in a 5-5 League Cup draw with Brentford. It was a fitting way to begin what has been a roller-coaster period for the club. Promotion in 1993 to the unprecedented heights of what is now League One was followed by an immediate and humbling relegation after Barnet had survived a Football League recommendation that they be kicked out for rule breaches. Given that flirtation with expulsion shortly before the season started and the fact that the squad had been ripped apart and hastily rebuilt as the League handed free transfers to the players from the promoted team, even managing five wins from 46 league games was no mean feat. "We are nothing more than raggy-arsed rovers," the then player-manager, Gary Phillips, said at one point.

There has been pride at seeing several Barnet players, including Clarke, Dougie Freedman, Linvoy Primus, Maik Taylor and Marlon King, reach the Premier League. More remarkably two former England internationals have managed the team over the past 15 years in Ray Clemence and Tony Cottee, though sadly the latter's brief spell in charge will not be remembered fondly.

His first home game, in November 2000, provided a rare opportunity for me to report on the club for the Guardian and bias turned out to be the least of my worries as Blackpool were trounced 7-0, with Cottee marking his debut as player-manager by scoring the first goal. The attendance was up by almost 1,000 on the previous home game and optimism abounded. With the team eighth, the play-offs seemed a realistic target – but it proved a false dawn. Barnet won only three of their next 18 games, Cottee departed in mid-March and relegation back to the Conference ensued.

Typically the club which refuses to die returned to the Football League in 2005 under the existing manager, Paul Fairclough, and has stayed there. Even long-standing problems with the stadium which have led to battles with the local council, fresh threats of expulsion from the League and provisional ground-sharing schemes have found at least a temporary resolution, with the building of two new stands giving the club the 2,000 covered seats required to help satisfy regulations.

It says something about the uncertainty surrounding the long-term location that the design of the recently built South Stand allows it to be moved in the event of leaving for fresh pastures. But under the chairmanship of the dedicated Tony Kleanthous the club appears to be in good hands.

My level of attendance has dropped over recent years, first due to living in the north of England for three years and more recently due to commitments as a newspaper reporter, but not even the privilege of attending Premier League, Champions League and international matches for work has diluted the enjoyment of an afternoon or evening at Underhill. Crowds may be smaller than they were when the club were going well as a non-league team but the past two relatively nondescript League Two seasons have been spiced by runs to the fourth round of the FA Cup and Barnet continue to find novel ways of staying in the public eye.

At a time when dissent and the crowding of match officials have been major talking points, Barnet showed a way for others when, amid a poor disciplinary record, they decided that on the pitch only the captain would talk to the referee. Sadly there are no extra points for good behaviour and the play-offs have eluded the team again but stability, Football League survival and just being in existence are not to be sneezed at after the turbulence of the past.

Jon Brodkin is the night editor on the Guardian's sports desk and was a football reporter for the paper from 1999-2007.

Favourite player: *Herbie Smith (Barnet 1987-89). Looked more like a cruiserweight boxer than a footballer and mostly played like one but he terrified opponents and enlivened the crowd.*

Most memorable match: *Fisher Athletic 2 Barnet 4, May 1991. Barnet needed only a draw to clinch promotion to the Football League but flirted with disaster by twice going behind before securing a win.*

SIR BOBBY ROBSON IS A KNIGHT TO REMEMBER

"There is nothing I enjoy more than talking football with him" – Sir Alex Ferguson

By Bob Cass

SIR BOBBY ROBSON does not just grace the managerial profession, he graces mankind. He is one of that rare breed who are able to stretch the limits of respect and buffoonery at the same time.

There are few who have not dined out on stories of Sir Bobby's apparent absent-mindedness, especially when it comes to remembering names and faces. He seems to be fair game for every celebrated mimic – one in particular squeezes every last vestige of poetic licence in his celebrated after-dinner routine, recalling Sir Bobby's time as coach of "PVC Eindhoven", where he became fluent in "Hollish."

But even in his and the repertoire of like-minded others, there is a bottom line of total admiration for the bloke. And if there isn't, there should be.

Sir Bobby and his wife Lady Elsie now enjoy the trappings associated with a distinguished career in the game. But, if he needed a reminder of his roots among the mining folk of County Durham his magnificent stately home is barely a 15-minute drive from the terraced colliery house he grew up in.

It was there where his dad Philip and mum Lilian instilled in him values which, in a sport too often defiled by scandal and corruption, make him a shining beacon of honesty and respect.

Fellow football knight Sir Alex Ferguson says quite simply: "I am privileged to call him a friend." The Manchester United manager broke a self-imposed pledge never to appear again on the BBC to present Sir Bobby with a Lifetime Achievement Award at the Sports Personality of the Year show in December 2007. His unscripted acceptance speech brought the house down.

"It was an honour which cut across any personal feelings I might have," said Sir Alex. "I first met Bobby in 1981 when I was manager of Aberdeen and he was at Ipswich Town. We knocked them out of the European Cup Winners' Cup, which they had won the previous season.

"Bobby was typically magnanimous in defeat, telling me he hoped we went on to win the competition. We did – eventually – the following year, but we have remained friends ever since.

"He is a great football man with a depth of knowledge about the game which is phenomenal. There is nothing I enjoy more than talking football with him. People tell me I get too involved in the game and should start slowing down but I just hope my enthusiasm for the game gets close to his.

"Time catches up with all of us and Bobby has had more than his fair share of health setbacks. But there aren't many who have conquered adversity like he is and kept smiling. His courage is amazing. But if body has borne the scars of too many operations his brain is still as active as ever."

Sir Bobby's battle against the evil disease of cancer which has attacked his body in various places – his face, his brain, his lungs – on no less than five occasions, typifies a fighting spirit which has constantly left his critics with egg on their faces. No more so than when much of the media celebrated the end of what they regarded as an unproductive spell as manager of England.

I remember interviewing Sir Bobby in the cosy front room of his parents' house in Langley Park on the outskirts of Durham City just after he was appointed in August 1982. His enthusiasm was matched only by that of his dad. In the eight years he was in charge, Philip, well into his eighties, rarely if ever – certainly when they were played at Wembley – missed a match, always insisting on returning to Durham on the night train back from King's Cross.

Had even the worst of those who judged Sir Bobby harshly been granted even a morsel not only of objectivity but also hindsight, they surely would have sung from a very different hymn sheet. After all, in the 1986 World Cup in Mexico when his team was hit with injuries to key players such as influential skipper Bryan Robson, did he not come close to salvaging what seemed a lost cause with his inspirational striking partnership of Gary Lineker and Peter Beardsley?

Diego Maradona may have clinched the quarter-final victory for Argentina with what was described as the "goal of the century", but the England manager still maintains that the foundations of his team's exit were laid when the celebrated striker cheated. "Hand Of God indeed," he said later. "More the hand of a rascal – God had nothing to do with it. That day Maradona was diminished in my eyes forever."

The euphoria of qualifying for Euro 88, dropping only a point in their qualifying matches which included an 8-0 win over Turkey, was only temporary, with what at times was venomous vilification in the sports pages after England failed to reach the later stages. Again Sir Bobby provided the perfect riposte to those who clamoured for his head.

Many, including one or two who are still hailed among certain observers as coaching geniuses, have followed him in the job but none has come closer to emulating the success of Sir Alf Ramsey in winning the World Cup – albeit on our own turf – in 1966. Already under sentence of the sack, England's semi-final penalty shootout defeat by West Germany in Italy was a bitter pill that the redoubtable Robson found difficult to swallow.

If it was back to square one ... back to what was, in effect a proving ground similar to what he encountered in 13 years establishing Ipswich Town as one of the top clubs in the country ... he revelled in the challenge.

And if there were few club chairmen in England willing to offer him a route back into football, there were plenty on the continent who would.

PSV Eindhoven first, where he won successive Dutch league titles in 1991 and 1992; then to Sporting Lisbon, where an acrimonious battle with the club president Jose Sousa Cintra ended with him being axed in December 1994 with Sporting leading the league table for the first time in 15 years, before more success at Portuguese rivals FC Porto, where he again won successive league titles in 1995 and 1996.

His subsequent appointment as coach at Barcelona was agreed on one major condition – that he took with him one Jose Mourinho who had begun their association as a translator at Sporting and Porto before being recruited to the back-room staff as a coach.

Mourinho put his time under Robson to good use, learning enough from his mentor to develop his own individuality as one of the top managers in world football. But he will always be grateful to the start he had after being a little known failed footballer.

"Bobby was a great inspiration and a wonderful man to work with," he said. "He ignited in me the passion that I feel for the game. Obviously without his help I would not have had the opportunity to achieve the success I have had since we were together."

A glowing accolade, surely equalled by one from another world "great". Brazilian goalscorer Ronaldo, signed by Sir Bobby for Barcelona for £19 million. "As a trainer without doubt he is one of the greatest in the world," he said. "The best thing about him is his personality; his character. He was like a father to me. Bobby Robson helped me to be consistent and helped me a lot with my career."

It is one of Sir Bobby's greatest regrets that he was not given more time to enjoy the fruits of his labours at the club he supported as a schoolboy. His achievement in taking Newcastle United from the bottom of the Premier League to Champions League qualification in the space of just two seasons did not spare him from what was surely a premature P45. But he maintained his dignity when others shed theirs.

It is typical of Sir Bobby that, in enduring the ravages of what have been for him a debilitating disease, he should try to spare others the same agonies. In March 2008 he launched the Sir Bobby Robson Foundation, a charity designed to raise money for research and equipment at the Freeman Hospital in Newcastle. Money and messages flooded in, varying from kids donating their pocket money to fund-raising dinners which contributed thousands.

Of course the target will be reached. His message to those who have played their part displays the gratitude of an unlikely lad whose greatness is almost an embarrassment. "Thanks to you, the Sir Bobby Robson Cancer Trials Research Centre at the Freeman Hospital will be up and running on schedule and the people of the north-east will be the very first to benefit from this state of the art facility. I am absolutely honoured and proud to have been involved in this project."

Sir Bobby Robson is indeed a Knight to remember.

Bob Cass has been a football writer with the Mail On Sunday for a quarter of a century. Before that he was north-east football correspondent for the Sun for 17 years. Earlier he had spells with the Sunday Sun and the Journal in Newcastle. He is a lifelong Darlington supporter.

__Favourite player:__ Kevin Keegan, a great player with Liverpool and Hamburg. He made a significant contribution to Southampton's later success but, even at the end of his playing career, he was still good enough to make a tremendous impact at Newcastle United. A great example to any young footballer.

__Most memorable match:__ Without doubt the 1973 FA Cup final and Second Division Sunderland's 1-0 win over a star-studded Leeds United side. I'll remember it for the Ian Porterfield winner; the magnificent Jimmy Montgomery save and, having watched it several times since, the effort, work-rate and skill of an under-rated side.

THE WIZARD OF OSSIE

Osgood had it all – except discipline

By Nigel Clarke

YOU can be too close to a football club, you know. My enthusiasm for Chelsea in my early days on the Daily Mirror not only saw me banned but sent manager Dave Sexton red faced with apoplexy.

Chelsea had been my club from the earliest days I can remember. I cut my teeth on Millwall, just up the road from where I lived in south east London, but among my friends there was a massive support for the Blues, chiefly instigated by a mate named Bogey Payne. When it became too dangerous to support the Lions any longer, I switched allegiance.

The kick-off at The Den in those days was 3.15, allowing the dockers to "sup up" and leave the pubs at closing time – 3pm – lubricated and ready for action. I used to jostle among them on the banking behind the goal, strong men with flat caps and booze-fuelled breaths. They also carried wicked stevedore hooks inside the pockets of their overcoats. When they began to use them on each other I thought it was time to seek my soccer entertainment elsewhere. I witnessed some horrible scenes, men slashing each other with these hooks, the St John's Ambulance volunteers too terrified to venture into the heaving masses to attend the injured.

Stamford Bridge was a verdant watering place in comparison, but never with quite the same atmosphere. The dog track that ran round the pitch was too intrusive, but because Chelsea were semi-hopeless in those days it added to my sense of affinity for the underdog (no pun intended). It has been with me ever since.

I was on the West Bank when Chelsea won the title in 1955, Stamford Bridge a far cry from the glamorous place it is today. For years I stood there wondering if they would ever be a force in football again. I soon became hooked and even took one of my first girlfriends there, then my wife, daughter and son. The first words my daughter spoke were "square ball" followed quickly by "Chelsea for the Cup." By then I had graduated to covering Chelsea for the Mirror after working for a now deceased agency. What joy. The then chief football reporter, Ken Jones, didn't have much of a relationship with manager Tommy Docherty and the number two Harry Miller didn't mix with the players. That left me to indulge myself with Terry Venables and George Graham, who both sent handsome wedding presents, then later Peter Osgood whose book Ossie The Wizard I ghosted. Ossie, a genuine Berkshire boy with an accent as outrageous as his talent, liked a drink, kept a ferret and loved to enjoy himself. We met every week after training to put together the next chapter, only after a pint or two. Ossie didn't want to talk, preferring another bevvy ... and another after that. "We'll do it later," he would laugh.

That was Chelsea in those heady days of the late 1960s and Sexton, by now the manager, did his best to discourage the so-called Kings Road culture. But Ossie was the King of the Bridge, aided and abetted by Alan Hudson, very much the local boy, with Tommy Baldwin, John Boyle and Charlie Cooke in eager attendance. After a Saturday match at Stamford Bridge, reporters were allowed to congregate in an area just outside the dressing room. There were very few restrictions and we could talk to whoever we liked, a far cry from the almost censorship set in place by most clubs now. As the players came out, the usual suspects would whisper out of the corner of their mouth: "Markham Arms, Clarkie." An hour later there they would be, with a few thirsty scribes and it was all good natured fun. Yes, a few too many drinks were taken on board, but there was no breathalyser then with less awareness of the realities of such excesses. The players were mates who were paid for what most of us had always wanted to do.

The after-match celebrations were something that dear old Dave Sexton tried hard to stamp on, but what happened at Chelsea was not an exception – it was the behaviour of most players in most teams in those days and not only in London. Better still were the away trips. On a Saturday evening, coming back to London I would be invited to join the team in the restaurant car for drinks and dinner. There was lots of gossip and joshing, but at no time did I ever betray a confidence or reveal in my paper one or two little indiscretions that might have taken place. The players trusted me, which made it all the better because, as a bye-line reporter, I had also become a confidant and friend.

It wasn't always easy. The wind-ups that were perpetrated were not always funny and most people became victims, especially from Ossie. But to see him pull on a Chelsea shirt was to see him transformed. He was totally brilliant and had he not suffered a broken leg I believe he would have gone on to become one of England's most talented footballers.

"This boy Osgood," Sir Alf Ramsey would say. "Tell me about him as a person. I don't understand him. He could be anything he wants to be, so why does he act like a clown?"

That was Ossie, a man who rarely took things seriously. Playing football was so easy for him, but the problem was he lacked desire and, too often, discipline. Recovering from that broken leg he became so bored he would play golf, balancing himself on his one good leg and still hitting the ball miles. One day I noticed, with some alarm, that the plaster on his injured leg was cracking and breaking.

"All that talent trying to get out," he observed.

It was more serious, of course. The leg did not have the support a proper plaster would have provided. This is not to necessarily condone such flippancy, but you could get away with things like that in those days when medical attention was nothing like it is today.

Ossie's search for a good time took in everything. One day, when the book research was going well, John Boyle and Charlie Cooke found us in a nearby bar. They joined in rather vigorously. Dave Sexton found out and ordered everyone back to the ground – someone said 14 bottles of wine had been consumed. We beat a hasty retreat and Sexton arrived to find Charlie sticking out of a hedge because he could no longer walk, Boylers asleep on the medical couch and Ossie contentedly singing his heart out.

Guess who got the blame? The story appeared in the Evening Standard the next morning, and Sexton even thought to give me a mention. He also banned me and once when I turned up at the training ground Sexton sprinted 400 yards to tell me, not too politely, to leave.

When Chelsea won the FA Cup in 1970, Ossie scored in every round. They also went on to lift the European Cup Winners' Cup the following season, beating Real Madrid in a replay. These were unforgettable European adventures during which Chelsea blazed a glorious trail with me remaining neutral a serious challenge. My heart would pound and palms sweat as I watched good mates put themselves on the line.

And Ossie. On a Sunday morning he would be up early, out with his dog ferreting, a star blessed with genius but so ordinary. My affection for him made me forgive him for ringing at mid-night and singing down the phone.

I helped him over the later years, ghosting articles for him so he could earn a penny. I also watched him struggle with the pain of arthritis to both knees that made walking painful and difficult. I laughed at his exploits, like borrowing the FA Cup when he was at Southampton when they beat Manchester United in the final. Ossie drove back down the M3 and stopped at a road-side café, where he filled it with tea and shared it with a motley crew of disbelieving bikers and lorry drivers. That was Os, the heartbeat of Chelsea. It broke him when he left Stamford Bridge for Southampton. He left his soul at Stamford Bridge and how fitting that his ashes are buried beneath the pitch now.

He had his heroes too, notably George Best. Ossie would meet me in George's bar in London's West End and many an afternoon was spent in joyous recollection with the player he rated higher than Pelé. He even asked George for his autograph.

Those crazy but wonderful days with players who became friends make it hard to accept what Chelsea has become. In those days watching and covering them was fun. Now it is strictly for business, where contact with players is at a minimum.

Ossie loved to walk down the Kings Road with Huddy by his side. They never had to buy a drink. I sometimes wonder what it would be like if they were around now. They were popular and in touch with fans, with Ossie the working man's hero and Huddy ever willing to support him. Football was different then. Chelsea chairman Brian Mears would invite the likes of myself and Jimmy Lawton (now of the Independent) into the board room after a match. Players would drift in too. When most had gone home, upon seeing we had not finished our champagne Brian would throw us the keys and say "lock up after you."

Those were the days for us and Chelsea. And especially Peter Osgood.

Nigel Clarke is ex-deputy chief football reporter for the Daily Mirror and football editor Daily Mail; now assistant sports news editor Daily Express.

__Favourite player:__ Peter Osgood. Because Ossie wasn't just a football star, he was also a human being. Great talent, great company.

__Most memorable match:__ 1970 FA Cup Final replay Chelsea 2 Leeds 1. The end of big bad Leeds, in a match so suffocatingly tense it was at times difficult to draw a breath. Why? My mates were playing and I knew what it meant to them to slay the Leeds dragon.

JAMIE REDKNAPP: THE LAST OF HIS KIND

Harry told his players to pass like his son

By Lee Clayton

GEOFF HURST'S three goals won a World Cup, Jamie Redknapp's England hat-trick is not so glorious.

Redknapp was the modern football icon. Able to pass a ball with either foot – long and short – he was the stylish captain of his club with the poster-boy looks. Until his crumbling knees wouldn't carry him any further.

Three times he was carted off on a stretcher while representing England. But he kept coming back. That is until doctors forced him to accept he was finished at 32. No more crying out in pain, or being helped out of bed. Jamie can pull on a pair of jeans unaided now and doesn't have the daily grind into London for injections and lubrication to stop the bones rubbing together.

He misses the game – of course he does – and the game has changed without him. Midfielders are now machines; athletic powerhouses who race across the ground with ferocious aggression. Redknapp was the last of his kind. Where are the playmakers, the old-style number 10s, now?

Jamie was brought up watching a game where gliding midfield artists were on every team sheet. From Glenn Hoddle and Liam Brady in England's First Division to further afield, where Michel Platini was Europe's box office star. A gifted schoolboy from the South Coast, he could also pass a ball with some flair. Modelling himself on Hoddle's graceful manner, as well as admiring Bryan Robson's swashbuckling, box-to-box technique, Redknapp soon found himself under the wing of John Barnes at Liverpool.

"He was such an incredible footballer," Redknapp later insisted.

"John could play, really play. I used to love playing in central midfield with him. He had such balance. I played with him at Liverpool towards the end of his career, but he was a class act. If there had been the same hype around the game in the late

Eighties as there is now, people would have been making the same fuss about him as they do over Thierry Henry."

Redknapp had joined Liverpool at 17 for £350,000, after Kenny Dalglish refused to take no for an answer. "My dad was at a football dinner dance. He was trying to dance with my mum but Kenny Dalglish, the Liverpool manager, kept following him around the room. Eventually, he butted in and said: 'I want to sign your son'."

Dalglish marvelled at young Redknapp's ability to manipulate the ball and signed him after just 13 games for Bournemouth's struggling first team, where he was being guided by his dad, Harry. It was to be Dalglish's final signing as manager of Liverpool before his unlikely and sensational resignation 38 days later.

I first met Jamie under the main stand at Bournemouth after a Second Division match; even standing there under a leaking roof, you could tell that he just loved his football. Just like his dad.

He told me then how he would skip school to join training sessions with the Bournemouth first team. "That's how I want you to pass the ball, just like Jamie," Harry would say to the senior pros. Much to the embarrassment of his son.

"I wasn't proud of missing school and my mum wasn't best pleased, but my education was football – being around the club, being around my dad," Jamie later acknowledged. "I loved being there, they were very happy days at Bournemouth. I didn't care if I was washing boots, sweeping out dressing rooms or cleaning the toilets. Dad should have been driving me to school, but he wanted me there too."

The next time I caught up with Jamie was during my first trip with England. Lawrie McMenemy was in charge and he demanded that his players should sing the national anthem, wear the three lions with pride and be locked up in their rooms rather than falling victim to the inviting Toulon nightlife (leaving that to the rest of us).

"We are England," he would remind them at every opportunity – England Under-21s, but England nonetheless. McMenemy, a warm and generous man, rich in football history, was eager to bring home the trophy and to achieve some positive newspaper headlines. No Turnips in Toulon.

The senior team under Graham Taylor were losing on tour in America ... and so some newspaper attention fell on the next generation. This tournament had previously conditioned talent such as Paul Gascoigne for the big stage and, included in McMenemy's squad this time, were Redknapp, Chris Sutton and Darren Anderton.

England came powering through their group, beat Scotland, despite Paul Dickov's attempts to kick them all around France and then won their semi-final. All they needed was someone to buy the drinks.

Unlike most England trips, where there is a cast of a thousand commentators, there were only three journalists covering the tournament. As a result, access to the players was excellent.

Still, despite their progress through the competition, McMenemy refused all pleas for a night off. So how about finding a young journalist with an expenses account who was willing to make new friends? I was only two years older than most of the players – and keen to show that I could be trusted.

After beating the hosts in the final, a well-earned night of celebration was in full swing, until McMenemy and his No. 2 Ray Harford raided Jamie's room in the early hours to find most of the squad and plenty of evidence, as well as a sheepish journalist and proof from the head barman.

Redknapp was the outstanding player and went onto make 18 appearances for the England under-21s, including one strange game as an over-aged player, soon after Hoddle became England coach and tried to make a case that his protégé could play as a sweeper.

Hoddle, who had finished his career playing in that position between two defensive markers for both Swindon and Chelsea, argued that a talented midfielder should fill the roll in order to help overcome the English disease of lumping the ball from back to front. He saw Redknapp as the answer.

"Jamie won't have to head the ball," said Hoddle, insisting one obvious weakness would be overcome. "I just want him on the ball and to get us playing."

The plan didn't work. On a cow-patch of a pitch, Redknapp had to endure his own team-mates coming short to take the ball from him. Nobody told Nigel Quashie that Redknapp was there to make the play.

There were no TV pictures beamed back to England and so his dad, Harry, had to rely on regular mobile phone calls from me to report on his son's progress.

"Er ... he's doing okay ... yeah, he's getting the ball, but they keep getting it from him." It was an odd evening.

Redknapp played 17 times for the senior team, including an impressive cameo performance in Euro 96 against Scotland, when he changed the direction of the game. However, he finished that match on a stretcher (again) with a broken ankle and his tournament was over. He rates this as the biggest disappointment of his brief international career.

Watch out for this pub quiz question, however. From whose shot did Rene Higuita make his "Scorpion Save" for Colombia against England at Wembley? The answer is Jamie Redknapp.

Though injuries continued to damage his progress for club and country, Jamie still managed to score on his Liverpool league debut, became the youngest player to play for the club in Europe and went on to captain them successfully, following in the footsteps of Anfield heavyweights such as Alan Hansen, Greame Souness, Emlyn Hughes and mentor Barnes. He collected medals in the 2000/01 season as Liverpool won the treble, although he missed the whole campaign as injury struck again and his Anfield career came to a premature end the next season after a 2-0 win at Charlton, following 308 games and 41 goals for the club.

Next he captained Tottenham and then Southampton, which meant he had started and finished his professional career playing for his dad.

Redknapp the younger's next transfer took him into the media where he has become part of Sky Sport's first team and contributes a regular column for the *Daily Mail*. He is what you see on TV — charming company, sharp, dedicated, smart and still loves to talk football.

Having retired so recently, he can help our readers to understand what it takes to play against the modern heroes such as Steven Gerrard, Wayne Rooney, Michael Owen and Cristiano Ronaldo.

It is a privilege to write about the game and there are some who do it with some style, but few actually know what it's like to stand in the tunnel at 3pm. Redknapp qualifies on both counts.

Lee Clayton is sports editor of the Daily Mail.

*   **Favourite player:** *Thierry Henry. In a league of his own. As a West Ham fan, Trevor Brooking, Alan Devonshire, Alvin Martin and Ray Stewart's penalties must get a mention too. Sorry.*

*   **Most memorable match:** *England losing to Argentina in the 1998 World Cup: Beckham's red card, Owen's goal, England's effort with 10 men … I spilled Diet Coke over my laptop in the stadium as I was about to file. Do cry for me Argentina.*

WEMBLEY CUP FINAL HEAVEN

In a snack bar across the road

By Mike Collett

THERE was nowhere quite like the Collette Restaurant & Snack Bar on FA Cup Final day at Wembley Stadium in the 1960s. Nowhere. It is the kind of place people no longer eat in. Actually, even when it existed there weren't too many places like it that people ate in, but on Cup Final day it was absolutely magical.

It stood less than half a mile away from the Twin Towers, opposite the entrance to Wembley Stadium mainline station and for me, for a time, it was even more magical and exciting than actually being in the stadium itself.

Well that's not quite true, because all I longed for was the chance to find a ticket. I used to imagine, as I poured out another Kia-Ora orange from the huge dispenser or prised open the top of another bottle of Coke or Seven-Up that I would find one carelessly discarded amongst the empty cups or plates, or that someone would just walk in, and offer me, a gawky teenager, a ticket for the final. You think like that when you are 15.

Without realising it at the time, the Collette gave me a privileged position among football fans, because I went to Wembley for the Cup Final every season. The Cup finalists often stayed not far from where I lived, either at the Brent Bridge Hotel off the North Circular or at the Hendon Hall Hotel and I learnt very early exactly what the magic of the Cup meant, both to the players and the fans.

We used to go to the hotels to get the players autographs. Then on Cup Final day I'd find myself among the fans, listening to their conversations about their heroes I'd been with the day before.

The optimism of fans never changes before a Cup Final. No matter what colours, or rosettes then, they happened to be wearing, it was always thrilling. No-one ever admitted they were going to lose, ever.

The desolation of the losers never changed either. Losing fans don't stick around for cups of tea afterwards. Winning fans would come back and order steak and chips.

Forty years on, and no matter what else the big clubs may be aiming to win today, there is still nowhere quite like Wembley on FA Cup Final day and those days at the Collette helped me fall in love with the world's greatest cup competition.

My Uncle Jack ran the place and added the final 'e' to the Collett name on the tiled shop-front sign to give it an air of refined European sophistication. But you cannot imagine a place less likely to attract refined European sophisticates.

"What's that last 'e' for, Uncle Jack?" I asked him once as I carried a huge pile of empty plates back to the kitchen where the amazing El Greco, the one-armed washer-up, worked on match days. In fact, he was about the nearest thing the Collette Restaurant & Snack Bar ever got to the European game. And despite his nickname, he was Italian and told me he used to play for Inter Milan.

"But you've only got one arm," I would tease him.

"I was not the goalkeeper ... and I've got two feet," he'd reply, and there was no arguing with that.

I never asked him how he lost the arm, but he was certainly the most effective one-armed professional dish washer I've ever seen.

While El Greco stayed year after year and did the washing up, cooks came and went, but none could match Vi. She was formidable with a mane of jet black hair and a personality that could fill a room, or even Wembley itself. There were often so many people in the tiny kitchen you had to walk sideways to get anywhere.

"We need more plates, Greco," she would scream at the one-armed dishwasher. "So hurry up."

Another arm wouldn't have gone amiss.

Uncle Jack had thought about the final 'e' on the end of the name and as I walked out of the kitchen, through a little corridor where he had his 'office' and used to type up things like '1965 FA Cup Final Menu Special', he was waiting with his answer.

"People will think it's Italian. Then it should have an 'i' on the end then and be Colletti," replied his precocious nephew.

"They'll think it's French then," he explained, as if that made a blind bit of difference.

All they wanted was a steak and kidney pie and chips, or steak and chips or beans on toast or egg and chips. I don't think they'd heard of pasta at Wembley in 1965.

But you had to hand it to him, Uncle Jack was certainly a showman with an engaging style. Small, balding and with a fine moustache and a wonderful sense of humour, he would also usually wear a long white coat while on duty on Cup Final day. It made him look like a cross between a doctor and a butcher, which perhaps wasn't a bad thing.

He was a cross between Arthur Lowe of Dad's Army fame and the great Spurs fan and actor Warren Mitchell and had been something in the City before a career swerve occurred. He ended up running this madhouse.

There were in fact three very distinct sections to it. The Snack Bar part, where I began working on match days as a 13 year-old, was at street level. The restaurant was up a winding staircase where about 25 tables occupied the whole floor.

There was a Juke Box in the corner and every time I hear Otis Redding's Dock of the Bay I can picture the sounds and smells of that restaurant as if it was yesterday. In 1968 an Everton fan put in about £2 – a fortune at the time – and keyed in Dock of the Bay which played non-stop about 25 times for more than an hour. It must have been the high point of his day. West Bromwich beat them 1-0 with Jeff Astle's extra-time winner.

One floor above the restaurant were the mysterious rooms which were let out to all kinds of equally mysterious people. I found out later that El Greco lived up there where he had a box with a wooden, gloved arm in it.

I rarely ventured to the rooms, but in 1965 Uncle Jack had a brilliant idea. Years before Sky TV came along, Jack, although he didn't know it, I reckon, invented Pay Per View TV. There was no satellite technology involved here however. He just put a TV in an empty room and charged all those without tickets still in the restaurant at kick-off time five shillings to watch the match. He made a killing.

There wasn't a lot to do while the game was actually on, and once I had cleared up the empties, he let me sit in with the world's first Pay Per View TV audience. There might have been 100,000 actually in Wembley across the road to see Liverpool beat Leeds, but it seemed to me there were almost as many in that bedroom, all of them Liverpool fans as I recall, all of them in suits and all of them delighted to be seeing the match on a tiny black-and-white Rediffusion TV set. However 'seeing the match' might be something of an exaggeration. After a while the room became so full of smoke, wild language and Liverpool fans going crazy, it was amazing anyone could breathe, let alone work out what was being beamed live from 200 yards away.

My lasting memory of the 1965 Cup final is actually 'seeing' Ian St John's winning header through a dense fug of Woodbine cloud and an ecstatic Scouser hugging me half-to-death celebrating Liverpool's first ever FA Cup win.

The following year, 1966, saw the Collette decked out in World Cup Willie paraphernalia and the place moved into overdrive with so many matches at Wembley. Everton and Sheffield Wednesday came to town for the Cup Final and the Snack Bar was doing a roaring trade.

The tea urn was being drained in record time, the sandwiches were selling like hot cakes, which of course, we didn't sell, bottles of Coke were going by the crateload. A Sheffield Wednesday fan came up to the bar.

"How much is a ham sandwich ?"

"Two and six," I replied

"How much is cheese sandwich ?"

"Two and three."

"And how much for teas?"

"Six pence."

He thought for a moment or two. I didn't know whether he was gonna hug me like that Scouser had or belt me.

"I'll have two teas. I'm not paying your thieving London prices."

I served him two teas. He drank one after the other and walked out. Strange people football folk. Wonderful people too.

It was April 11, 1970, about half past two and the Cup final between Chelsea and Leeds was less than half an hour away. As was usual, the Collette was emptying as fans went across to the stadium.

I was cleaning up the Snack Bar when I heard the words I'd dreamed of for years.

"Oi, mate, you don't know anyone who fancies a ticket do ya? Face value."

"What? I do. Wait there one second."

I bounded upstairs and found Uncle Jack to tell him of this stupendous, earth-shattering opportunity.

"You can go if you find someone to stand in for while you've gone," came his less than encouraging reply.

Half an hour before kick-off and Where on earth was I going to find ANYONE to do that?

"But it's the FA Cup final and some bloke is offering me a ticket."

"Ok, go on, I'll do it. Off you go, but be back here five minutes after the game ends or else you're sacked."

Twenty minutes later I was IN Wembley.

I'd been there before but never on Cup Final day, and yes I had to admit it. It was JUST a bit better than seeing the match on the black and white telly upstairs at the Collette.

The old place was pulled down many years ago and replaced by a bland office building. I've been a journalist covering matches at Wembley for over 35 years now and often wish I could just pop in there for a cup of tea and a bacon sandwich.

And put Dock of the Bay on the jukebox. Over and over again.

Mike Collett is the author of the Complete Record of the FA Cup and the soccer editor of Reuters.

Favourite player: Jimmy Greaves, one of the greatest goalscorers ever. He created a wave of anticipation and excitement whenever he got the ball in a scoring position and finished with an assured elegance that no one has ever bettered.

Most memorable match: Happened on my birthday and in a FA Cup final at Wembley when Ricky Villa's goal gave Spurs their famous 3-2 win over Manchester City in 1981.

ORDINARY PEOPLE

Charlton fans have experienced it all – even a rubber shipment from Bangkok

By Patrick Collins

H E WAS an elderly man with a taste for full-strength Capstan and a hacking cough. I met him on a November afternoon in 1982, as he stood against a crush barrier in the Valley's North Stand and watched Charlton Reserves play Swansea Reserves. The game had attracted a crowd of 2,578 – around 2,500 more than usual – and most of them had come to watch one man.

Allan Simonsen had arrived at Charlton with a reputation. In 1977 he had been voted European Footballer of the Year – Kevin Keegan finished second and Michel Platini third. And he had left Barcelona in order to make room for Diego Maradona. Plainly, he had kept exalted company. Yet somehow a fee of around £325,000 – negotiated by a chairman whose ambitions were greater than his resources – had brought him to London SE7, and the reserve match was seen as a suitably low-key opportunity to introduce him to the English game. My friend in the North Stand was not overly impressed. He stared down impassively, offering the briefest nod as I arrived breathlessly late. "What's he like, then?" I asked.

"Who?" he said.

"Simonsen," I said.

He stared down at the man who had made way for Maradona. Then he sucked at his Capstan and narrowed his eyes. "He takes a decent corner," he said. "I'll give him that."

I remember thinking that this sage embodied that philosophical serenity which characterised the authentic follower of Charlton Athletic. After spending perhaps half a century staring down from that same spot, nothing could surprise him. He never despaired, but he distrusted optimism. Instead, he meekly hoped for better days. And if somebody like Simonsen could help deliver those days with his decent corners, well, wouldn't that be nice?

Simonsen didn't deliver them, of course. He played as Ronaldo might play were he to be loaned to, say, Leyton Orient or Leicester; skilfully but fitfully, aware that his talents had been designed for higher things. The signing was more a grandiose gesture than a solid investment, and his stay was brief. The fans reacted with a collective shrug. Why did they taunt us with signings like Simonsen? We enjoyed being ordinary. Ordinary suited us.

There was a time when we might have been something more, when the FA Cup was won in 1947 and the crowds began to cram into that great bowl of a football ground. With a splurge of brave investment, we might have done something wonderful. But it didn't happen, and we decided that it wasn't meant to happen. And so, year by year and decade after decade, we were thankful for small mercies. Most modern fans will find such forebearance difficult to understand. We live at a time when success is all, when a home defeat provokes foam- flecked calls to 6-0-6 on Radio 5Live.

"The manager's lost the plot, Alan! He don't know what he's doing! I'm gutted!"

I don't recall us reacting like that at the Valley. It wasn't that we lacked respect, even awe. I remember my childish reverence for players like Eddie Firmani, John Hewie, Derek Ufton, Stuart Leary and the glorious Sam Bartram, whose statue now stands at the main entrance and who engaged the affections like no Charlton player before or since. And I remember, more vividly, a later generation; the side managed by Firmani. It was a team touched by eccentricity. Charlie Wright, the goalkeeper, was once the Hong Kong Footballer of the Year. A good friend of mine, he never let a goal in that was his own fault. I recall asking him why he had failed to keep out a scuffed penalty which bounced twice before crossing the line. He told me it had taken a deflection.

Ray Treacy was not only a distinguished Charlton striker, he was possibly the only player in the English League player to record a song which finished top of the Irish Hit Parade. While Matt Tees played the role of jostling, threatening, belligerently physical centre-forward, while weighing around 10 stones in his overcoat. Firmani was succeeded by Theo Foley, another friend and an outstanding manager. Long before managers began to rehearse their pitch-side poses, Theo's Dublin vowels could be heard bellowing above the crowd. I once saw him warned by the referee for abusive language. He was sitting in the directors' box at the time.

And his transfer dealings were inspired. He recognised the possibilities of fine players like Derek Hales, Mike Flanagan and Colin Powell, bought them for about a fiver and sold them for hundreds of thousands. As soon as they had finished counting their profits, the board sacked him. And so Charlton started to drift, scarcely registering on the radar.

Until the really bad times arrived, and something happened which would raise us above the ordinary.

First, we went broke. Being Charlton, there was an Ealing Comedy aspect to our poverty. The chairman Mark Hulyer – the same genius who had recruited Simonsen – at one stage offered the Revenue a deal which involved delaying payment until urgent funds were freed by the delivery of a quantity of rubber from Bangkok. Don't ask. Anyway, the judge ordered that Charlton Athletic be formally wound up. I remember looking in to see Lennie Lawrence, the bright new manager, on a Spring morning in 1984 in a cabin at the rear of the grandstand. There were padlocks on the gate and a crowd of mourners outside, awaiting the noon deadline which would signify extinction.

"Morning, Len." I said. "How's it going?"

How I well remember his answer. He said: "You taking the piss, Patrick?"

Lennie was one of our greatest stars. He was manager when oblivion was narrowly averted, and he was in charge when the new board closed down the Valley in September 1985 and moved the club to Selhurst Park, that singularly charmless football ground which stands in the shadow of a supermarket. Somehow, and despite the fact that everyone hated the new home, he won promotion to the old First Division. It was an extraordinary feat of management.

But even Lennie's contribution did not match that of the Charlton fans. That philosophically serene bunch, those people with low expectations and a love of the quiet life, they slowly and stirringly transformed themselves into revolutionaries. Within a few months of exile, they made it clear that they loved the old place more than they had ever admitted. They knew that if the club was to survive, then it had to return to the Valley, and they fought and schemed and marched and agitated to secure that objective. They took on everyone who stood in their way, from bone-headed directors to foot-dragging local councillors to the dreary legions of defeatists who told them their cause was hopeless. The petitions were effective, the poster campaigns quite brilliant.

But, as the years of exile slipped past, their most stunning coup was reserved for the local elections of 1990 in the London Borough of Greenwich. Fighting on a single-issue ticket of taking Charlton back home, the Valley Party stood in 60 of the 62 seats, received 10.9 per cent of the votes and trounced a stream of other parties, including the Lib Dems and the Greens. Two years later, they were back home. True, it was a greatly reduced home, with lots of scaffolding and temporary stands; not quite coats for goal posts, but certainly cabins for dressing rooms. But it was home and we were heart-thumpingly proud, and everything was possible.

Besides which, we had found a worthy successor to our Lennie. Alan Curbishley was always suspicious of notebooks, cameras and microphones. He answered questions the way English batsmen used to play Shane Warne. But he remained a considerable talent; a man who could prepare football teams and build football clubs. He stayed for 15 years, and some of us still curse the day he departed.

Curbishley enabled us to live above our means for season after improbable season. He made us believe, absurdly, that the Premier League was our natural home; that we who were used to counting the pennies belonged in the company of billionaires. But best of all, he gave us that Wembley occasion in 1998, the play-off final with Sunderland, and perhaps the most thrilling game ever played before the twin towers. They knighted Geoff Hurst for scoring a Wembley hat-trick which wasn't in the same league as the one that Clive Mendonca scored on that incomparable day.

It was after that success that people started to speak about "the Charlton way." It really was possible to hold down a place in the top stratum of English football through a combination of shrewd management, intelligent administration and supporters who played a full part in the general strategy of the club. Add to that a keen sense of social awareness and an eagerness to play a part in the community, and it was small wonder that Charlton were seen as an example of what the jargon calls "best practice."

In the face of all that admiration, the temptation was to become smug. Sadly, we succumbed. Curbishley left, the board at large took its eye off the ball, poor decisions were made and much of the good work of 15 years was undone by the relegation of 2007. I remember hearing one glib pundit argue that we were just too nice and that, as nice guys finish second, so nice football clubs eventually bite the dust. Nonsense, of course, since it implies that success belongs only to those who are feared and despised. But I can see where he was coming from. Charlton are the club who raised a statue to Sam, because he was a lovely bloke as well as being the best goalkeeper never to win an England cap. Charlton are the club who, for more than half a century, have been taking the field to the strains of the wonderfully soppy The Red, Red Robin played by Mr Billy Cotton and his Band.

And Charlton are the club who, on a whim, signed the former European Footballer of the Year; a man who could take a decent corner.

Like the old chap with the Capstan and the cough, I love them dearly. And I continue to hope for better days.

Patrick Collins has been chief sports writer of the Mail on Sunday since the paper was launched in 1982. Previously, he worked for London evening and national Sunday newspapers.

__Favourite player:__ Bobby Moore: style, grace, vision, intelligence and a sublime technique. Allied to a ruthlessly competitive spirit and an extraordinary ability to bring out the best in those around him.

__Most memorable match:__ Nothing comes close to that 1998 First Division play-off final, Charlton v Sunderland. Best match ever played at Wembley, and the happiest ending.

THE DAY DIEGO WAS DONE FOR DRUGS IN DALLAS

And gave me a World Cup scoop

By Gerry Cox

WHEN MOST people think of Dallas they think of JR Ewing, JFK and the grassy knoll – but I always remember being deep in the heart of Texas when the world's greatest footballer was kicked out of the World Cup for taking drugs.

There was no doubt that the diminutive Diego Maradona stood head and shoulders above the rest when it came to his ability with a ball, but his control was sadly lacking when it came to dealing with his inner demons, and nothing demonstrated it more starkly than his spectacular fall from grace in the summer of 1994. It was an astonishing story at the time, but that was then, albeit not that many years ago. Can you imagine what sort of coverage it would generate now, in the relentless world of 24-hour media, always-on sports TV stations and with the internet voraciously feeding off anything that moves?

In an age when dozens of camera crews and reporters are despatched around the world at the drop of a hat to broadcast 'live' whenever anything even slightly out of the ordinary in football happens, it is hard to imagine that the only representative of Fleet Street's daily newspapers at this momentous event was me, a relative newcomer to reporting. I had been working for national newspapers for only four years, initially for the famous Hayters agency and then with Teamwork, the agency I had set up with Nick Callow and Mark Irwin a year earlier. To get myself to the 1994 World Cup in the USA I had done a deal with the Daily Telegraph that guaranteed to cover my expenses. It was a package of matches that were mostly the runts of the litter – South Korea versus Saudi Arabia, for example. I would be based in Dallas, Texas, where the world's greatest sporting event was invisible to the naked eye. But one of the best lessons I learned under the tutelage of the great Dennis Signy was that the best stories originate from the least likely sources – and so it proved in Dallas.

As well as covering matches for the Telegraph I was attempting to freelance for other outlets to fill in the rest of my time and a yawning gap in income. Yet there had been little appetite for stories such as the Belgian team's secret weapon against the intense heat of Florida – reflective hair-gel. No, I needed strong stories, I needed a result or I was on the next flight home – much like Diego Armando Maradona.

Dirty Diego, as we knew him after giving England a good fisting in 1986, was in decline. Eight years earlier, just south of the border down Mexico way, he had effectively won the World Cup for Argentina single-handedly, but in the intervening years his fortunes had been up and down. Still a great player, he had come under competition as the best in the business from those such as our own troubled genius Gazza, whose reputation mushroomed at Italia 90 just as Maradona's was starting to fall apart. Diego was dogged by tales of high-living in Italy – women, drugs, the wrong 'friends'. It showed on the field, where his effectiveness waned as his explosiveness diminished, though his personality was no less combustible. So he arrived at USA 94 like a boxer who has taken one battering too many, but still capable of the killer blow to put him back on top of the world.

The signs of desperation were there, especially after an astonishing celebration –wild-eyed and straight-to-camera – after scoring in the Argentinians first group match against Greece. That picture of the tortured genius's face, close-up, contorted in equal measures of rage and relief, and spattered with mud and grass, remains an enduring image. We knew then that all was not right in the life of Diego Maradona.

It was barely a week later that his life really began to unravel, after the subsequent game against Nigeria. I was in the media centre by the Cotton Bowl, Dallas, on a quiet afternoon, researching a feature on fellow Argentina star Claudio Caniggia. Like Maradona, the striker had been suspended for cocaine use before returning to his national side. Back in those days, when the internet was still in short trousers and our American hosts' idea of useful media information consisted of a thicket's worth of meaningless stats on 'turnovers, steals and shutouts,' the only way to find out more about an overseas player was to talk to him or to people who knew him. The former was impossible and the latter was not easy, given that I spoke no Spanish and the Argentinian press did not exactly like the English after the Falklands War. So I spoke to a dozen or so journalists before I found one prepared to help. He had long hair, like many of the players, and was waiting for a training session with the squad ahead of the forthcoming game against Bulgaria. We started talking about Caniggia, and I was putting a piece together when there was suddenly a flurry of activity among the Argentinan press. You did not need to be a hard-nosed newshound to know that something was up, and the ripples spread across the rest of the international media – drugs was the word. Rumour and counter-rumour flew until a terse statement appeared on the official media wire – a player or players unknown had tested positively after the Argentina v Nigeria match.

Of course the word was immediately that Maradona and Caniggia were two of them. I got straight on the phone to London to see if the desks back home knew what was going on. One editor said the rumours were rife, but no-one would run with any names unless there was official confirmation. My challenge was to get an official prepared to name names on the record, and file it before the other agencies. I had no competition from the nationals – the only other English newspaperman there was Steve Stammers of the Evening Standard, whose paper would not hit the streets until mid-morning the next day. We went down to the terraces of the Cotton Bowl for the mid-afternoon training session, which was inevitably delayed. Even if we were to gain confirmation, because of the 6-hour time difference it would be close to deadline back home.

When the players finally arrived, we were surprised to see Maradona trooping out sheepishly on the pitch, but he sat against a goalpost looking disconsolate. We could not get near them – they still had tall fences at pitchside. So there was our man, 100 yards away and clearly not in the mood to talk. The Argentinian press were cagey with us, even my new friend with the long hair, but we were joined by Michael Robinson, the former Liverpool player who worked in Spanish TV and knew several of the squad. He said the word was that it was Maradona and he had taken ephedrine, a banned substance often found in cough medicine. "I can't believe they are going to hang him out to dry for that," said Garth Crooks, who was working for BBC Radio. Really, Garth?

Eventually the players mooched back to the end of the pitch, and the hundreds of reporters caged behind bars started baying at them like animals. No response as they all walked off, and with them went our hopes of getting a story. But then, clearly having had second thoughts, a figure in a blazer re-emerged and came straight towards us. It was Julio Grondona, not only the head of the AFA, but also a vice-president of FIFA – as good a source as you could get. Everyone started firing questions at him, some reporters hanging from the fencing, and you did not have to speak Spanish to understand when he said the words "Si" and "Diego". I had not let go of my long-haired friend and got him to translate quickly before he rushed off to file his own story. "Yes it is Diego, the drug was ephedrine. It is a tragedy for Maradona, and he will be going home tomorrow." That was all I needed – apart from a phone.

By now it was almost midnight back home, normal deadlines had passed but I had rung round the desks earlier and they had all said file whatever I got, at whatever time. Of course there were few transatlantic mobiles back then, and to get a phone in the media centre would have involved a re-enactment of Goose Green, but I knew there was a payphone deep in the bowels of the stadium and got there as quickly as I could. Ten calls, a lot of dimes and an hour later, having dictated copy on the spot, in some cases straight to news desks, I was done.

I drove home, exhilarated that I had got the biggest scoop I could have wished for, and stopped at a diner to ring my wife. Her response put me in my place: "You wake me up at two in the morning to tell me that –what's the big deal?"

The next day showed what it was about – back page lead on just about every national paper, and on the front pages of most, too. The subsequent press conference in Dallas that day was mobbed, every newspaper sent anyone within flying distance, and I could barely get in the door. No-one needed my services that day, and we hardly made a mint from what had been a major scoop by any standards. But I had done enough to get the story out, helped put Teamwork on the map, and my career was in the ascendant – in start contrast to Maradona's.

Sent home in disgrace, it was the beginning of a very sad and rapid decline that is not over yet for Diego Armando Maradona. It was difficult to sympathise with him at the time, given his history with England, and it is always hard to feel sorry for drugs cheats. The day they are allowed to get away with their offences is the day we have to stop loving sport and begin telling our children to steer clear.

But sometimes you have to understand what drives great sportsmen to desperate measures. If there had been a drug that could prevent brain damage in boxers, who would have castigated, say, Muhammed Ali if he had taken it in his latter fights, knowing what we know now? Whatever we have thought of Maradona over the years – boy wonder, genius, cheat, lunatic – the overwhelming sense now is of sadness and pity for the decline that began on that day in in Dallas. And I was there to tell the story.

Gerry Cox was Chairman of the FWA from 2002 to 2005. He started his career at Hayters before co-founding Teamwork Sports Agency in 1993. He returned to Hayters in 2003 as chief executive. He has written for most national newspapers in the UK, particularly the Observer and Daily Telegraph and has over a dozen books to his name.

__Favourite player:__ Jimmy Greaves. Greavesie was my first football hero and is still my favourite player of all time – skill, speed, a smile on his face and goals in his boots.

__Most memorable match:__ The 1981 FA Cup final replay, Spurs 3 Manchester City 2. Ricky Villa's winning goal has a special place in the heart of every Spurs fan who was at Wembley that night.

RUTHLESS, PASSIONATE, DEDICATED, UNCOMPROMISING AND LOYAL

Fergie is an impossible act to follow

By Steve Curry

AGE has not withered Sir Alexander Chapman Ferguson CBE, nor has custom staled his infinite variety as he pursues his passion to become the greatest British manager in football history.

Arguably he already is.

With apologies to William Shakespeare's description of Cleopatra, there is no sign yet that the man universally known as Fergie is about to abdicate his own throne while 76,000 fans regularly worship at his feet, or more precisely at the feet of the teams he creates. Now well into his third decade at Old Trafford the man from the Govan shipyards has used his acute brain to create teams with a good deal more grace than the oil tankers his father helped to build in Glasgow. He chases his goals with a Machiavellian zeal, understanding fully the intrigue and deceit in the game. To his fellow members of the League Managers' Association committee, to every player moving into management he is a Godfather figure, dispensing wisdom and warnings to an increasing number of colleagues, one of whom might someday replace him.

Sometimes those who ring him don't always like the advice they are given but the one thing he commands from the up and coming is a huge respect. One of those managers to have sought his advice is Birmingham's Alex McLeish and he claims that Fergie has made and broken the careers of many young men in the profession because of his frankness on their suitability for a job.

Willing ears will be advised that the qualities he believes make the best coaches are observation, perseverance, imagination and communication (the latter with the players rather than the media) but for him the most important of these is observation.

He believes that to coach and watch at the same time is difficult; that if you are coaching alone, you miss other things. This is why at United he has always employed a strong assistant and why you rarely see him scribbling on bits of paper. It is about delegation.

Those who aspire to become his successor at the Theatre Of Dreams have an impossible act to follow. No manager has had greater control over his club and his team, not even Brian Clough. Fergie is perhaps the last of the managerial generation for whom hands-on means what it says.

Yet whoever is destined to take over may have to wait. In an occupation where longevity doesn't enter the vocabulary, he has proved the antidote to any discussion of an ageing society. His decision to do a U-turn on his initial retirement plan in 2002 was met with scepticism by those who felt he had run his term. But subsequent events have proved he made a sound decision, that reaching the pensionable age of 65 need not be a time to take to slippers.

Like most driven men, he doesn't need to work. His near £4 million salary, his carefully selected endorsements have enabled him to build a fortune estimated at £30 million, the kind of sum not to be hugely disturbed by his love of a flutter on the horses. It is a matter of record rather than rumour that he would get his then young winger Keith Gillespie to run his bets to a nearby bookmaker. What continues to motivate Ferguson is a desire to add the catalogue of successes by creating a side that he can bequeath to a successor he will no doubt have a hand in appointing.

Ferguson, 67 on New Year's Eve, 2008, continues to have a work ethic that would exhaust a younger man. He is regularly the first to arrive at fortress Carrington, the club's state-of-the-art training headquarters. He is happy in that environment, where his sergeant-major style dressings-down can be handed out to his millionaire players without a prying lens or a journalist's notebook. That is his power base, where his unremitting will to win is conveyed to his players. Just a few of his outbursts have filtered through for public discussion. Famously at Aberdeen, his last port of call before moving south, he flung a pair of sweaty underpants across the dressing room where they handed on a young player's head. The youngster sat like a statue, so frightened, he didn't dare remove them.

And when David Beckham emerged with a cut above his eye, inflicted by a flying football boot Fergie had kicked, stories emerged from his former charges of flying teacups and nose-to-nose confrontations which have entered football folklore as the 'hairdryer treatment'.

These have usually been conducted in the privacy of the dressing room but more public displays of Fergie's invective have occurred for all to see, invariably against a journalist or commentator who has written or said something to offend him. Even those who have enjoyed a cordial relationship with him are not spared. I can vouch for that having been subjected a blast from the hairdryer at a Football Writers' Association Gala Tribute Night function at the Savoy Hotel for daring to debate during a television discussion whether the time might have come for him to consider retirement.

I was lucky. Two days later I took a call from him apologising for the outburst. Others, notably the BBC and for a period my own employers the Daily Mail, have had much lengthier periods of isolation. At the time of writing the BBC remain on his banned list.

He has, too, a penchant for goading those managers whose teams are set to play United in vital matches and you can be sure that Arsene Wenger and Rafa Benitez are not on his Christmas card list.

With 10 Premiership titles, four FA Cups, two League Cups and two European Champions trophies to his name as 2008/09 began, he is almost irreplaceable. And though no-one is bigger than their club, he must come very close.

Four years after Fergie took over as manager in 1986, and before the glut of trophies began pouring in, United might have been sold for a mere £20 million. He has made them football's most valuable franchise. When chief executive David Gill finally has to come to terms with finding a replacement – and Fergie maintains it will not be until he has reached 70 – then who knows who might have emerged as a potential successor?

You can be sure the Baron of Old Trafford will be invited to have his say and both he and influential director Bobby Charlton will be involved in the consultancy process. Bear in mind that it took United five managers and a dip in fortune to replace Sir Matt Busby. Immediate replacement Wilf McGuinness lost his head of hair during the brief period he held sway with Sir Matt 'upstairs' as general manager. Then Frank O'Farrell, Tommy Docherty, Dave Sexton and Ron Atkinson all had their turn.

Though it is claimed that the club had sounded out England manager Sven Goran Eriksson before Ferguson changed his mind about calling it a day, the preference might be in four year's time for another British boss. If they continue to impress then David Moyes at Everton, Martin O'Neill at Aston Villa or one of their own, Steve Bruce may have the right credentials by then, but then you cannot discount Fergie's former right-hand man Carlos Queiroz from the reckoning. It will have to be a man who can identify with the United fan base, stretched as it is across the globe. Though Ferguson may be difficult with the press, who on the whole he has little time for, he does communicate with the supporters and, of course, as a winner they love him.

Fergie has long claimed that you need to have a special temperament to be a United player. But the same applies equally to the manager. Fergie IS United at the present time and though he and the club's bosses are like a battle-weary married couple they depend on each other.

Now he has assembled a new generation of Ronaldo, Tevez, Nani, Anderson and Rooney, most of who were not even born when Fergie joined United. It has been an exceptional journey but it is those self same players who keep him young.

Ruthless, Passionate, Dedicated, Uncompromising, Loyal. These are the Ferguson qualities that must be found in his successor; a man who can handle the very best players yet treat them equally. He won the respect and loyalty of giants of the game, Bryan Robson, Roy Keane, Peter Schmeichel. The list is endless.

Fergie always claims that the football pitch is the judgement place for every one. But that is not quite true. The training ground and the dressing room have been Ferguson's places of valuation and evaluation. They are still a drug to him, so for the time being forget about retirement.

A former chairman of the FWA, Steve Curry was chief football writer of the Daily Express for 20 years. In 1996, after briefly working for the Sunday Times, he joined the Sunday Telegraph before joining the staff of the Daily Mail, where he still works.

   Favourite player: *Pele. It was a privilege watching him.*

   Most memorable match: *The 1966 World Cup Final which he covered from the press box*

RONALDO IS A UNIQUE TALENT

But CR7 must prove himself over again

By Neil Custis

CRISTIANO RONALDO had established himself in the pantheon of greats at Manchester United.

Even the man who currently holds that unofficial title, Sir Bobby Charlton, admitted it.

Charlton still watches United games as an avid fan and director of the club. He used to sit back relaxed with his elegant fedora on. Last season he would ease himself to the edge of his seat watching wide eyed as the young Portuguese star electrified stadiums.

For Charlton it brought back images of the late, lamented George Best with whom he won the European Cup in 1968. Charlton said: "Cristiano is a marvellous player. He is one of those players who draws you to the edge of your seat. Cristiano does things with a football that I have not seen.

"Sometimes he has been over-ambitious. When he first came over he just seemed to want to show people how many tricks he could do - and that was a little embarrassing sometimes. Now he is getting better than we ever imagined. Ronaldo is a unique talent. He can be remembered here as one of the best."

As Ronaldo collected his second successive Footballer of the Year trophy in May, 2008, to suggest that he could be booed by the Old Trafford faithful who had elevated him to icon status after a 40-goal season the following campaign would have been farcical. Unthinkable.

Yet a summer of growing discontent as Ronaldo pressed the self-destruct with a stream of quotes saying he wanted to join Real Madrid proved that while it takes time to become a hero, becoming a villain can be fast-tracked. And whether Ronaldo can even become a true United great must now be in serious doubt - just weeks after such a status had seemed inevitable.

United fans, particularly, will never understand how a player at his peak (and Ronaldo has probably not reached his best yet) could want to leave Old Trafford.

From there the only way is down, to second-best yourself. How can you do better than the Champions of the most popular league in the world who a few weeks earlier won their second European crown under Sir Alex Ferguson? Even the most successful club in European history cannot currently compete with United. Real are the past, United the present.

Old Trafford's stance was immovable. Ronaldo was going nowhere. His ankle injury compounded an already complicated situation while Sepp Blatter came out with his ridiculous "slave" quote that will be a tattoo for life on the FIFA president who rarely wastes a chance to make a fool of himself.

If Blatter will always be remembered for his summer attack of foot-in-the-mouth disease, has Ronaldo lost the chance to become the greatest Red of all?

Eventually, belatedly he ate some humble pie saying he was staying with United for at least this season. Hardly a statement of commitment. And when he said he was staying he had no say in the matter. He was under contract to United who had no intention of becoming involved in any Real deal.

As public relations campaigns go the summer of 2008 for Ronaldo made Gerald Ratner's public statements seem shrewd. CR and PR don't go hand-in-hand.

Ronaldo will have to win the United fans over again which will not be easy but in football time, goals and silverware have proved to be great healers. When Steven Gerrard was on the verge of joining Chelsea a few years ago they were burning effigies of him on Merseyside.

However the Ronaldo cards ultimately fall, in terms of skill, technique, movement and magic he remains a player made for the venue dubbed by Sir Bobby as the Theatre of Dreams.

He houses all the ingredients that make a Manchester United player though he should let his feet rather than his mouth do his talking. He has a star quality and a lust for the ball that is unquenchable.

When he first arrived as a gangly teen in 2003 he was a one-trick pony that had some raising doubts about his true effectiveness. It's alright doing three stepovers but no good if the end product is not there.

But as with so many raw recruits Sir Alex Ferguson used the best of Ronaldo and moulded him into the superstar player he became. He used to fall over too easily and complain at a sense of injustice faced with hatchet men on the opposition who wanted to dull his colourful play. Some may say that is still the case but his critics would probably also admit that he has become a warrior who will not be defeated on the field of battle no matter what comes his way.

The last thing Ferguson wanted to do was eradicate the thrills and spills from his game which make watching Ronaldo worth the entrance money on its own.

As United won their 10th Premier League title in 2007/08 Ferguson said: "As far as I am concerned he can carry on doing what he does. He's a winner. Opponents can't kick him out of the game because he will always get up and play.

Ronaldo is a player who wants to express his talent, which is why people are prepared to pay £40 to £50 to watch him play.

"We encourage him to do that, we encourage it of all our players. It's an expression of play, of having confidence in the way you play. In this modern day it's a breath of fresh air to see players with expression in their game, and Ronaldo won't be intimidated by opponents who want him to stop doing that. We don't encourage our players to humiliate opponents. But fans want to see players like Ronaldo who are prepared to show talent.

"I think it's great that a player like Ronaldo is able to develop his game to such an extent that he's prepared to try all these tricks and skills in big games."

In 2007, Ferguson paid Ronaldo the highest accolade, one that certainly did not weigh heavily on his shoulders. Ferguson claimed that at Ronaldo's age he had "... the same skill factor as Maradona and Pele. He is one of the best signings I have ever made."

Ronaldo has improved with each season he has been at Old Trafford. Ferguson used to have bets with him about how many goals he would score. First he challenged him to 15, then 20. It was as well in 2007/08 that Ferguson decided all bets were off, because he knew he was on a loser. Ronaldo was a cert to meet any challenge the manager gave him and thus he crashed through the 40 goal barrier.

A good-looking lad, Ronaldo has won his share of headlines in the front of newspapers for his wooing of a string of beauties (not just in Los Angeles as he recovered from his ankle operation) but football for him has always come first. A teetotaller, despite some recent claims, he looks after himself and when out in Manchester he is a retiring figure who prefers a meal with friends than a wild night out.

The strength of his character has seen him overcome many hurdles. The death of his father, an unfounded rape allegation and then the bust-up with Wayne Rooney in the last World Cup that lead to the England player's sending-off. Ronaldo has shown great strength of character to bounce back. Many fans continued to boo but even they had a grudging respect for how he plays the game.

Ronaldo admitted: "I'm used to the booing. Last season I was booed in all the stadiums in England. The booing doesn't kill me."

Far from being at odds with Rooney the pair remain strong friends. Their link up play on the pitch is almost telepathic. Ronaldo said: "With Wayne Rooney, everything's going well. Despite what happened between us in the past there are no problems or worries between us. He has his own personality, his own style and has much to learn. And like me, he has chosen the ideal club to progress with and to lead a solid career."

Ronaldo has become a student of United history watching black and white pictures of George Best. He also relives the 1999 Champions League final triumph on the club's own TV station when David Beckham drove the team to victory.

Ronaldo adopted the famous number seven shirt worn by both those afore-mentioned players and in terms of skill he is a worthy successor.

The nightmare summer of 2008 has knocked Ronaldo back in the Old Trafford popularity stakes. If 2008/09 proves to be his last as a United player we can at least marvel at a winger who in full flow is to watch a sportsman at his very best.

He is an Ingemar Stenmark swerving between the slalom rods.

A Carl Lewis bursting from a standing start with breathtaking speed.

Michael Jordan leaping to the air with power and great athleticism as Ronaldo did with that astonishing header in Rome this season.

Shane Warne would do tricks with a ball never seen before in the spinner's art. Ronaldo makes the larger spherical object move in ways we have not seen.

Witness his incredible free-kick at Old Trafford against Portsmouth which went up and down over the wall with incredible pace.

He has a huge house in Alderley Edge but how long he will live there remains to be seen. For purely footballing reasons United should keep him as long as possible.

Golf coach Butch Harman once commented that fans of the sport should be truly grateful to be alive in the era of his former pupil Tiger Woods.

The same can be said of Ronaldo and football. His talent is unquestionable but we shall have to see how the fallout from his ill-advised public desire to go to Madrid affects the way he is remembered in Manchester.

Neil Custis has been a football reporter for the Sun since 1993. After starting in London and moving to the Midlands he took over as their Manchester United correspondent in 1999.

Favourite player: Roy Keane. The greatest midfielder of all time. His performance against Holland at Lansdowne Road to help Ireland into the World Cup play-offs in 2001 was stunning. His early tackle on Marc Overmars shook the ground.

Favourite game: Manchester United v Bayern Munich (Champions League final 1999) Bizarrely people forget that the actual 90 minutes were pretty dull. But stoppage time made up for that. The most thrilling finish in a big game ever in the most beautiful stadium in the world. I still get goosebumps thinking about it and I'm a Newcastle fan!

RIO HAS TURNED OUT GRAND

Free speaker is now centre stage at the Theatre of Dreams

By Shaun Custis

RIO FERDINAND – just mention the name a couple of years ago and hackles would start rising around the country. You could almost feel it. What's he done now? Can't stand that bloke. Thinks he's great him.

This was one of England's most naturally gifted footballers of the last 25 years, a gazelle of a player who would be a starter at any of Europe's major clubs. Were he a Brazilian – as he ought to be with a name like that – he would be their centre-back, no arguments. But he was ours. How lucky was that? We were blessed to have such a talent yet there were few English sportsmen who polarised opinions so starkly.

Even at his own club, Manchester United, the love for Rio was a slow burner. Having been bought for £30m from bitter rivals Leeds he was already on the back foot. He had to be twice as good as he actually was just to earn grudging acceptance. United won the title in Rio's first season but being his own harshest critic he honestly admitted he had not pulled up any trees. The following campaign, United were top at Christmas, but then Rio was famously banned for missing a drugs test and Arsenal's "invincibles" went on to claim the title. The fans were not happy and Rio bore a chunk of the criticism. When he later took too long to sign a new contract at Old Trafford, he was branded ungrateful after the club had stood by him in his darkest hour. He got it big style from all angles.

Only in 2007/08 did Rio win the United fans over as he ended an unforgettable season by captaining the team to Champions League victory over Chelsea 10 days after pipping them to the Premier League title. Before then he was probably more popular at his first professional club, West Ham, than at the Theatre of Dreams. The same old stuff was trotted out time and again. Flash Cockney, arrogant, selfish and plenty of other unprintable labels. For years Rio was perceived as the stereotypical modern day footballer with too much money, too little sense and a detachment from real life. The accusations were levelled at him largely by those who barely knew him and it drove Rio mad.

When Ferdinand penned his autobiography Rio: My Story he was slaughtered for daring to have a point of view of his own which didn't tally with that of his critics. He spoke out against what he felt was an injustice by the FA in banning him for eight months for missing the drugs test. Ferdinand felt victimised because there were no strict regulations for taking the test and his excuse that he forgot to take it was not believed. He fought to prove his innocence, including a test on his hair follicles which is clinically accepted as evidence of whether or not someone has been a drug user in the previous six months. He passed but it was to no avail. Although the tribunal which banned Rio clearly acknowledged in its official statement that he had not taken drugs, that was glossed over by his detractors. So too was the fact there were precedents which the FA had set for missed tests including one for Manchester City player Christian Negouai, who was given a £2,000 fine and a slap on the wrist for the very same offence. Rio felt there were those determined to make an example of him, who believed he was the epitome of football gone wrong. FA chief executive Mark Palios seemed to want his head on a plate.

The England players almost went on strike to support Ferdinand with the cause led by United skipper Gary Neville. It was Ferdinand who actually told them not to strike but nobody cared about that either. And when Rio exercised his right to free speech he was hammered for doing so by our free Press. Veteran football observers like Scotsman Patrick Barclay slammed Ferdinand for defending himself in his book while later admitting he had never read it. "It irritates to no purpose," he argued. How did he know? Barclay once taped over the Three Lions badge when he turned out as a guest for the England Press team – a good indication that he was never going to play fair with an England footballer. Then there was Rod Liddle, who wrote a page in the Sunday Times systematically ripping Ferdinand apart then brazenly confessing in the very same piece that he would rather "read my own death certificate" than Rio's side of the story. This was a former editor of Radio 4's Today programme, who vehemently defended a reporter he hired named Andrew Gilligan over the story that the dossier on Iraq's weapons of mass destruction was 'sexed up'. Liddle argued that Gilligan always checked his facts and his integrity should not be in question. Yet here he was destroying Ferdinand and unashamedly admitting he could not be bothered to read his defence. No wonder Ferdinand felt he was badly treated.

Rio has been a daft lad in his time. He is not unfamiliar with the front pages of the tabloids, but the other side of Rio is one which is not heard as much as it should be. And that is because Ferdinand refuses to blow his own trumpet.

Much of his life away from the football field has been spent helping others less fortunate than himself. He grew up on a tough council estate in Peckham but made the best of it with the help of loving parents, good friends and local youth leaders who were always there for him. Rio knows better than most that kids need encouragement to turn their lives around. His ambition is to establish youth centres around the country for youngsters from all walks of life. His Live the Dream Foundation is an initiative he is working on with the Government to help children discover a career path by giving them practical training in a range of activities. He sought help from previous Prime Minister Tony Blair to get the project off the ground and it has been taken on by Gordon Brown.

Ferdinand also co-founded White Chalk Music giving aspiring musicians a chance to sing professionally then organised a talent contest in Manchester with the prize of a recording contract. He has campaigned for justice in the cases of murdered schoolboys Stephen Lawrence and Damilola Taylor. Teenager Stephen went to Rio's school while 10 year-old Damilola was stabbed on an estate near where he used to live. He has become an active campaigner against knife crime, following a spate of murders around the capital and has been urging kids to hand in their weapons and understand there is another way in life. Rio knows what makes these disaffected youngsters tick and what can be done to get them on the straight and narrow. Rio does not just play at it, he gets out there into communities preaching the gospel. He does not expect thanks, he does it because he believes in it. The close friends Rio grew up with on the Friary Estate are still his mates today. He has never forgotten his roots and he keeps in touch with what is happening on the streets.

Football gave Rio a way out for which he will always be grateful. Never a day goes by when he does not realise how lucky he is. As a 15-year-old at West Ham he feared he might never become a pro footballer. A sudden growth spurt led to a loss of co-ordination to the point where he could barely run without falling over. Banished to the sidelines as a sub in the youth team he feared West Ham would dump him. But the Hammers kept faith and it all came right in the end.

Rio's playing style makes it seem like the game comes easy to him. But he has worked hard to get where he is today. There are some footballers who play for money without truly loving the game but Rio is obsessed by it. He was captivated from the moment he watched the 1986 World Cup on TV and would run round the grass on his estate, his mini-Wembley, trying to emulate the great players.

At home he has a wall covered with shirts of the artists of the game. He can spot talent too. When a youthful Cristiano Ronaldo played against him in a pre-season friendly he begged Sir Alex Ferguson to sign the Portuguese wizard for United. Ferdinand had been mesmerised by him and now he gets to play in the same team. He would secretly admit he would love to have been a player like Ronaldo.

Rio's doing alright, though. The proudest night of his career was when he led England out as captain in Paris. The day before the match he addressed the media resplendent in suit and tie. The last time many of us had seen him in such attire was when he turned up at his FA appeal hearing to have his ban for the missed drug test confirmed.

Captaining his country was a moment he had always dreamed of but one he feared would never happen when he was banned and vilified. Pulling on the armband made Rio's rehabilitation complete but as he often says: "No matter what I do some people will always have it in for me." That may be true, but the Society of Rio Haters no longer has to book the Royal Albert Hall for its meetings – a phone box will suffice.

Shaun Custis is the chief football writer of the Sun. He is also a former sports editor of the Daily Express

Favourite player: *Malcolm Macdonald – a barnstorming centre-forward with pace and power who scared the living daylights out of opposing defenders. A knee injury prevented his career reaching the heights it deserved.*

Most memorable match: *Germany 1 England 5 – a 2002 World Cup qualifying result no-one could have predicted. Michael Owen netted a hat-trick on a night everything went right for manager Sven-Goran Eriksson. Even Heskey scored.*

SHIRT HAPPENS

Almost as much preparation goes into goal celebrations as scoring

By Christopher Davies

"IT DOESN'T matter who scores as long as the team wins" – a popular statement made by players before a game.

If that is the case why are so many goalscoring celebrations an exhibition in self-indulgence? Surely if it was all about the team the scorer would immediately join his team-mates to receive their appreciation?

Gerard Houllier told his Liverpool players: "When you score, run to the player who laid on the goal." An admirable instruction, but one which now seems as dated as Brylcreem.

What do we see instead? Visiting players cupping an ear with a hand or putting a finger over their mouth to the home supporters. That should bring an immediate yellow card for unsporting behaviour which is likely to incite the crowd. The scorer's sarcasm-heavy message is obvious and, rather than show joy after scoring, he is celebrating in a negative manner. And it is so, so unoriginal, like a V-sign or a hand shuffling a dice response from another driver after you have pointed out you have just been cut up big time.

Wow – a cupped ear. How did you think that one up? If goalscoring is the ultimate aim of football why celebrate it by baiting opposing fans? Supporters of teams who have just scored throw their arms in the air, pump their fists and hug each other when the ball goes in the net. The guy who put it there is more likely to have some unoriginal routine rehearsed and ready for public consumption.

It is difficult to pinpoint when goal celebrations changed from handshakes and hugs to choreographed dances or gynmastic acts. In 1979 Arsenal's Sammy Nelson was suspended for two weeks by his club and fined two weeks' wages for lowering his shorts in front of the crowd after equalising in the 1-1 draw against Coventry at Highbury. Nelson's bum rap came after he had been barracked by the crowd for scoring a first-half own-goal. But that was something of a one-off.

We have now reached the point where goal celebrations are rehearsed almost as much as the moves that led to scoring. When we talk about "a triumph for the training ground" it means not just the way the goal was executed as the equally precise nature of the celebration.

The 1994 World Cup was probably the tournament when team-mates mobbing a goalscorer was not enough. Julies Aghahowa of Nigeria performed a magnificent seven back-flips at USA 94 after scoring his country's first-ever World Cup finals goal. Lomana LuaLua and Obafemi Martins have made it a Premier League art form even if LuaLua was injured performing his speciality for Portsmouth and missed five games.

Rocking the baby has since become cringe-worthy but maybe, just maybe, the first time we saw the celebration it was fun. This was started by Brazil striker Bebeto at USA 94 when he scored against Holland and was joined by Romario and others. Perhaps the first guy to wear a baseball cap the wrong way round looked good, too.

The baby routine reached rocking-bottom when Manchester United's Carlos Tevez took it one step further and put a dummy in his mouth to celebrate his daughter's birth. Dummy and dumber. He looked like any adult with a dummy in his mouth would – ridiculous. He continued the dummy run, presumably oblivious or uncaring about how a grown man with a dummy in his mouth looked.

Another first that was fun was Roger Milla's samba by the corner flag after scoring for Cameroon against Colombia at USA 94. Trouble is, there have been more imitations of this theme than Sepp Blatter has had bad ideas. It was also in the USA that Diego Maradona ran like a madman at the television camera after scoring against Greece. So much for The Verve saying the drugs don't work.

The Aylesbury United team, nicknamed the Ducks, must have had Soccer AM in mind as they went down on their knees, waddling in a line, with their elbows flapping after an FA Cup goal. Sadly Peter Crouch will probably be remembered more for his 2006 Robo-crouch celebration than any of the goals he scores.

There are some celebrations that question the sanity of the scorer. When Cuauhtemoc Blanco was with Mexican club America, he once took off his boots and matador-style used them as swords, thrusting them in the back of a team-mate on all fours playing the part of the bull. As you do.

Some are individual and inoffensive. Raul of Real Madrid kisses the ring finger of his right hand to salute his wife while AC Milan's Kaka, a devout Christian, raises his arms to the sky to thank God. Jurgen Klinsmann's famous diving celebration after his first goal for Tottenham was a brilliant self-parody after the constant jibing about his propensity to hit the deck too easily, but the bad and ugly tend to outweigh the good.

Robbie Fowler was fined £60,000 for getting down on all fours after scoring for Liverpool against Everton and pretending to snort a touchline of cocaine. We can only hope manager Gerard Houllier's claim that the striker was imitating "a cow eating grass" was tongue in cheek. Mike Channon's windmill celebration or the raised arm of Denis Law (finger pointing up) and Alan Shearer (flat hand) would be considered naff by today's goal artistes. Such celebrations are not seen in other sports. It is hard to imagine Brett Lee producing a dummy after claiming a Pommie wicket or Phil Vickery urging his team-mates to join him in a Twickenham tango.

It is surprising managers don't ban their players from sliding along the turf on their knees to celebrate. The risk to ligaments and cartilages performing this must be high. On the other hand, when Thierry Henry scored for Arsenal he often had the expression of a guy who had just realised he'd lost his lottery winning ticket. As Arsenal fans were delirious the downbeat Frenchman would show the passion of an undertaker.

The most brainless celebration is surely the removal of the jersey which is a mandatory yellow card offence. Professionals earning more in a week than most make in a year know the punishment yet they STILL do a half monty.

Like speeding restrictions, it doesn't matter whether we agree with the ruling – it's in place and everyone should know the consequences. Against England in March 2008 Franck Ribery had made a T-shirt with a personal message – in effect going into the game knowing he would be cautioned if he scored. And players tell us we don't know the game because we haven't played it. A yellow card for shirt removal in the 20th minute means a mistimed tackle in the rest of the game means a dismissal. I refuse to believe it is a natural, spontaneous act after scoring. More natural is to run to the guy who laid on the goal and celebrate with team-mates rather than going topless.

The powers-that-be made it a mandatory caution to (a) stop secondary advertising on the undershirt (Nike swoosh etc) and, (b) as football is a global game, a bare chest is offensive for religious reasons in some countries. Yet still the jersey is whipped off. If clubs don't fine the strippers they are condoning the illegal celebration. A manager who is unhappy a player was subsequently sent-off for a second yellow card offence should have left his team in no doubt that taking off the jersey after scoring would not be tolerated.

That's that off my, er ... chest.

Some may argue that celebrations are part-and-parcel of football, they are harmless and what fans love to see. Some are not harmless, they are designed to incite while others have become repetitive and unoriginal.

The best, most memorable and spontaneous goal celebration was by Italian midfielder Marco Tardelli after he scored Italy's second goal against West Germany in the 1982 World Cup final. No player has equalled Tardelli's outpouring of happiness as he sprinted away, fists pumping and beating against his chest, tears pouring down his face and screaming his name. As an exhibition of sheer joy and happiness it gets no better than this.

"The emotions inside me were like a volcano exploding," said Tardelli.

If you get the chance watch his celebration on YouTube and compare it with the premeditated, farcical dances or what have you players now perform for television cameras, you'll see. It's no contest.

Christopher Davies was sports correspondent of the Daily Telegraph for 20 years before joining the freelance ranks in 2006. He has also written for Shoot, the Daily Star, the People, Sunday Mirror, Observer, Sports Illustrated and Japan Times.

Favourite player of all-time: *George Best . He had every skill a world-class player needs and more.*

Most memorable match: *World Cup Final Italy 0 Brazil 0, USA 94. Brazil won on penalties. The first World Cup final I covered for the Daily Telegraph. A dream as a young lad growing up in south-east London.*

THE WRITER IN THE BLACK

I am thanked more often than I am sworn at

By Mick Dennis

YES, I am the w****r in the black. I referee kids' football matches, and I know you'll have two questions. So let me answer them.

Firstly, yes, my parents were married.

Secondly, why on earth do I do it? Well, someone asked me that a couple of years ago, halfway through a game which was only just the legal side of open warfare, and I gave a revelatory response. It was an end of season fixture between two teams of 18 year-olds who were fighting for the league title, and I do mean fighting. The natural, macho bravado of young men of that age was heightened by the occasion and by the presence of pumped-up parents and two rival gaggles of girlfriends. I didn't have a good first half. The intensity of the tackling took me by surprise. Some of the challenges were assaults, but I let too much go early on, and by the time I had raised the tempo of my own refereeing to match the fervour of the players, it was a real challenge to impose any semblance of order.

At half-time, I jogged over to the sideline, where my kitbag sat on its own, away from the knots of spectators. I had a quick slurp from a bottle of water and tried not to relax too much, because I knew I would need to be up to speed from the moment I signalled the start of the second half. A grey-haired bloke with fewer tattoos than most of the other adults wandered over to me. From his age I presumed he was granddad to one of the testosterone-fuelled young warriors in the teams. I braced myself for a volley of insults. Instead, granddad shook his head and said: "Why do you give up your time for this? It's murder out there, isn't it? Terrible. And they'll all be causing mayhem in the town centre later tonight."

Without thinking, I replied: "No. I don't think they will. I think they're getting it out of their system here."

The second half finished without any serious crimes and the game was won by a spectacular goal – a darting run and a good, deep cross from a lad on the right and a leaping, thumping header at the back post. I drove home, emailed reports of six yellow cards to my local FA, had a long, slow bath and reflected on what I'd said to granddad. I thought then, and believe profoundly now, that unwittingly I had hit upon a truth. At its worst, football for kids is a catharsis for them (and for their parents). It channels their frustrations and aggressions into sport. That, in itself, is a significantly good thing. But most of the time it is much more than that; much better. Most games are not exercises in savagery. Most of the time, it is just football, with all the good and all the enjoyment that involves – two sets of players straining and striving, yet often managing to produce moments of real skill. It is beneficial exercise, it provides lessons about team-work and about dealing with success and failure. And, if the ref is as useless as I am, kids' football teaches the participants that life is not always fair.

Despite all the publicity about abusive players and parents, there is not as much of that as you might imagine. I am thanked more often than I am sworn at. I referee most weekends during the season and can count the matches in which there is an unacceptable level of "commentary" from the sideline or from players on the fingers of one hand – although it is true that, from time to time, the fingers of hands are raised towards me.

Of course the Football Association should work to improve the behaviour of players and spectators at grassroots matches and, yes, there is a critical shortage of mugs like me who give up a couple of hours to referee. But every weekend in our country there are thousands and thousands of matches which take place without a hint of trouble.

The numbers are impressive. There are 40,000 clubs in this country below the level of the professional leagues, more than 9,000 of which are clubs exclusively for youths. Many clubs run up to 20 kids' sides. All that amateur football is sustained by an army of more than half a million regular volunteers, including about 27,000 qualified referees.

All of us who love football know that the game can lift the soul sometimes and when two teams of good players contest a high-calibre match then it is enormously rewarding for the bloke (or woman) who has helped make that possible – the referee. To meet the physical and mental challenge and facilitate a proper game of football is very worthwhile. It is a catharsis for the referee as well. For the duration of the match, he or she cannot think about anything else. Professional or personal anxieties have to be locked away in another bit of the brain for a while.

I became involved because of a commonly held, but entirely erroneous, opinion. When I turned up to watch my own sons playing football when they were very young, I was often asked to help out by referring. People assumed that, because I was a football journalist, I knew the laws of the game. Hah! After a few months of wrecking decent jeans and trainers (and ruining the matches, probably) I started turning up in tracksuit bottoms and took my boots. But the parents of the opposing team knew I wasn't a qualified ref and frequently gave me a hard time. So I decided to do things properly and take the referees' course.

That was when I realised that, despite having been a sports journalist for 18 years at that time, I did NOT know the laws. I'd played football for decades, coached teams and worked as a football writer for national newspapers. But I did not know the laws properly. Football is basically a simple game, so I'd just picked up the rudiments of the laws as a young kid from listening to adults. As the years had passed, I'd absorbed all the myths and misunderstandings which I now know are commonplace.

Anyway, to help my sons and their football clubs, I became a 'proper' referee and I learned that there was a lot more to it than putting on a black shirt and spoiling everyone's weekend. Now, 14 years later, I am still refereeing kids' games.

I never wanted to take it more seriously than that, to move up the grades and the leagues. I had neither the time nor the inclination. But I have become a refereeing anorak. Without much prompting, I will list the seven reasons a player can be cautioned, for instance. Sad, I know.

Another reason to avoid me at a party is that you might get a lecture about the unfair, ill-informed and constant carping about referees on radio, TV and in newspapers.

My Sunday sessions have helped me appreciate the guys at the pinnacle of the refereeing pyramid and made me despair of many of my friends in football journalism, who make highly-critical judgements about the match officials, but frequently display a shocking misunderstanding of the Laws of the Game and the way they are supposed to be applied.

My Sunday morning runabouts also provide considerable contrasts with my work at top games. On a Saturday I might be at the Emirates Stadium, with its state-of-the-art media facilities, composing what I hope is an entertaining and informative essay about a top Premier League encounter. Then, on Sunday morning, after emailing that essay to my newspaper, I'll pitch up at a park somewhere, put my boots on besides my car and hope the dog mess has been cleared up. Instead of walking out with two highly-trained, neutral assistant referees and a fourth official, I am on my own. So, while the two teams are reluctantly complying with my pre-match instruction to remove jewellery and body-piercings – a process that can take several minutes and produce an impressive, if garish, booty – I stand in the centre circle with a flag in each arm and shout: "Two linesmen, please".

The volunteers vary in keenness, but often the ones who run over enthusiastically and tell me that they, too, are qualified referees, are more trouble than the overweight, heavy smokers who have obviously been press-ganged into 'helping'. The keen ones tend to have a hair-trigger response to what they believe to be offside decisions and tend to be partial. All right, some of them cheat.

It just adds to the challenge for the writer in the black. Why do I do it? Well, not for the £20 match fee, that's for sure. But let me leave you with one thought: let's go back to that match between two teams of warring 18 year-olds and imagine what would have happened if I'd fancied a Sunday morning at home and not turned up.

Mick Dennis is the Football Correspondent of the Daily Express. He has worked for four other national newspapers and was Sports Editor of the (London) Evening Standard.

__Favourite player:__ Iwan Roberts. Legendary scorer of 96 goals for the club I support, Norwich City.

__Most memorable match:__ Burnley 4, Norwich 4. 1975. The first match from which I sent a 'live' match report to the Norwich 'Pink' football paper.

ENGLAND PAY THE PENALTY FOR POOR PREPARATION

Germany are cooler and mentally stronger

By Matt Dickinson

O NLY IN England could a book be written about penalty shoot-outs because only in England has the task of placing a ball into a net from 12 yards come to be regarded with the same difficulty, and complexity, as brain surgery. In the rest of the world, you take them and, mostly, you score. In England, you fret, you hesitate and then, all too often, you fail.

Then you get to star in a commercial for Pizza Hut.

If a whole nation can possess a phobia, England has developed one towards the penalty shoot-out. Our record in World Cups is three defeats out of three. We have won only one of the three in European Championships and that, against Spain at Euro 96, was quickly followed by the resumption of normal service with an agonising shoot-out defeat to Germany in the semi-final.

When Owen Hargreaves was the only member of Sven Goran Eriksson's team to score against Portugal on the last such occasion, the 2006 World Cup quarter-finals, the joke went round that he was a German anyway courtesy of his years at Bayern Munich. Except it was not really a joke. Give Steven Gerrard the most knicker-wetting last-minute penalty to take for Liverpool and he will drill it into the top corner: give him the same opportunity for England and he will look like he has been asked to walk naked along Albert Docks. Ditto Frank Lampard, who scored a spot-kick for Chelsea days after the death of his beloved mother but who has been known to step up for the national team with all the certainty of a 16-year-old trying to order a round of beers in the local pub.

Roberto Baggio, who famously missed in the 1994 World Cup final, once said that the only way to guarantee not missing a penalty is to not to take one. To which we might add that the best way to be sure of missing is to give the ball to an England international.

So what is the cause of this national failing? Why do we have such a pathetic record and Germany have won four shoot-outs out of four in World Cups? In his book, On Penalties, Andrew Anthony writes that "the penalty is unique in sport because of the emphasis it places on conscious choice. For a brief period the game stops and the penalty-taker enters his own chamber of truth, a place where actions have ineluctable consequences." To which a golfer might say that he enters the same chamber every time he steps up and waggles a five-iron. In golf, though, there are no active variables such as a goalkeeper, Anthony counters. "With a football penalty, the taker is confronted with a genuine decision. And that presents a distinct problem." Particularly for English players, it would seem.

Does the breakneck speed of our game, the chaotic pinball, count against English players more than other nationalities when the game is reduced to a static set-piece? Does slowing the game from 100mph to a standstill make our players freeze more than the Spanish, Italians or Germans? There might be more to that argument if England was the only country which has developed a hang-up about penalties. But we are not alone. During the 1990s, the Italians lost a quarter, semi and final of successive World Cups. More recently to Spain at Euro 2008. And the Dutch, supposedly the kings of cool and of technique, lost a quarter-final and a semi in European Championships as well as the semi-final of a World Cup. Dennis Bergkamp should be the greatest penalty take ever born, a man with awesome technique who can control a ball like the Old Masters could control a paint brush. Yet he developed one of the most notable phobias of penalties (to go with his fear of aeroplanes) after failing to beat Peter Schmeichel in the 1999 FA Cup semi-final replay. And many of the greatest names in the sport, including Pele, Diego Maradona and Zico, have failed to convert from 12 yards in big matches.

Can practice make perfect? In England, it has been the cause of great debate. The idea that you cannot replicate the pressure of a penalty shoot-out is a theory which has been advanced by Glenn Hoddle, among others, but then the former England manager had a few wacky ideas, not least the idea that the disabled are living out the sins of a previous life. To some extent, his explanation about the uselessness of rehearsal was an excuse for England's failure to overcome Argentina in the 1998 World Cup shoot-out when David Batty failed with the last, fateful kick. "That's the first penalty I've been asked to take," the midfielder said afterwards. "I've never even taken one in training." Given that Hoddle, for all his failings, could never be accused of lack of preparation, it seemed a shocking admission.

More than one coach went out subsequently to prove Hoddle categorically wrong. Sir Clive Woodward's contribution to football may have been roundly scoffed but he came up with a small, but clever innovation when he advised Aidy

Boothroyd, the Watford manager, on how to prepare for the eventuality of penalties in a play-off final. On Woodward's advice, at the end of a regular-season game, Boothroyd sent his players to one end of the pitch while the stand was still full of spectators and staged a penalty shoot-out in front of thousands. As it happened, Watford never endured a shoot-out and, in any case, the benefits of practice would have been hard to quantify, but it at least showed an enlightened approach, the search for every little advantage.

As a nation, we can hardly afford to turn our back on any advance.

Other suggested remedies have included making penalty-takers practise from 14 yards, rather than the regulation 12, so that the target looms large when the pressure is at its greatest. Other managers have experimented with forcing their shooters to tell the goalkeeper which way the ball is going to go to try to instil a certainty of thought and a firm strike. From the goalkeeper's point of view, there seems little doubt that, while confidence can play a huge part, practice and research can make a big difference.

You will not be surprised to hear that the Germans are a step ahead. "I just think we're a little bit cooler in front of goal. It is a ruthless streak Germans show when they take penalties," Tim Borowski, their midfield player, said during the 2006 World Cup finals after another successful shoot-out, this time against Argentina.

Yet victory owed as much to Jens Lehmann's saves which were not just a tribute to his athleticism and reactions but to meticulous research. Lehmann saved two of Argentina's four and guessed correctly on the other two – although guesswork actually had nothing to do with it. When at Schalke, his manager, Huub Stevens, had compiled a personal database of 13,000 penalty kicks. Lehmann had used the archive to help win the 1997 UEFA Cup against Inter Milan and, prior to facing Argentina, made sure that the German FA carried out the same checks. Stuffed down Lehmann's socks was a piece of hotel notepaper on which was written such instructions as: "Julio Cruz – stand tall, don't move, dive right." For Roberto Ayala, "look at shooting foot, left low." Simple but, as it transpired, very effective.

All of this forms part of the picture of why England missed more penalties in one shoot-out (against Portugal in the 2006 World Cup) than Germany have done in their entire history (scoring 16 of their 17). But the causes are perhaps not to be found in the detail but in the broader scope. "Too many things go through your mind if you keep losing at penalties," Hoddle argued, with some justification. "If you keep winning them, like the Germans, psychologically they feel that it is going to go their way. The confidence is there. It's just a mental thing." We have become so accustomed to crushing disappointment that we arrive at shoot-outs with dread already swamping our minds. "They are masters at it, masters of winning on penalties. We have to develop that mentality at make-or-break moments in tournaments," Gary Neville said in 2006 as England headed home to contemplate another disappointment. And as Neville appeared to be hinting, the problem goes wider than the spot-kicks themselves. They are just a symptom of our mental weakness, the feeling of inadequacy, the worry that we do not quite belong in the latter stages of tournaments, a deep-seated doubt that we are quite good enough. It is years of accumulated failure – and it only shows signs of getting worse.

Matt Dickinson is chief sports correspondent at the Times, for whom he has worked since 1997. He spent seven years as chief football correspondent having previously worked for the Daily Express.

Favourite player: *A childhood thing, was David Crown in the days when the dashing striker stuck them in for Cambridge United. Premiership honours go to Patrick Vieira.*

Most memorable match: *A personal favourite was England v Argentina at the 1998 World Cup even if England did lose. Michael Owen's goal, David Beckham's sending-off, 10-man heroics and penalties; about as memorable as a defeat gets.*

HAMMERS FANS LET DOWN BY BUNGLING BOARDS

The soul of West Ham should not be sold – for any price

By John Dillon

THE JOKE used to be that so many of the reporters in Upton Park's press box were West Ham supporters that they would sway in time to Bubbles with the old boys on the Chicken Run.

It's partly true. There has always been a wide streak of claret-and-blue running through Fleet Street. Some of the journalists with the Irons in their soul have even been around long enough to have written pieces about the club winning something. Others, who are pushing into middle age now, were still at school in 1980, when Arsenal were beaten in the FA Cup final. It's a long time to have been Holding The Back Page.

A thousand more one-liners have been cracked about this phenomenon of mass allegiance to the Hammers in national newspapers, but some in the business don't find it funny. They think it leads to bias in their favour. They suggest it means West Ham have had an easy ride through the years.

This isn't true. If only for the reason that most of the time, this is a team which isn't involved in the truly big stories.

Arsenal, Spurs and, in recent, ruble-laden years, Chelsea are the serious headline-churners in London. In the North, Manchester United and Liverpool have won and achieved so much more on a global scale that they have commanded miles more column inches.

West Ham have their moments. But the journalists who support them are respected enough and experienced enough to be able to refute quite easily any serious suggestions of partisanship. And these days they spend most of their time trailing the Big Four around Europe in the Champions League or watching them carve up the Premiership, so they rarely get to the Boleyn Ground, anyway.

It's all just a matter of geography, really. Look around the Premier League and calculate how many top level players and coaches have emerged from the fertile breeding ground of east London and Metropolitan Essex. John Terry. Frank Lampard and Ashley Cole were all raised on the opposite end of the District Line to Chelsea, for example. A certain D. Beckham is from Chingford, as is the recently-retired Teddy Sheringham. Sol Campbell, Tony Adams and a certain R. Moore all knew a thing or two about defending. The list is copious.

As with players, so with newspapermen. This area is densely populated and football-mad, so its stands to reason that it has thrown up so many journalists as well. You can tell who they are if they do get to write anything about West Ham. They are the ones whose copy avoids all that pie 'n' mash, Knees Up Muvva Brahn guff. The truth is that the club isn't even in the East End. The distinction is subtle, but it's a cultural and historic one.

Upton Park is in East London, an area that sprawled out in the late 19th century as the might of the Thames docks grew up. You can sense it simply by walking along Green Street and observing that the ground is surrounded by small Victorian terraces. The East End, further in towards the City, is older. It had different industries, like the furniture and rag trades. In places like Bethnal Green and Shoreditch, the old Cockney population was as likely to support Spurs, Arsenal or Orient as West Ham.

This little lesson in social history all seems like stuff which is peripheral to modern football. But, actually, it is what makes clubs like West Ham critically important to the future of the sport, even as it becomes increasingly dominated by the wealth and glamour of the big-time elite. They are not alone in representing a particular social and cultural tradition. Football clubs up and down the land do that, even while the core of the support has moved away from its old homelands and new, massively diverse populations have taken their place in the streets surrounding the older stadia.

The temptation to over-romanticise West Ham should be studiously avoided, of course. Yes, they are easy to love. Their ideals and their style have often been fine and innovative. Have I mentioned 1966 yet? Ron Greenwood and John Lyall were among the finest of English managers, who each took a small-ish club to a European final. Harry Redknapp's passion and smartness is only now being recognised belatedly at Portsmouth. Billy Bonds and Trevor Brooking should both have been in the House of Lords long ago.

But West Ham have also been among the most feeble-minded and uncompetitive clubs in top-level football on far too many occasions. Their DNA is noble, but is fatally, infuriatingly flawed too. Before Alan Curbishley saved them from the drop in the remarkable conclusion to the 2006/07 season, they were facing their fourth relegation from the top flight in 18 years.

Still, they are unique, at least, among London's Premier League clubs in having the strongest regional identity. As the movers and shakers at the top of the pile look ever more ravenously towards emerging global markets and the Los Angeles Galaxy begin to get more coverage here than, say, Sheffield Wednesday, the preservation of the customs and ideas with which the ordinary people of England that built all these grand institutions for themselves, must be preserved and respected.

Ironically, it is West Ham who provide us with one of the most stark examples of recent years of how such ideas are being corroded by the lust for wealth and power swirling around football now. The shameful Carlos Tevez affair stunk from start to finish. I said it would in my column in the Daily Express, the day after Tevez and Javier Mascherano signed in their most unlikely and convoluted loan deal. And the Premier League commission agreed when, in their inquiry, they concluded that there had been "dishonesty and deceit," and directors had told "direct lies" to the League.

The £5.5 million penalty imposed on West Ham for the chiselling which surrounded the signing of these two brilliant Argentine players was a world record at the time. It seriously besmirched West Ham's good name.

Money was the cause, of course. West Ham's board were attempting to sell the club to an agent, who just happened also to have a share in the future of the two players. Such "third party ownership" of footballers was against the rules. But there was a lot of cash to be made. This was modern football in rapacious microcosm.

In the end, West Ham was sold to an Icelandic consortium instead and the chairman, Terry Brown, walked away with around £20 million.

This led to another stark lesson in the realities of modern football. The fans of every club cry out now for the arrival of their own Roman Abramovich. West Ham supporters were no different. They imagined foreign money would catapult them into the real big time.

Instead, they got the striking sight of the gleamingly bald Eggert Magnusson, leaping around the directors box claiming the club was "in his blood." Then departing after a year, presumably with the club no longer in his blood because as far as I know, he hasn't been at any matches since.

Now the Icelander Bjorgolfur Gudmundsson is in control. The club talks about a new stadium and attempting to get into the Champions League. Well, of course, football is about ambition. West Ham have as much right to aim high as anyone else. And, yes, it's a business and we all know where the big money lies. But am I being old-fashioned by wondering what right a team which has never won the title might have to be in the Champions League?

A year before the Tevez affair, West Ham played Liverpool in Cardiff in one of the most remarkable of all FA Cup finals. It was utterly typical of them to allow Steven Gerrard to equalise two minutes from the end and then lose on penalties.

But that day under Alan Pardew, they were a club which made a fabulous stand for something precious and enduring about the people's game. They played in the expansive West Ham way. In the stands, supporters who had been given nothing serious to shout about in 26 years, created a fervent, cacophony of noise and colour as soulful as anything emerging from the travelling Kop, which is rightly famed for its veneration of its team, but has had its fanaticism nourished by five European Cup wins. It was a truly moving day.

A year later the Tevez affair tarnished all that. And in the summer of 2008, after a rare, uneventful season when safety was secured early, West Ham stand at the crossroads of the modern game. They are in middle tier of the Premiership's order of power and wealth, but they have big ideas. How they go about achieving them is just as important as whether they succeed or not. Along with so many of the old 'people's clubs', the soul of West Ham is far more important than their brand or the wealth they might chase. It has no price and it should never be for sale.

John Dillon has been chief sports writer of the Daily Express since 2002. Previously, he was with the People and then senior football writer at the Daily Mirror from 1998.

Favourite player: *Billy Bonds epitomised the best of West Ham and also offered them a competiveness not always apparent elsewhere at the club.*

Most memorable match: *West Ham 3, Eintracht Frankfurt 1. ECWC semi-final second leg, 14 April 1976. Bunked off school to queue up, paid 20p to get into the old North Bank, 39,000 bursting out of the place and a brilliant comeback from a first leg defeat. With gallons of mud and rain thrown in. A lifetime memory.*

QUESTION: "WHAT DO YOU DO FOR A LIVING?"

ANSWER: "I shout footballers' names."

By Peter Drury

AND THAT, essentially, is it. I have 1,500 words to write here about preparation, research, technique etc. – which is fine, as long as we realise from the start that a television commentator's function is limited. It is, as they say, not rocket science.

When you listen to a game on the radio, the commentator is essential. Without him, you wouldn't have a clue. When you read a match report in the paper, you rely on the writer to impart the flavour and communicate the essential facts. But, when you sit down to watch a match on the telly, you can see for yourself what's happening. The pictures tell the story. The essential facts are self-evident. The commentator's role is at best marginal.

This is not some exercise in pseudo-humility. It's just a fact. In an occupation where an unchecked ego is dangerous, it is always worth a commentator reminding himself that no viewer (with the exception, perhaps, of his mum) has turned on the TV to hear him. The match is the attraction.

A TV commentator exists only because, on balance, it is still broadly accepted that he is in some sense a worthwhile 'part of the furniture'. And, as long as you hear children in the park 'commentating' on their jumpers-for-goalposts games, that's probably right. When a goal is scored, they expect that it should be articulated by a raised voice ... a sharp, staccato phrase ... the bellowing of a name.

Commentary is an accompaniment. I have heard it fairly described as "audio wallpaper." But, of course, people get very worked up about their wallpaper. It can enhance or ruin; it can set a tone; it can blend or clash; it divides opinion. One man's favourite is another man's greatest irritant.

There are three main questions with which commentators regularly have to deal. The first is: "When the hell are you going to shut up?" ... but we'll gloss over that one.

The second and third are, however, linked and more easily-addressed. Very often, the same person, within the same conversation, can ask, on the one hand: "You only work for 90 minutes once or twice a week – what on earth do you do for the rest of the time?" And, on the other: "How do you recognise all those players and know so much about them?"

Of course, the answer to both questions is the same: "I prepare."

If it's to be worth anything, commentary has to be 'instant journalism'. It is about anticipating and identifying the story of a match while it is in progress, articulating that story, putting it into context and bringing it alive. In order to tell the story, the most important thing is to have a grasp on its characters and background. The days before a big, live game are spent researching those.

Identification is the first and most important base to cover. If nothing else, the viewer has a right to expect that you will be able to tell him the name of the player in possession.

The great, late Brian Moore once said to me that he attempted to mention the name of every player inside the first five minutes of the game, as if ticking them off on the back of the match programme. This is particularly important for a European or international match where the majority of viewers may not be familiar with one or both of the teams involved.

If, for instance, Chelsea are due to play Shakhtar Donetsk in the Champions League, I would make it my business to have watched a couple of Shakhtar's recent games on tape and, ideally, to attend one of their pre-match training sessions to familiarise myself with the players. It would be extremely embarrassing if the players in question ever got hold of the rather personal notes I jot about them (e.g. "Long nose" or "Balding" or "Bow-legged" or "looks like a Bull Terrier/the mother-in-law") but those are the sorts of things for which you're looking out ... particularly if you stumble across a team whose players – from 75 yards away – 'all look the same'.

Incidentally, there are times when all of this preparation is rendered pointless. As a practical joke at the French World Cup of 1998, the Romanian players all had bleached crew cuts on the eve of their match against Croatia. In those days, fewer players wore flashy, multi-coloured boots. There were almost no distinguishing features. Commentators the world over were frozen with fear.

That occasion apart, on the night of the game, it's worth studying the warm-up closely. If you can't distinguish between the two centre-backs, then perhaps one has white boots and the other black ...one may have short sleeves and the other long. Just the other evening, I commentated on Manchester United's Champions League match in Rome; Cristiano Ronaldo scored with a magnificent header. No problem, you might think ... one of the most famous and recognisable players in the world. But, from the distant commentary position at the Olympic Stadium, it wasn't Ronaldo I saw soaring into the penalty area, it was just the blur of his bright red boots. Thank goodness I'd bothered to check – that would have been a bad one to get wrong.

So, recognising the players is by far the most important thing. Knowing about them comes next ... and yes the stereotypical image of the nerdish student surrounded by reference books (and, these days, the internet) is pretty close to the mark. For a major game, I have a file with five or six A4 pages of hand-written notes which would include biographical details on every player on each squad ... the managers ... the form of the teams ... various points of historical interest ... records that are ripe for breaking ... and various 'just in case' information – like quickest goal, biggest score, penalty shoot-outs etc. All possible eventualities must be covered.

Compiling that information can be dull. Overusing it can be duller. Most commentators will tell you that they use less than 10 percent of their homework. The aim should be to deploy the information only when it becomes relevant. However, show me a commentator who claims to have a perfect record in this regard and I'll show you a liar. If you've spent an hour researching a 'knock-out fact', the chances are you won't resist the temptation to broadcast it ... regardless of its relevance. Sorry.

Occasionally, you're glad to have put in the hours. Week after week for more than a decade, I've written and re-written the various Champions League records without ever referring to them. Finally, last October, Arsenal beat Slavia Prague 7-0 and all that information came pouring out. A fortnight later, as I sat down to prepare for my next European assignment, the temptation was huge not to bother with that page of notes. It couldn't possibly happen again! In fact, at the very last minute, almost out of superstition, I scribbled it all out before climbing up to the Anfield gantry for Liverpool 8 Besiktas 0.

One bone of contention amongst commentators concerns the extent to which we prepare our words. Is it wrong or, in some sense, cheating to pre-consider or script words for a particular occurrence?

Opinions vary. My own is that only the very cleverest commentator (and there are few, if any) can make a scripted line sound spontaneous ... and, during the course of the game, it's infinitely better to rely on spontaneity. Invariably the best lines are of the moment. I'm pretty sure Kenneth Wolstenholme hadn't written down "they think it's all over", nor had Barry Davies prepared to say "interesting ... very interesting."

Personally, I will have words ready for the pre-match stuff (taking the teams out of the tunnel etc) and for the lifting of trophies. I will also tend to write down bullet-points for the final whistle so that in the excitement of the moment I have a clear note about the significance of a particular result. But to try to script a game or a moment is dangerous, not least because the moment doesn't always happen as you imagine it.

At Euro 2004 in Portugal, my first live game was Italy v Denmark. Keen to make the right impression at the start, I had written some grand lines to use off the back of the Italian national anthem. Pompously, I delivered the words: ". . . a major international tournament has never properly begun until we get our first glimpse of those iconic **blue** Italian shirts . . ." At that moment, the Italian players unzipped their track suit tops ... to reveal that they were playing in **white**! Lesson learned.

The role of the commentator is essentially to articulate what he actually sees – to deal with facts. Opinion is the exclusive terrain of the former player or manager who sits with him – David Pleat, Mark Lawrenson, Andy Gray et al. They have 'done it' and so understand in a way that qualifies them to impose an opinion on the broadcast. A good commentator facilitates that; it is an impertinence, however, to trespass onto the expert's view.

Anyway, the commentator's is a simpler role. What does he do for a living? He shouts footballers' names.

Peter Drury has been a commentator for ITV Sport since 1998, having previously spent 8 years with BBC Radio (and – briefly – TV). Prior to that, he served his apprenticeship at Hayters Sports agency.

__Favourite player:__ Trevor Brooking. Wonderful vision and range of passing, two-footedness, a stately elegance, loyalty, humility and impeccably behaved on and off the field.

__Most memorable match:__ Doncaster Rovers 3 Halifax Town 4, 21 April, 1990. Halifax, desperate for points to stay in the League, had been three goals down with 25-odd minutes to play. Raw sport that really mattered to people.

__Favourite commentator:__ Brian Moore . For his glorious voice, simplicity of words and transparent love of the game.

A 22-HEADED MONSTER

But it became the most popular league in the world

By Alex Fynn

ASSAILED by the Football League whose proposal 'One Game, One Team, One Voice' called for the Football Association to join them and create a new executive body to run the professional game, the FA turned to me in their hour of need [the football authorities along with many in government and business wanted to believe that Saatchi & Saatchi had the answers to their problems].

Already canvassed by David Dein of Arsenal and Noel White of Liverpool as representatives of the 'big five' – Manchester United, Tottenham Hotspur and Everton made up the number – on the idea of a breakaway First Division, I inadvertently provided the FA with the reasons to support their plans. I explained to Sir Bert Millichip, the chairman, Graham Kelly, the chief executive and Charles Hughes, the national director of coaching and education, that professional football from top to bottom needed restructuring: a showcase top division and regional divisions at the base. The common denominator was the recognition of the inherent event-like quality of all football. With no more than 20, ideally 18, clubs in a division, the number of events [title, promotion, Europe, play-offs and avoidance of relegation] would be maximised and non-events [mid-table, nothing to play for games] minimised. So Arsenal v Manchester United would be a national event and Exeter v Torquay a regional event.

On the other hand, Oldham v Coventry at the top [it is difficult today to believe they were founder members of the Premier League] and Torquay v Carlisle at the bottom would be non-events and should be eliminated.

However, what really opened the FA's eyes for the first time was the idea that the England national team and the FA Cup could be positioned alongside the top division at the apex of the game. With fewer, albeit more important, league fixtures the two properties of the FA could enhance their special scarcity value. Moreover, for the first time the national side for friendlies and competitive fixtures alike would have the field to themselves; there would be no top division games cluttering up the mid-week or weekend respectively.

The FA now had a reason to produce their own counter proposal in order to destroy the League's bid for power sharing. The result was the Blueprint for the Future of Football, the centrepiece of which was the support for a breakaway Premier League of preferably 18 clubs. Armed with quantifiable information, probably the first time the fans had ever been asked what they wanted in an authentic research study, one of the main reasons for the vote of approval was that an 18 club league would be beneficial for the national team.

"The prospect of an autonomous league would be questionable," said Kelly, "If the FA does not sanction a new league it cannot operate."

Precisely. But the FA lost its nerve. It could, and indeed, should have told the rebels: "You start with 18 clubs or you don't start at all. Oh and by the way, as it is our name up front, we will be taking 25 per cent of the broadcast revenues."

I told the FA the rights should fetch £22.5 million for 30 live games. My estimate was derided by the media and the football authorities alike. BSkyB actually paid £35.5million for sixty games in season 1992/93.

Ironically, the catalyst on behalf of the breakaway clubs, Dein, the Arsenal vice-chairman, was about to be marginalised as his long time adversary, Ken Bates, the Chelsea chairman, explained: "When we had the founders' meeting David Dein was so over the moon at getting his little Premier League and couldn't understand why Ken Bates was being so supportive. We got a few things in there ... he is only now beginning to realise what hit him. One club, one vote, no committees, only self-liquidating working parties so you had no permanent chance to be in the corridors of power or have committee influence."

Further, with 22 members, the size of the First Division at the time, it was the ultimate irony that the big clubs who had agitated for change, now found themselves in the minority. And the first bitter experience of being out-voted was the decision to award the first television contract to BSkyB – "The 22-headed monster", according to the players' union chief Gordon Taylor who had bared its teeth. Taylor subsequently threatened to bring his members out on strike unless the Premier League paid the PFA their agreed share of the broadcast revenues. A satisfactory compromise was reached. If only the FA had shown such fortitude.

Dein's jaundiced view was: "It was a lost opportunity [a league of 18 clubs]. I'm increasingly embarrassed when people ask 'what is the difference between the Premier League and the old First Division?'

"I have to face them and say 'nothing except there is more money swishing around.'".

Like most of his fellow directors and chairmen, he was unaware of the revolution that was about to break. Sky's presentation did indeed create as they claimed "a whole new ball game" initially, providing an antiquated product with a new, garish image. More importantly though, in time the broadcaster added substance to the proposition and changed the way that football is financed, promoted and indeed played.

Thanks to Sky the Premier League is the richest and most popular league in the world. Untold riches for its members; penury for those outside. The annual revenue for the 20 Premier League clubs is just under £1,500 million; the revenue for the 24 Championship clubs a mere £320 million.

In England more people go to watch professional football in more divisions than any other country in the world. Yet life outside the Premier League exists in spite of the system, not because of it. But spare no pity for the Football League with their overblown 24-club divisions and their short-sighted maxim of "play more games, earn more money'" with the inevitable by-product of too many unavoidable non-event encounters.

A country's football strength cannot be measured by 20 clubs alone. They are unrepresentative of the omnipresence and popularity of the sport. Worse, a situation has been created whereby due to the indolence of the FA, the Premier League has been allowed to disappear over the horizon with all of the hype and all of the money. The Premier League has become the only competition that matters. Success, whoever you are, is mandatory. For today's big four it is defined by the title and the Champions League. For some like Aston Villa and Tottenham success is qualification for the UEFA Cup. And for Sunderland and half a dozen others, it is the avoidance of relegation.

But the answer is the same for all of them. As fast as the money comes in to the bottom line, particularly from the huge broadcast rights fees with absolutely no costs attached to them. Over £500 million is shared out annually between the top 20 and their six former colleagues now plying their trade in the Championship. It goes out again to be spent on players' transfers and salaries with an increasing preponderance of foreign investment.

In the 2006/07 season less than 40 per cent of players who started Premier League games were English. We no longer have an English league. We have an international league that happens to be played in England. So with club, not country, driving and dominating the game, the lack of success for the national team is the reverse side of the Premier League high value currency.

The answer? Well, if Premier League II was formed so that there would be 40 clubs who mattered, the stigma and cost of relegation would be mitigated. There would be more fluidity to the system. Clubs, players and coaches would move up and down and there would be an overall raising of standards with many more English-born players coming through.

Money would not be the be all and end all [in any case it could be more equitably distributed between I and II, perhaps on an 80:20 television fee split between the two divisions] and there would be more opportunity for talent, both coaching and playing to emerge. And England, at last, should be able to choose from a larger group of candidates than are currently available to the national selector.

Back in March 1991, there was a meeting between the FA and the big five clubs in the boardroom in Goodison Park at which the FA pledged their support to the breakaway top division. In conclusion, Philip Carter, the Everton chairman, said: "Well, gentlemen, that seems to be satisfactory. All that remains to do is to elect our chief executive."

"But we already have a chief executive," Charles Hughes interjected pointing to Graham Kelly. But Kelly said nothing and the moment was lost.

Gone forever.

As a director of Saatchi & Saatchi, Alex Fynn advised the FA, the Football League and British and continental clubs on media and marketing. He has written on the business and politics of football for the Observer and the Sunday Times and has co-authored several books on the subject.

Favourite player: Michel Platini. 41 goals in 72 internationals and three times the leading goalscorer in Serie A when it was indisputably the best league in the world: a midfield genius whose goalscoring record is the envy of most world-class strikers.

Most memorable match: c.1960, Christ's College, Finchley, U-14s 12, St. Aloysius College U-14s 0. A.E. Fynn (9).

WHEN BEING NEGATIVE DELIGHTED CAPELLO

An unknown boy gave the England manager his most tense moment

By Michael Hart

A LIFETIME spent covering football around the world was no preparation for an afternoon with Fabio Capello watching African youngsters being tested for the HIV/AIDS virus. The England manager and Football Association coach Ray Clemence, along with a small group of media representative from London, had travelled to Lesotho to see at first hand the work the FA was doing in one of the poorest countries on earth.

Life expectancy in this part of Africa is just 40 years and the prevalence rate of HIV/AIDS among adults is 28 per cent. The FA established links with its counterparts in Lesotho, Malawi and Botswana as part of the UEFA-CAF Meridian Project in 1998 and agreed development plans for each nation. These projects range from administration and refereeing to youth and women's football.

The FA was particularly keen to encourage the growth of grassroots football, believing that the elite game needs a solid base to prosper. It was while developing this area of their programme that they recognised the valuable social impact modern football can have in countries like Lesotho. So, in partnership with charities like Coaching for Hope and Kick4Life, the FA is now using football to empower vulnerable young people in the developing world and make them aware of the dangers of HIV and AIDS through an integrated education programme. Enter Fabio on his whistle stop tour.

Exhausted after 15 hours in planes and airports, he was nonetheless captivated by the sight of dozens of smiling African youngsters playing barefoot matches on the undulating dust and scrub pitches they often share with grazing cattle. "If I can make only one percent of difference it will be worthwhile," said the England manager.

Capello and Clemence, the former England goalkeeper, spent a busy two days in Lesotho, monitoring the progress of the FA's coaching programme and promoting football as an educational tool in the fight against disease.

On a warm, sunlit autumn afternoon they watched 12 schoolboy teams playing in a tournament for Under-14s in Maseru, the capital of Lesotho. Each school had about 50 supporters with the winning team determined not just by results on the pitch but by the number of children attending HIV education sessions and undergoing an HIV test.

Capello and Clemence chatted to the children and their coaches – they all speak English – handed out gifts, signed autographs, posed for photographs and adopted the two teams that contested the final. Ray's team beat Fabio's in a penalty shoot-out. Desperately poor by UK standards, the children were enchanting. They were painfully polite and greeted questions with a shy smile. They danced and sang their tribal songs between matches and when you asked which of the big clubs they supported they almost all replied: "Manchester United."

Among them were some seriously talented young footballers. "When you look at the pitches they play on you realise how important it is for them to learn to control the ball well," explained former West Ham midfield player Geoff Pike, head of the FA coaching team working in Lesotho. Pike is in the process of establishing a coaching infrastructure in the country. "I'm teaching the coaches to become tutors so they can go out into the rural areas and put together their own coaching programmes," he explained. "If we do the job properly here we can really make a difference – on and off the pitch."

For Capello the most profoundly moving moments of the day were spent in one of the 14 tents erected around the football pitches for the purpose of testing the children for HIV/AIDS. The Italian coach, Clemence and members of the English media contingent were invited to watch the first little boy undergo the test that would tell him whether he was likely to die before the age of 40. The test takes a matter of minutes and a counsellor, speaking softly, explained to the barefoot child in an England shirt, what was about to happen. There was no obvious sign of his parents. The little boy was clearly anxious and when the counsellor asked him to sign a consent form tears began to flow. He wiped his eyes and then dabbed his thumb onto an ink pad before signing the form with a thumbprint. Talking gently to relax the boy, the counsellor then pulled on surgical gloves and removed a lancet and micro-pippette unit from a sealed package. With the needle he pierced the boy's middle finger and then drew a miniscule amount of blood for the test.

The blood was carefully transferred to a small, flat disc. A chemical solution that reacts to HIV 1 and HIV 2 antibodies was added to the blood. Then it was simply a matter of waiting. The reaction of the blood to the solution determines the presence of the virus. A colour change means that HIV antibodies are present. The boy had been told this. He stared at the little red spot of blood on the disc. Capello, a father of two sons, sat just feet away. He stared. We all did.

How would I feel, I thought, if this was one of my own children?

No-one said a word but everyone felt for the little boy. He was about to be told whether he had the disease that was cutting such a tragic swathe through big parts of Africa. It must have been an ordeal for him, particularly as this sensitive and potentially devastating moment in his short life was being monitored by foreign strangers with TV cameras and notebooks. The atmosphere in the tent was claustrophobic and Capello, familiar with plenty of highly-charged, emotional situations during his distinguished career as a club manager, admitted later that he'd never felt such tension.

Finally, after a wait of two or three minutes, the counsellor spoke softly to the little boy. There had been no colour change. Without a word, the boy bounced to his feet, wiped his eyes and wriggled his way through the throng and out of the tent. "He's negative," the counsellor announced with a smile.

That day more than 400 children were tested for the virus. Nineteen were positive and were immediately introduced to the nearest antiretroviral clinic for evaluation, treatment and care. Capello was quite visibly moved by the experience. "I've never known anything quite so emotionally intense," he said. "I was quite afraid for the little boy waiting for the outcome. Fortunately, we scored a goal, so to speak, because he was negative.

"It was a good experience for the soul because it makes you understand the hardships in the world. I feel enriched because I have seen things that make me think. Football is a rich sport and I think it has an obligation to use some of its wealth to help the poor and make a difference in the world. I believe some of the big personalities in sport should ask themselves if they can help."

When I began my career in Fleet Street more than 40 years ago the influence of football and footballers was limited. The big football personalities, for instance, advertised things like jars of Brylcreem, the benefits of Marmite or, if you were Jimmy Hill, a fur-lined hat for the winter called the Kossack, retailing at 30 shillings.

In those days football had no significant role to play in the world beyond the confines of sport. Could you imagine, for instance, Sir Alf Ramsey leading an FA missionary expedition to Africa? Of course not. In those days few in Africa would have even heard of England's World Cup-winning manager of 1966. The power of the media has changed that. Today, even in the remotest enclaves in Africa, they gather to watch Premier League football. Television has given football and footballers the power to change lives for the better. It's extraordinary that the popularity of the modern game in England can be used successfully to target vulnerable groups for HIV education and testing in an informal and entertaining setting.

This helps to create an environment of positive peer pressure and encourages young people to know their HIV status because there are still rural areas in countries like Lesotho where most forms of sickness are blamed on witchcraft. The FA has played a major role in lending expertise to develop the game in Africa in the last ten years and, in doing that, they have given fresh impetus to the fight against HIV/AIDS.

"We are very grateful to you for your assistance and support," said Mafole Sematlane, head of the Lesotho FA. "We're proud to be associated with one of the great football nations and we will always be your best friend."

Leslie Notsi is a former coach to the national team and – a rarity this in Lesotho – a Tottenham Hotspur fan. He was delighted to hear the latest White Hart Lane gossip from former Spurs goalkeeper Clemence. "It is wonderful to see people like Ray Clemence and Fabio Capello here because they will help young people realise the dangers of AIDS," he said. "In the long term helping us fight this problem is the best thing you could do for us."

A strong greed element exists in European football but there was clear evidence, here in the middle of Africa, that the modern game is not just about big transfer fees, big salaries, big TV ratings and big revenue. Football and the iconic stars like David Beckham can be forces for good in the wider world in the future.

The government of Lesotho has launched a programme called "Know Your Status" to test for HIV in everyone in the country who wants to be tested. The programme is funded by the Clinton Foundation and two years ago Bill Clinton and Microsoft chairman Bill Gates visited Lesotho to assess progress in the fight against the disease. Prince Harry has also founded a charity, Sentebale, to deliver a range of initiatives for vulnerable children throughout Lesotho. But the FA, embracing the power of modern football, arrived here a decade ago to begin their good work. Of course, their missionary zeal may produce an unexpected bonus when the African countries come to vote for future World Cup host nations but that was the furthest thing from Capello's mind when he stood in that tent watching the trembling little boy await the outcome of his test.

"I'm very proud of what the FA is trying to do in Africa," he said. "I want to be part of this sort of thing. It's very important for us who live comfortable lives to go into the wider world and realise that there are a lot of problems still to be solved."

Michael Hart joined the Evening Standard in 1969 and has been football correspondent since 1976, having previously worked for Hayters Agency.

Favourite player: Bobby Moore. Anyone who watched him as much as I did will know why he remains my favourite player.

Most memorable match: World Cup Final 1966. Couldn't be anything else! As a Hayter's messenger boy at Wembley that day I could see nothing but England glory and success stretching ahead of me for years. How wrong can you be?

OUT OF AFRICA

Europe's elite benefit from Africa's finest

By Ian Hawkey

THE 2007 Carling Cup final had turned into a hot-tempered affair. Being a contest between the Chelsea of Jose Mourinho and an Arsenal who had accumulated an alarming number of red cards under the management of Arsene Wenger, that was always a possibility. It had been close, too, and tense. After a mêlée during an extended period of stoppage time, Chelsea's Mikel John Obi and the Arsenal pair Emmanuel Adebayor and Kolo Toure were dismissed by referee Howard Webb.

One national newspaper ran a headline the next day: 'Three Africans sent-off as Chelsea triumph.' Nothing inaccurate in the observation – Mikel is Nigerian, Adebayor Togolese and Toure Ivorian – but it seemed a peculiar sort of lens through which to view the events.

Were many of the stories of English football to be told only through that lens they would be obliged to produce headlines like 'Africans dominate Premiership goalscoring charts' – first in 2006/07 was Chelsea's Ivorian, Didier Drogba, with 20 goals; second Blackburn Rovers' South African, Benni McCarthy, with 18 – or 'Redknapp ponders all-African attack for FA Cup final' as Portsmouth, the club of Kanu, Utaka, Muntari, Bouba Diop and Lauren prepared for Wembley in May 2008. Or even 'Redknapp rues diminished African presence': a year earlier, Pompey also had a Zimbabwean, a Zambian and a Congolese striker on their staff. While we're at it, we might as well note that even after Webb had removed the brawlers from last year's Carling Cup final, there were still four Africans left on the field.

The point here is the vast impact African football has had, not just on the English domestic game but across the elite leagues of Europe, and how rapidly that has come about. Spain's La Liga has become accustomed over the last three years to expect the Cameroon striker Samuel Eto'o who found fame with Barcelona and Sevilla's Malian centre-forward Frederic Kanoute to be contesting the 'Pichichi' award, given to the leading scorer in the top division.

On a typical domestic weekend in France, not far short of a third of the players in action in Le Championnat will be African, or the sons of parents from Africa. Do not forget that Zinedine Zidane was of Algerian descent. Nor can it any longer be said that most of these players are arriving with the advantage of being cheap to recruit because they have come from impoverished countries where a five-figure sum in dollars or Euros or pounds might sustain the selling club for years. They are as pricey as any of the best.

The first thing Fabio Capello did on joining Real Madrid in July 2006 and assessing the handsome budget available for transfers was to insist that the biggest tranche of it – over £25m – go on Mahamadou Diarra, the defensive midfielder from Mali, whose vendors, France's Lyon, were still whooping with joy over the £24 million they had received from Chelsea for the Ghana midfielder Michael Essien 12 months earlier. Essien, like most of the African players in the Premiership, arrived via a western European club, so that is the economy they are trading in, and usually they come without some of the advantages of the hundreds of others who make up the so-called foreign invasion of the Premiership.

They might have work-permit frontiers to hurdle, and they might very well be asking for six weeks off in the middle of every alternate season. It is at these times that the Premiership does its audit of the African impact, and finds a greater and greater number of its best players disappearing off in January and February to play in the biennial African Cup of Nations, now the international football tournament with a worldwide television appeal bettered only by the World Cup and the European Championship. Close to 40 footballers from the English leagues went to the competition in Ghana in early 2008. Sixteen years earlier, when it was hosted in Senegal, the number of English league players who made the journey stood at: one.

Naturally, English clubs complain long and loud about the exodus of stars for a tournament that sits awkwardly in the calendar, but they would also acknowledge the upside. The Premier League is no longer lagging behind Spain and Italy in the European Cup, and the Drogbas, Essiens, Toures and Manu Eboues have something to do with that.

Where Serie A, La Liga and German Bundesliga clubs have long held a decisive edge over the Premiership in their ability to snare the best South American footballers, English clubs are now attractive destinations for the best Africans. Just as some leading European clubs have thrived on establishing a culture of, say, Brazilians – like Milan, or the strong Deportivo La Coruna of five years ago – or a strong nest of Argentinians – like the 2007 and 2008 Serie A champions, Internazionale – Chelsea and Arsenal have become places where good Ivory Coast players will encourage talented compatriots to come and join them.

The difference is that it will be very long time indeed before the African continent has gathered as many World Cups as Brazil and Argentina. No African country has ever gone beyond the last eight of a World Cup finals, and we long ago passed the deadline of Pelé's often-quoted forecast that an African country would be world champion by the end of the 20th century.

True, for most of that century they weren't given much opportunity. Between Egypt's invitation to the 1934 tournament in Italy and Morocco's qualifying for Mexico 1970, no automatic berth was granted to Africa in the World Cup finals, despite football's significant part in the growing sense of sovereignty among North and West African countries who had regained their independence from colonialism during that period. African football's potential for the rest of the world had to guessed at, from watching players like the Mozambican Eusebio excel for Benfica and Portugal in the 1960s, or seeing Albert Johanneson, a South African, sizzle down the wing for Leeds United.

Morocco did okay in Mexico in 1970 and even took the lead against West Germany in their group match. Alas, the most resonant image of the African challenge at World Cups during the 70s would be left by Zaire, who travelled to West Germany in 1974 full of hype, wearing vivid shirts with a leopard's face printed across their chests. They conceded 14 goals and scored none in their three defeats. They also had a man sent-off for breaking out of the defensive wall out of frustration that Brazil, who beat Zaire by just the three goals, were taking so long to strike the ball. It's a comical moment often replayed.

That Zaire team had some good players but, despite offers to some of them to come to European clubs, they were prohibited from moving abroad by their national association, under instructions from the government. And, naturally, there was no compensation in a hero's welcome when the humiliated Leopards returned home from West Germany. Their leading striker would end up, 20 years later, trying to make ends meet by ushering drivers into car-parking spaces in return for small tips.

Zairean football doesn't make much of a noise, even in Africa, any more. The vast country is now known as the Democratic Republic of Congo and has been at war for most of the last decade. Its best footballers have been those who grew up outside its borders, like Lomana LuaLua – once of Newcastle, Portsmouth and a school in Colchester – or Shabani Nonda, who played for Blackburn after a long journey that took him from a refugee camp in Tanzania to Monaco and Roma.

Nor do you hear much from the national team of Algeria, the country who made the most consistent impression on World Cups in the 1980s, thrillingly beating West Germany in the Spain tournament of 1982 and qualifying again for the 1986 finals in Mexico. By the 1990s, Algeria was mired in horrific civil conflict, costing over 100,000 lives. During that decade one of the heroes of the '82 and '86 World Cup campaigns served four years in prison for his alleged association with a banned political movement.

Against that sort of background, it's hard to build and fund a sporting ethos that will make you the Brazil or the Italy of your continent. More stable African nations have not managed it. Ahead of the last World Cup, African football seemed to suffer a sporting equivalent of a massive coup d'état when Cameroon, quarter-finalists at Italia 90 and the continent's most regular World Cup participants, Senegal, who had reached the last eight in Japan 2002, and Nigeria, qualifiers for successive World Cups from 1994 to 2002, were all dumped out in qualifying for Germany 2006. A quartet of newcomers, Ivory Coast, Ghana, Angola and Togo, displaced them. Only Ghana reached the second round.

These debutants gave the tournament an extra variety, but novices don't tend to go too far. Countries who win World Cups are those with an accumulated, sustained history of excellence, the Brazils, Italys, Germanys and Argentinas. If any of those are in a slump, they will still make the starting line-up at the 2010 World Cup.

The tournament will be the first to be hosted in Africa. About time, too, given its contribution to the world game. But placing the great juggernaut that is the World Cup in a continent of ragged infrastructures is not without difficulties. South Africa was the only viable candidate. It should overcome the scepticism about its ability to host the event, but we can be absolutely sure their rather ordinary team will not win it. Five other African countries – a record turnout – will take part, too, and among their numbers by then may be dozens of Premiership players. Enough good footballers, in other words, that a headline like 'Three from Africa make World Cup semi's' ought to be plausible. One semi-finalist would do. It would mean progress.

Ian Hawkey is European Football Correspondent of the Sunday Times, based in Barcelona. He has also lived in Nigeria, Zimbabwe, Egypt and South Africa. His book about African football is published in 2009.

Favourite player: George Best. I only saw him live at Craven Cottage with his best days gone, but that was enough to persuade a very young Fulham fan. Seeing the older footage just confirmed it.

Most memorable match: Juventus 2 Manchester United 3, Champions League semi-final second leg, 21 April 1999. In many ways a more inspired comeback than the final, because the deficit after ten minutes in Turin was greater. Awesome spirit.

PARKLIFE BLURS PROBLEMS OF ENGLISH FOOTBALL

Youngsters need to learn the vocabulary of football

By Paul Hayward

ANY OTHER country would have hoisted the white flag by now, slunk off home to find something it was good at. In our case – art-rock, comedy, and selling things to foreign speculators. I'm referring, naturally, to the long trail of tears that has been England's road from 1966 to today, when, for the second time in three appointments, the Football Association have raided Italy's Serie A to cure the congenital failings of the national team.

In between Sven-Goran Eriksson and Fabio Capello, an Englishman stood under an umbrella at Wembley and clutched a paper cup of tea as chaos unfolded. Contrary to the apocalyptic reviews of that wet autumn night, the mother country did achieve something from the final Euro 2008 qualifier against Croatia: Steve McClaren kept his hair dry.

I think I know where the problem starts. Forgive the pomposity, but if you stare at something for 20 years to make your living you ought to be able to work out what's going right, and wrong. A mistaken belief that importing foreign experts who are unfamiliar with our unique culture (eg Super Sunday, Big-Four clashes three days before England internationals) is certainly high on the FA's crimesheet. So is the policy of purchasing a whole county in the Midlands and then having to mow it while FA board members argue over the feasibility of a National Football Centre, which, thankfully, now looks certain to be built. English football's HQ has the potential to be like Oxford or Cambridge: a repository of wisdom from where a national curriculum can be imposed, with tanks, if necessary, so that the country that invented the world's favourite game can have an agreed philosophy, a way of playing, that is coached by properly qualified experts, rather than dads with vans, thus bringing us into line with France, Holland or Portugal.

The problem is the system, but it's also us. It's in the parks and schoolyards and Recs of England, where you can often a hear a game a mile away, such is the volume of medieval and often contradictory shouting. In a typical season, I will watch live games at local club, schoolboy, Conference, League One, Championship, Premier League, Champions League and international level, and it's my contention that there is a Great Unwritten Book about our national game, just as there is the elusive Great American novel. The synopsis is as follows. We don't teach, value or understand well enough the vocabulary of the game: touch, balance, agility, spatial awareness, passing, ball retention, two-footedness, skills. We go straight to the other bit: the tackling, battling, lumping, booting, hustling. Our grass-roots football is still largely a trial of strength, of spirit, not the athletic arts of a physically subtle game, as practised by Cesc Fabregas of Arsenal and Spain.

More and more these days you see fields of cones and coaches in bibs and "proper" coaching going on. There are some good teachers out there. Some, though, are mistaking cones and clipboards for good technical instruction. More seriously, the few skills learned at 10-and-under are being swept away in the maelstrom of competitive league action, where boys and girls are encouraged to "get the ball forward" to achieve "results". In English youth football, you can feel the intensity of touchline urgings and see children tumble into the trap of booting the ball "long" and failing to control or pass it properly. It's mortifying. It makes me think the English game will never climb out of its pit of penalty shoot-out calamities and quarter-final exits.

Here are some of the things people still shout at youth games: Get rid of it. Be first. Send it. Get it forward. Get stuck into him. Win this, lads, and we can get up to third in the league.

You may think this a dated view of English parklife. It's not. The language may have become more jargonised since people would shout, in my youth, "cut out the fancy stuff," but there remains an astonishing schizophrenia in the English game. Dads, mums, coaches will sit in front of HD screens and eulogise Arsenal's symphonic football. "Look at the way they pass the ball. Beautiful," they'll coo. And then they'll head down to the park on Sunday morning and exhort boys to launch the ball upfield as quickly as possible and crunch-tackle the opposition to a standstill. Our football is a test of machismo, not the mind. It's a game of subjugation, of excitement and power, of accidents and courage.

As Arsene Wenger once remarked, the warrior tendencies of the British island race find their natural expression on a football field, which is why our players are feared abroad, though seldom for the right reasons. Italian, Spanish and German clubs fear the top English players, but they rarely buy them. The trepidation stems from the knowledge that an English player will keep coming at you. To graduate from local football to millionaire's row, the top English footballer must be relentless in his work-rate and hunger. But from long experience, his equivalent in Portugal, France or even Croatia will fancy his chances of finding a way round the John Bull bearing down on him. It's called tactical and technical prowess.

One of the few things I'm sure of is that England's best players make it to the top despite, not because of, the culture in which they grow up. A few, like Aston Villa's Gareth Barry, are freaks, mastering the art of economical passing. Others, like Steven Gerrard, are a force of nature, well taught by their clubs but also blessed with a fierce resolve to impose their personality on a game. John Terry, Michael Owen, David Beckham: these men scored highly in the self-motivation stakes to get where they are. Arguably the most technically gifted of the current generation all play at Manchester United: Wayne Rooney, Rio Ferdinand and Paul Scholes. From these promising ingredients, no England manager for 42 years has been able to fashion a tournament-winning side, perhaps because the technical deficiencies of the average English footballer are disguised by the presence of so many foreign colleagues in Premier League and European combat.

And now we reach the part that really caves my mind in. England crash out of major tournaments and we don't ask why. We don't investigate. We blame a Swiss referee, hound the sent-off player, ostracise the guy who missed the penalty, curse the goalkeeper who let one fly over his head or round on the foreign agent provocateur. Here, you have only to think of Cristiano Ronaldo's tiny and inconsequential intervention during Rooney's dismissal at the 2006 World Cup.

Because our football industry and media are personality driven, there is a compulsion to reduce everything to the level of which famous player did this or that and who we can find to punish. In the meantime, no-one looks for the real reasons why England have been riding a roller-coaster of anti-climaxes since 1966. Equally, their record in international tournaments prior to Alf Ramsey-and-all-that was also pretty dire. What we have is more than half a century of under-achievement, punctuated by one great afternoon at Wembley, when England were at home.

Journalists love to call things a scandal, but I consider it an outrage that nobody at the FA has ever sought to commission a study to look for evidence and patterns of inadequacy in all those early blow-outs. In the last 12 years alone, the English have wept over Euro 96, France 98, Euro 2000 and 2004 and the 2002 and 2006 World Cups, not to mention the debacle of non-qualification for Euro 2008. Did anyone think there might be common denominators, things we might be able to put right, even if it was only penalty-taking techniques?

When McClaren took charge, I asked him whether he would use any of his many spare days to examine the central failing, which is England's ability to come through the really big, high-intensity knock-out games at World Cups and European Championships. He agreed it would be a good idea. Next – radio silence.

Problem, cause, solution. It's not hard. If a town flooded every two years, you would probably invite a government agency down to have a look, to work out why and suggest remedies. Instead, England float along on the same river of self-regard. Amnesia takes us on to the next fiesta. 'This time it's going to be different. Why should we change? We invented the game. Have you seen our Premier League? Best in the world, old son." This self-deceit is a road to nowhere.

I propose a year-zero imposition of a national curriculum and the kind of coaching standards they have at Clairefontaine in France, where, in mitigation, the good work can proceed without the French FA having to defer to clubs that are worth half a billion quid, and throw their weight around accordingly.

My guess is that we'll all settle for the entertainment splashed out by an enthralling Premier League, and go on hoping, in defiance of logic, that a foreign messiah can deliver a winning England team, without us having to face the truth about our grass-roots culture, which is that it's mostly poorly taught, and largely crude, ugly and naive.

I hope I'm wrong. I hope one day we can engage the head as well as the heart.

Paul Hayward is chief sports writer at the Daily Mail. He has held the same position at the Daily Telegraph and the Guardian and has also worked for the Independent, Independent on Sunday and Racing Post. He co-wrote the autobiographies of Michael Owen and Sir Bobby Robson.

Favourite player: Zinedine Zidane, despite 'le butt'. I didn't cover Pele, Best or Maradona (in his prime), so it has to be Zizou for his skill, elegance and talent for orchestration. A brooding genius.

Most memorable match: France winning the 1998 World Cup final against a comatose Brazil. A multi-ethnic triumph, inspired by Zidane, followed by mass-euphoria on the streets of Paris, where I stayed until dawn.

I SET UP PETER REID FOR SUNDERLAND

But was the last to write about the story

By Paul Hetherington

FOOTBALL REPORTERS sometimes aren't in a position to write their best stories – particularly if they are part of the actual tale.

It's not just a case of a newspaperman being unable to file copy at times because he has been sworn to secrecy, been given information which is strictly off the record, had a legal problem on a story or been asked to delay publication. Occasionally, the reporter is a key figure in the story through being asked by a club to use his contacts to set up a transfer – or help secure a managerial appointment.

That happened to me in 1995, when I working for the News of the World, based in Manchester but with a special responsibility to cover the area in which I had learned the journalistic trade – the north east. I was asked by Sunderland to set up the appointment of Peter Reid, the former Everton and England midfield player and ex-Manchester City boss, as the club's next manager. I did just that and was more than happy to help two friends – Reidy and Sunderland director Bob Murray, who had two spells as chairman of the club. The fact that Sunderland was the club I had always supported and Reid was, in my opinion, ideal for the job, made my initially hush-hush role even easier for me to undertake. The downside for me was that I ended up effectively being the last to write a story I had known about first.

Reidy, as he is known to everyone in football, became manager of Sunderland on 29 March 1995, but the background to his appointment goes back a few months earlier to a lunch I had in Harpers restaurant in Manchester with Murray. The Sunderland chief asked me then who I saw as a potential manager of the club and I recommended Reidy, available after being harshly sacked by Manchester City two years earlier after three seasons in charge in the wake of top-flight finishes of fifth, fifth and ninth. An inspirational dressing-room character, who would instantly command respect, I saw Reid as a manager who would galvanise the club.

It was March 27, a Monday night, when the call came from Murray to my home. He told me the club had decided to end Mick Buxton's two-year reign as manager and they wanted Reid to replace him. Could I contact him and arrange a meeting the following day in Sheffield with Sunderland director Graham Wood?

I was happy to help and after a flurry of phone calls, leaving messages for Sunderland's manager-elect, Reidy rang me back at 11pm and I gave him the news he was back in management – if he wanted the job. His only concern was for Buxton, but I assured him that Mick was out of the job, regardless of whether he accepted it. If Reid said "no" someone else would be approached. Reidy wanted the job all right – and I wanted the story. But as a Sunday newspaperman, I knew this one wouldn't last from Monday night for another six days.

Sure enough, Reidy's appointment was announced on the Wednesday of that week. He was unveiled at a press conference for evening and daily newspapers, radio and television and I ended up attending a briefing with him with my fellow Sunday scribes. So much for an exclusive.

At least I covered myself by keeping my sports editor at the time, Mike Dunn, now in charge of the sports pages at the Sun, informed of what I was involved in. I also, after the press conferences were concluded, had my own private, story-producing session with Reidy in a nearby hotel, where we celebrated his appointment with a couple of bottles of champagne. It was a story, though, that I knew about first and ended up writing joint-last. Such is the frustration at times of working for a Sunday paper, which means you have only one 'hit' a week.

My consolation was that my judgement was proved to be right, as Reidy was in charge of Sunderland for seven years and in that time, he became the club's most successful post-war manager in terms of league results. He immediately saved the club from relegation to the old Third Division, won two promotions as champions and had two Premier League finishes in seventh position, which is so high for Sunderland it was enough to give their fans a nose-bleed. Reidy was also named Manager of the Year in only his second season at Roker Park, Sunderland's home before moving to the Stadium of Light.

When I told him I would be revealing the background to his Sunderland appointment in this book, his reaction was precisely the same as it was when I first mentioned to him the possibility of going to Roker: "Just get on with it." But my role in his arrival at Sunderland soon became common knowledge on the soccer grapevine and I discovered seven months later that his predecessor as manager there – Buxton – certainly knew all about it. It was the Northern Football Writers' Dinner in Manchester and as I walked past the table on which Mick was seated, I heard him shout: "Paul."

I turned round to see Buxton holding a knife, which he handed to me and said: "Just stick that in my back."

Fortunately, his face then broke into a broad smile. He didn't bear a grudge against me or Reidy. He knew his time was up at Sunderland and he also understood, of course, how the football world worked.

Football writers are very much part of that world, of that fraternity. One of Reid's predecessors at Sunderland, Denis Smith, was appointed after another national newspaperman had acted as the middle man, brokering his arrival from a successful spell at York City. And if he was like me, an unpaid go-between, too. It's nothing new – certainly not to Sunderland. I know of another two journalists from the north east who were involved in clandestine attempts to secure managers for the club.

They were unsuccessful, but their ambition could not be doubted. The targets were two of the managerial world's greatest legends – Bill Shankly and Brian Clough.

Paul Hetherington worked on the Gateshead Post, as a freelance; Sunderland Echo, Newcastle Evening Chronicle, Sunday Sun as sports editor; the Newcastle Journal as chief football writer; the News of the World, Sunday Mirror and currently the Daily Star Sunday as football editor. He was Chairman of the Football Writers' Association from 2005 to 2008.

__Favourite player:__ One of my main regrets, both as a fan and a reporter, was not seeing Pelé play live. So I have to go for the greatest British footballer – George Best. If only I could have secured him for Sunderland.

__Most memorable match:__ As a fan – Sunderland's 1-0 win against Leeds in the 1973 FA Cup Final (well, it would be).

As a reporter – England's 5-1 win in Munich against Germany in September 2001.

"MA FEMME EST LAIDE"

Russian to get home from Moscow for the big moment

By Oliver Holt

I WAS nervous as hell when England went to Moscow in October 2007. Nothing went right for England as they lost 2-1, from being a goal in front, in a vital European Championship qualifying game. Plenty went wrong for the journalists, too. And I had other reasons for wanting to get out of there sharpish.

Paul Joyce, the chief football writer for the Daily Express, was mugged on one of the main shopping streets in broad daylight, caught in a sting organised by a bloke in police uniform. It was cold, it was slushy, it was grim. There seemed to be an awful lot of men in black leather jackets looking mean and moody and chain-smoking.

The press team had a nightmare, too. We played against a Russian press side in the Luzhniki Stadium complex a few hours before England lost in the main arena that evening. We got thumped 9-3. Jamie Redknapp played for us. He looked shell-shocked at the final whistle. Like a man who'd decided he'd made two appearances for the press team that afternoon: his first and his last.

Morale was low. Some of the boys – mainly the ones who haven't developed pot bellies yet – took it harder than others. It felt like an omen. That night, our result was announced at half-time and 80,000 Russians hooted their approval.

I just wanted to get out of Russia. It felt too far away. My wife was eight and a half months pregnant and I knew that if she went into labour unexpectedly, I was a four hour flight away and there were only two each day. I'd be struggling to get back in time for the birth. Most of the other lads were heading straight back to London, but I had a crack of dawn flight to Paris for the Rugby World Cup Final that Saturday. I thought I might make a Jonny Wilkinson press conference at the team hotel in Neuilly on the Thursday morning. But there was a transport strike in Paris. I missed it.

I felt happy to be in Paris, though. Just a Eurostar journey away from London, where we live. My wife sounded fine, too. Relieved that I was closer to home. I went to the final press conference the next day. Wrote a piece about Mark Regan and then went out with a few of the lads. I didn't intend to have a big night, but I was happy I was nearly home. And maybe I thought it might be my last chance of a bender for a while. I had a Thai meal with my mate, Paul Hayward, from the Daily Mail. Then we went to a bar to watch the end of the third-place play-off match between France and Argentina.

Then it gets a bit hazy. At least until I plucked my mobile phone out of my pocket at just after 3.30am in a bar in the Latin Quarter and saw a missed call from my wife.

The phone rang again while it was in my hand. Her waters had broken. She was in a taxi on the way to the hospital. I panicked. I wobbled up the street to a taxi rank across the river from Notre Dame. There was a long queue. I panicked a bit more. I waited.

The hotel was only ten minutes away by car. I could get my bags and then take the taxi straight on to the Gare du Nord to catch the first train to Waterloo. Eventually, I got to the front of the line. A cab pulled up. I tottered forwards. But before I got to the taxi, a woman sauntered out of the shadows and got in. The cab driver appeared to think this was fine. I was drunk and panicking even more. Now I was a little irritated, too. So I got in the cab as well.

I tried to express my outrage in my pidgin French. The cabbie looked unsympathetic. I desperately searched my mind for the French word for pregnant so I could adequately convey my desperation to get home.

I remembered it. "Ma femme est laide," I roared at the cabbie and the woman sitting next to me on the back seat. I paused for effect. It didn't seem to have had any. The cabbie wanted me to get out. He emerged from the driver's seat and tried to drag me out. I just kept screaming at him. "Ma femme est laide, ma femme est laide," I shouted louder and louder. "Je dois retourner a mon hotel tout de suite."

The woman didn't seem as affected as I thought she might have been and she didn't seem at all impressed by my plight.

Eventually, the cabbie got back behind the wheel and began to drive in the direction of my Marriott. I assumed he'd finally taken pity on me. More probably, he just thought he'd got a budding Dennis Wise in the back of his cab and decided to cut his losses.

"Ma femme est laide," I said, in more measured and meaningful tones now, to the woman on the back seat as we got close to the hotel. I wanted her to feel bad about trying to steal my cab. So I looked at her as sternly as I could through the alcoholic haze while I was saying it. How could you do that to me, I wanted to imply, how could you deprive me of attending the birth of my child?

The cabbie dropped me off. He wouldn't take any money. He just wanted rid of me. I was still full of self-righteous indignation about my treatment. Still panicking about my wife.

I got my bags, got another cab, got to the Gare du Nord, got a chocolate tart at a shop, got the first Eurostar back to London, threw up the chocolate tart and fell into an uneasy sleep. I woke on the English side of the Channel Tunnel. My wife had texted to say I was going to be in time. The birth was scheduled for midday. I was going to be at Waterloo by 10am. There was no-one else on the train. Everyone was heading in the opposite direction to watch the World Cup Final. I was the only Englishman going from Paris to London.

I started to think about the conversation in the cab and a kind of dread began to settle over me. What was the word for pregnant? Was it 'laide' or was it 'lourde' which, on reflection, I thought meant 'heavy'. It was after 9am by now, so I texted a mate of my mine who speaks fluent French. The word for pregnant, he said, was 'enceinte'. The dread deepened. The hangover was starting to take hold and I knew now that 'laide' definitely didn't mean pregnant.

So what had I been saying to that cabbie and the woman in the back of the taxi? Why had they looked so unmoved?

I texted my mate again. I got the answer. Turned out I had been roaring rather a different message to my companions. "My wife is ugly," I'd been shouting, over and over and over again. "I have to get back to my hotel, immediately. My wife is ugly."

Classy, I thought. Classy behaviour all round on my part. The kind of behaviour a footballer would have got panned for if he'd done it.

And you know what? My little boy didn't come into this world until the middle of the afternoon in the end. If I'd known, I could have waited for the next taxi.

Oliver Holt is chief sports writer for the Daily Mirror. He began his career on the Liverpool Daily Post and worked for the Times as motor racing correspondent, chief football writer and chief sports writer.

Favourite player: Dead heat between Micky Quinn, Peter Barnes and Norman Whiteside because I associate all of them with a lot of happy times in my childhood before watching football became a job.

Most memorable match: Manchester United v Bayern Munich in the Nou Camp in 1999 because of its unbelievable ending, the fact that it sealed the Treble and that it finally brought United another European Cup victory after more than 30 years of trying.

THE MAN WHO LAUNCHED LEGENDS

Argentina's debt to the man from Kent

By Tony Hudd

ENGLAND coach Fabio Capello calls him "il diavolo" – Italian for the devil – while in his native Argentina he is "la pulga," Spanish for the flea.

Samuel Eto'o likens seeing him play to watching "dibujos animados," Spanish for animated pictures. Ex-Barcelona team-mate Ronaldinho, describes him simply as the best footballer in the world.

Just as Zinedine Zidane and Ronaldo were icons to the previous generation, Lionel Andre Messi, all 5ft 5in – even with the benefit of growth hormones – stands on the cusp of becoming one of the greatest footballers of this generation. When this extravagantly gifted youngster has the ball at his feet he is blessed with the ability to move fans, irrespective of allegiance, to the edge of their seats.

Messi is the latest, most notable talent, to emerge from an English-founded footballing dynasty responsible for nurturing some of the world's greatest players. Out of that same, prolific Academy, poured Argentine legends Diego Maradona, Gabriel Batistuta and Jorge Valdano. Others who have contributed to the Argentina national side are former Serie A leading scorer Abel Balbo, ex-Manchester United defender Gabriel Heinze, Walter Samuel, Ariel Ortega, Maxi Rodriguez and Aldo Duscher, who was to gain notoriety for breaking David Beckham's metatarsal.

Like his predecessors, Messi, Barcelona's 10-stone talisman, has reason to respect Englishman Isaac Newell from Taylors Lane, Strood, near Rochester in Kent who founded a dynasty that was to become Newell's Old Boys. So rich has been the quality gushing off their conveyor belt of talent that Newell's established themselves in football history by having all their players fill the national team in a single game when they represented the country in a pre-Olympic tournament. Queen's Park of Scotland became the other when they represented the country in the first ever international against England.

Born on 24 April 1853, Newell, the son of Joseph Newell and Mary Goodger, was an adventurous youngster who developed a love of sport and with it a passion for football. After turning 16 he was accompanied by a group of his father's friends to Argentina on a ship bound for the industrial northern city Rosario, attracted by the sizeable English community that had taken up residence. Rosario, which lies 18 miles north west of the capital Buenos Aires, today revels in the distinction of being Messi's birthplace.

When Newell arrived he presented a letter of recommendation from his father to William Wheelright, the administrator of the British-owned Central Argentine Railway. Wheelright gave him a job as a telegraphist. In 1876, Newell married German girl Anna Jockinsen who bore him a son, Claudio and daughters Liliana and Margarita. By 1884, Newell had acquired a property and founded the Colegio Comercial Anglicano Argentina. His adopted college colours were a distinctive red and black, a mixture of the English and German flags which, to this day, remain the colours of Newell's Old Boys.

Argentina's early fascination with football started with natives watching British sailors playing the game. The country's dominant genes may be from Spain and Italy but the influence of Britain has arguably had the greatest influence on Argentina's football. In the year that Newell founded his college, the first football set of laws arrived in Argentina. As the game took a hold on the country, British railway workers, who had become crucial to the country's economy by laying tracks to ports where beef and grain could be loaded on to ships, formed Quilmes Football Club and they, along with Gimansia y Esgrima of La Plata remain Argentina's two oldest clubs.

By 1891, Alexander Hutton, director of the English High Schools, established the Argentine Association Football League and a championship was played a full five years before Sweden and Belgium became the first to do so on mainland Europe.

Education, and the teaching of the English language, gave way to football at the top of Newell's pecking order of priorities as he added his name to the number of the game's founding fathers in Argentina. Such was the growth of the sport's popularity, Newell decided to alternate study at the college with sporting activity. Resplendent with his trademark handlebar moustache, he became a familiar figure on the streets of Rosario, watching, always learning, from the matches involving street urchins who clogged the highways, kicking around rag balls. Coats were used as goalposts, just as they were in Messi's formative years in playground kickabouts.

Newell became addicted to street football, watching many matches on Entre Rio Street where the revolutionary Che Guevara was born in 1928. On 3 November 1903, he took the momentous decision to form Club Atletico Newell's, recruiting many of the street urchins whose skills he had admired. Fellow teachers and students made up the numbers. Newell appointed himself coach. It was the start of city rivalry with Rosario Central, a neighbouring club.

Newell's took the nickname "leprosos" (lepers) after their founder insisted the team played a charity match to raise funds for a leprosy clinic. Two years later, the equally renowned Boca Juniors was founded by Italians Esteban Baglietto, Alfredo Scarpatti, Santiago Sana plus brothers Juan and Teodoro Farenga. As the British and European influence gathered momentum, River Plate, whose most famous old boys are Alfredo De Stefano and Omar Sivori, was founded. In the same year, the British influence was felt again as English tea baron, Sir Thomas Lipton, donated a cup to be presented to the winners of internationals between Argentina and Uruguay.

In 1900, ill-health persuaded Newell to appoint his son Claudio and daughter-in-law Katie Cowell directors of the college. Yet still he maintained his slavish devotion to all matters football. Seven years later, on 16 October, this South American pioneer of football and the man whose club was to launch legends died at the early age of 54. His legacy to Argentine football remains indelible.

Today, the club calls home the 42,000 capacity El Coloso del Parque (The Colossus of the Park) where in 2003 they celebrated their centenary.

Newell's role of honour includes five Argentine Championship wins in 1974, 1987/88, 1990/91, 1992 and 2004. In addition they were runners-up of the Copa Libertadores de America twice in 1988 and 1992. Newell's also won a friendly mini-tournament called the Little World Cup in 1988 competing against River Plate, Milan, Juventus, Real Madrid and Manchester United. In 1941 they became one of a handful of Argentine clubs to tour Europe, defeating the likes of Valencia, Borussia Moenchengladbach, Real Madrid and the Spainish A national team.

Britain is a country towards which Argentines have mixed emotions, though the anti-British proletariat have no choice but to scream English words "Newell's! Newell's!"

Despite the emergence of the African nations, Argentina continues to be the world's most prolific producer of top quality footballers. Since the World Cup's inception in 1930, the famous light blue and white stripes have consistently figured among the favourites. As we Brits, numbed by continual failure at the highest international level, look enviously at their continued success, there is the consolation of knowing they could not have done it without us and especially the likes of Kentish Man Isaac Newell.

Tony Hudd is the Kent Messenger Group's chief football writer. After covering Gillingham for many years he has since graduated to reporting Charlton.

***Favourite player:** Zinedine Zidane. I was privileged to watch him during his formative years with Cannes and Bordeaux. Whenever he played I studied him rather than the game because he was the complete footballer.*

***Most memorable match:** Wembley, May 25, 1998. Charlton beat Sunderland 7-6 on penalties in the Nationwide League's First Division play-off final. If ever a football match squeezed emotions dry this was it on an afternoon of unparalleled drama.*

WRONG NAME BUT HUGHES MAKES THE RIGHT MARK

The "split-personality thing" that turns him into a rottweiler

By Oliver Kay

THE BIRTH certificate reads Leslie Mark Hughes. Somehow it is difficult to think of Mark Hughes as a Leslie. Whether in raging bull mode for Manchester United or Chelsea in his heyday as a player, or on the touchline these days as the belligerent manager of Manchester City, he never really seemed like a Leslie.

Away from football, though, he could hardly be more different: perhaps not a Leslie, but certainly quietly spoken, polite, self-effacing, the antithesis of the figure who once spread fear through the hearts of opposition defenders and is now the scourge of referees, linesmen and fourth officials on touchlines up and down the country. It is what Sir Alex Ferguson calls "a split-personality thing."

"Off the pitch you could not find a quieter guy," the United manager said. "But put him on the pitch and he's a totally different character – he was a rottweiler on the pitch, a real warrior."

And that is Hughes in a nutshell. Off the pitch, some would liken him to a poodle – and not just when his tight curls get wet in the Lancashire rain – but when that whistle blows at the start of every match he is involved in, he becomes the rottweiler that Ferguson describes, transformed in an instant from mild-mannered Dr Jekyll into the terrifying Mr Hyde.

It is a transformation that Hughes says he "can understand, but can't really explain." In his attempt to do so, he often harks back to his time in the youth teams at United in the early 1980s. As a teenager he was shy in the company of players such as Bryan Robson, Ray Wilkins and Frank Stapleton. Even Norman Whiteside, 18 months his junior, felt far more at ease, having been tipped for superstardom from an early age and played in the 1982 World Cup finals as a 17-year-old. Hughes, by contrast, lacked confidence and became frustrated at his struggle to break into Ron Atkinson's team. And it was this frustration that propelled him towards the first team. "I had felt I wasn't showing how good I could be, so I started lashing out a bit," he recalled. "And when I started getting aggressive, I started making progress, so I stuck with it."

That progress saw Hughes undergo a conversion from a box-to-box midfielder into a rampaging striker who, even at the age of 20, when he finally made the breakthrough to the United first team, belied his shyness by ruffling the feathers of defenders more than ten years his senior. He scored on his debut, in a League Cup tie against Oxford United in November 1983, and, more memorably, on his international debut for Wales against England six months later, but it was his gutsy performances, rather than his goals, that made his name.

Hughes was never a prolific goalscorer – not when compared to contemporaries such as Ian Rush, whom he played alongside in the Wales team, or Gary Lineker, with whom he was to team up in an ill-fated move to Barcelona – but the goals that he did score tended to be spectacular. Picture Hughes in his prime for United, Chelsea or Wales and, if he is not tussling with an opposition defender, he is airborne, perhaps horizontal, perhaps almost upside down, his right foot swinging back to unleash a spectacular volley past an incredulous goalkeeper, the power generated from the strength in those formidable thigh muscles. As Alan Partridge might have put it, Hughes had a foot like a traction engine.

And there we return to the great contradiction: how could an individual who appeared so meek off the pitch be such an animal – a ferocious, newly-uncaged animal – on it? That was a mystery during his playing days, but at least his teammates at United, Chelsea, Southampton, Everton and Blackburn and in the Wales national team knew that the great enigma would not continue to surprise them once he hung up or his boots. Or so they thought.

Many of Sir Alex Ferguson's former players at United have followed his footsteps into management – Bryan Robson, Steve Bruce, Roy Keane Paul Ince, Mark Robins – but nobody expected Hughes to do so. As Keane put it recently, "I thought Brucey would go into management and Robbo and possibly Paul Ince, but Sparky would not have been at the top of the list. He was fairly quiet until he was out on the social scene. I didn't necessarily think he would be a manager."

Nor did Hughes when he was thrust into the role of Wales manager in the summer of 1999, when he was still playing in the Premier League for Southampton. Asked to do the job to help his country, he accepted the challenge, but when he took sole charge of the team for the first time, in a European Championship qualifier away to Belarus, he freely admits now that he "didn't know what I was doing." Wales won, to his surprise, but he felt that it could only have been beginner's luck as he took time to adapt to the demands of management.

Suddenly, though, after two difficult years, things clicked for Hughes and Wales. After emerging unbeaten from an exacting series of friendly matches against Argentina, Czech Republic, Germany and Croatia in 2002, they started the Euro 2004 qualifying campaign with a bang, beating Finland, Azerbaijan twice and, most memorably of all, Italy at a packed Millennium Stadium. Wales, with a 100 per cent record from their first four matches, were dreaming of reaching the finals of a major tournament for the first time in almost half a century.

Sadly it was not to be, with Wales running out of steam and then harshly beaten 1-0 by Russia in a qualification play-off, but, while that might have marked the beginning of the end for Hughes as a national team manager, he had made such an impression that it became inevitable that he would be offered the chance to take charge of a Premier League club sooner or later. That offer arrived from Blackburn in September 2004 and, given that he had ties with the Lancashire club, having spent the final year of his playing career at Ewood Park, he had little hesitation in accepting the challenge, taking with him Mark Bowen and Eddie Niedzwiecki, his two loyal sidekicks from the Wales set-up.

There were those who felt that the quiet man would be found out at Blackburn, claiming that his reputation with Wales had been founded largely on a freakish victory over Italy, and the doubters were rubbing their hands gleefully when, within a few weeks of his arrival, they fell to consecutive 4-0 defeats at home to Middlesbrough and away to Chelsea. They had won just one of his eight matches in charge and for a time they were bottom of the Premier League, but then, suddenly, as with Wales, something clicked as his players began to adapt to his ideas and his methods and the team began to climb the table.

So what are those methods? To listen to some people, you would think Hughes is a manager whose ideas go little beyond telling his players to kick their opponents. Admittedly mud sticks in football, but this label is at least three years out of date, if indeed it was applicable in the first place. In his first season in charge, when Hughes needed his team to break the cycle of insipid performances that had put them at severe risk of relegation, they were certainly feisty and had their share of red cards – as you might expect of a team containing the likes of Lucas Neill, Andy Todd, Robbie Savage and Paul Dickov.

But the moment his first goal – survival – was attained, Hughes began to reconstruct his team on different lines, playing the type of football that belied their reputation for thuggery. He also showed that, on top of everything else, he was a shrewd operator in the transfer market. A look at some of his signings Ryan Nelsen (free transfer from DC United), Aaron Mokoena (£300,000 from Genk), Zurab Khizanishivili (£500,000 from Rangers), David Bentley (undisclosed from Arsenal), Benni McCarthy (£2.5 million from FC Porto), Chris Samba (£400,000 from Hertha Berlin), Stephen Warnock (£1.5 million from Liverpool) and Roque Santa Cruz (£3.8 million from Bayern Munich) reveals a record that few, if any, of his rivals can match over the past four seasons. With a budget far smaller than that of Newcastle, Tottenham, West Ham and others he somehow established Blackburn as a team that belonged in the top half of the Premier League. Now back in Manchester, Hughes more than most knows the challenge of making City realistic Premier League contenders in the shadow of his former home.

And that has always been the thing with Hughes. He has always had more strings to his bow than anyone has ever given him credit for. Motivator, organiser, tactician, genius in the transfer market – he appears to have it all. However, his current job may now preclude him from being amng the candidates when Sir Alex Ferguson finally vacates the manager's office at Manchester United. People may say that Hughes lacks the personality or the authority to take such an enormous role. Really, you would have thought they would know better by now ...

Oliver Kay has been a football reporter for the Times since 2000, covering the north-west of England. Previously he worked for Nottingham Evening Post and in the Manchester office of the Wardle Agency.

__Favourite player:__ Diego Maradona. An incredibly flawed individual, but a true genius with a ball at his feet.

__Most memorable match:__ Liverpool 1, Chelsea 0 (European Cup semi-final second leg, 3 May 2005). Not a classic game, but an unforgettable occasion. I have never known an atmosphere like it. The release of emotion at the final whistle is something I have not witnessed in a football ground before or since.

THE EXCUSE WAS A LOAD OF BALLS

The blame game includes a bald head and croaking frogs

By Des Kelly

THE WORLD of politics has always been awash with excuses. Former deputy Prime Minister John Prescott is apparently fat because he's bulimic. The married Liberal Democrat MP Mark Oaten only had a relationship with a rent boy because of a midlife crisis brought on by his baldness. And Gordon Brown was a master economist when Britain was thriving, but when the country fell into debt it was all down to a global credit crunch.

"Political language is designed to make lies sound truthful and murder respectable and to give an appearance of solidity to pure wind," said George Orwell.

These days that hot air is called 'spin', which is a dismal excuse in itself. Yet politics has nothing on sport when it comes to offering up ridiculous alibis. Our national game has a great history of farcical attempts at vindication, one where managers and players deserve medals for audacity.

For instance, they say clothes maketh the man. In football, they also maketh a handy excuse. Emlyn Hughes explained Liverpool's 1971 FA Cup Final defeat was caused by shirts that were "too heavy for the hot day", but that was merely a sample of the rag trade ingenuity that football legends are able to call upon.

Back in 1996, I was one of the reporters in Southampton when a bedraggled and unhappy Manchester United traipsed in at half-time at the wrong end of a 3-0 beating. The players certainly looked like strangers to one another, but little did we know sitting up in the press box that they were actually invisible too.

During that dismal 45 minutes, United had been wearing in a new kit that was battleship grey in colour. But then they trotted out for the second half clad in blue and white, having ditched their original strip. The quizzical laughter and derision of the crowd could not quite drown out the screams of the distraught kit manufacturer's marketing department many miles away.

Afterwards in the press conference manager Sir Alex Ferguson spelt out the reason for the quick change of outfit: "The players couldnae pick each other out against the crowd," he said.

Taking my life in my hands, I asked: "Er, can I clarify that you actually blaming the kit for defeat?"

"Aye," Ferguson replied, daring anyone to laugh, before trying to justify his bizarre explanation. Lord knows how much the decision to consign a kit to an instant firesale cost, but as collective excuses go it is priceless.

When accounting for defeat, a lack of talent or application rarely comes into it. So if it's not the kit, it must be something else. During his time as manager of Wimbledon, I remember the ever-entertaining Bobby Gould standing in front of the assembled media and growling: "You know why we are so poor? It was because of this!" he yelled, slamming a football into the floor for emphasis.

So how had this inanimate object conspired against him? Were the players unfamiliar with the strange orb placed before them? (Possibly). According to Gould, there was another reason; the ball was "too bouncy".

Hilariously, Kenny Dalglish trotted out the same claptrap during his time in charge of Newcastle United, when his massively expensive squad drew with non-League Stevenage in the FA Cup. Again, the ball had turned out to be "too bouncy." No matter that the balls in question had been the same for the humble semi-professional outfit pitted against his collection of millionaires.

The gripe led to a wonderful moment on BBC2's Newsnight when Jeremy Clarkson turned to Dalglish, and sneered: "Aren't you just a big girl's blouse?"

Footballers certainly can be delicate creatures. Did you know that a proud squad of World Cup contenders was once brought to their knees by tiny amphibians?

At the 2006 World Cup, Ukraine slumped to a woeful 4-0 defeat against Spain. Naturally, poor defending, slack marking or inept tactics had absolutely nothing to do with it. Hardly. In fact frogs wrecked their chances.

Ukraine defender Vladislav Vashchuk said the noise made by the little creatures outside the team's hotel in the Potsdam the night before the game had left the team tired and unable to perform. "Because of the frogs' croaking we hardly got a wink of sleep," the defender whined.

A German newspaper understandably decided this was "the worst World Cup excuse of all time." Ukraine croaked either way.

But if you want a demonstration of world-class excuse-making, then look no further than Scotland half-back Tommy Docherty. After taking part in a humiliating 7-0 defeat against Uruguay back in the 1954 World Cup in Switzerland, the Doc gave an early glimpse of the quotability that would mark out his managerial career as he struggled to pinpoint a reason for this national failure. Although the performances on the pitch were woeful, off it he produced a moment of individual brilliance. Docherty announced the players had let in seven goals because they had been physically drained prior to kick-off by the length of the Uruguayan national anthem.

We are all familiar with the affliction of temporary blindness that strikes managers when it comes to spotting the crimes committed by their own players. But it is rare to find a team-mate being blamed for causing that loss of vision.

Former Rotherham goalkeeper Chris Mooney was known as the 'Mad Monkey' for his habit of swinging from the crossbar like an ape as corners were about to be taken. He also made an absolute baboon of himself when he tried to find a reason why he had let a shot straight through his legs. Naturally, he blamed his centre-half as all good goalkeepers do. Only this defender hadn't been derelict in his duties. Instead, Nick Smith was accused of causing this embarrassing slip up by daring to possess a shiny bald head that reflected the sun's rays into the eyes of the keeper at the crucial moment, blinding Mooney as he reached for the ball.

Proof that football does not confine itself to itself to earthly concerns in the search for excuses. It doesn't even confine itself to this life. When Blackpool missed out on promotion in the play-offs against Bradford in 1996, someone who reads tea leaves in their spare time decided this wasn't a straightforward sporting setback but the work of supernatural forces. A story did the rounds suggesting that the ghost of Lord Nelson haunted the boardroom because the wood panels adorning the walls had been salvaged from his flagship.

Or it could have just been a bad dream I had.

That's my excuse anyway.

Des Kelly is a Daily Mail columnist, reporter and pundit, BBC1's Inside Sport, media consultant for Hill and Knowlton, director of Fast Web Media. Former acting editor and deputy editor of the Daily Mirror, head of sport Daily Mirror, head of sport Daily Express, chief sports reporter Today.

Favourite player: *Roy Keane. For his ultra competitive nature, no nonsense approach and his scorn of the celebrity football culture.*

Most memorable match: *Manchester United's 1999 Champions League victory in Barcelona. A thrilling end to a perfect trip with my dad and my brother. Unforgettable. Unbeatable.*

SAFER BUT QUIETER

Something has been lost from the modern game

By David Lacey

THERE WAS a time, before football grounds sprouted floodlights and no fan wore a replica shirt, when it was possible to arrive in a strange town and know immediately that there was a game on and where it was taking place. Men walking to a match had a certain step; not hurrying exactly but moving with the assured stride of people anticipating events. They usually walked in twos and threes, exchanging the odd word along the way but more often keeping their thoughts to themselves as they wondered what the afternoon would bring.

L.S. Lowry got it right when he picked out those dark figures going to a match at Bolton. That is the way it was for the best part of 100 years: no cars to speak of, no floodlights, no television highlights … just private images, personal memories.

For J.B. Priestley a game of football "turned you into a critic, happy in your judgment of fine points, ready in a second to estimate the worth of a well-judged pass, a run down the touchline, a lightning shot … it turned you into a partisan … elated, downcast, bitter, triumphant by turns at the fortunes of your side … and what is more it turned you into a member of a new community, all brothers together for an hour and a half."

Today's brotherhood is somewhat different. For a start it is part sisterhood given the fact that many more women go to games. It is also a brotherhood of conformity, all wearing the same scarves and the same shirts. Somebody, it may have been Jasper Carrott, has said that Newcastle United supporters look like bar codes.

Top-class football in England has never been watched in more comfort and safety, or at greater expense, than it is now. Spectators are seated with a perfect view of the play. Refreshment and toilet facilities are, for the most part, more than adequate. Even now it is mildly disconcerting, shortly before a big game kicks-off, to see the stands still half empty. Where are the fans? Finishing off their snacks and pre-match drinks before leisurely making their way to their allotted places.

Less than 20 years ago this seemed an impossible ideal in the English game. Even the major stadiums were hostile, claustrophobic, unsociable, insanitary places; not the sort of places to take mum and the kids. All that changed on a sunny April afternoon at Hillsborough in 1989 when after six minutes of an FA Cup semi-final between Liverpool and Nottingham Forest a policeman ran on to the pitch to tell the referee, Ray Lewis, that people were dying in the crush at the Leppings Lane end of the ground.

Ultimately the death toll among Liverpool supporters reached 96, with 200 injured. The subsequent report on the tragedy by Lord Justice Taylor savaged football for its complacency over safety matters, in spite of previous disasters at Bolton, Ibrox and Bradford, and summed up the overall slovenliness of the game's approach to its customers in scathing terms.

Taylor described facilities on the terraces as "lamentable" adding that "apart from the discomfort of standing on a terrace exposed to the elements the ordinary provisions to be expected at a place of entertainment are sometimes not merely basic but squalid."

In his view the absence of toilets at many grounds lowered standards of conduct. "The practice of urinating against walls or even on the terraces has become endemic," he said. "And is followed by men who would not behave that way elsewhere. The crowd conduct becomes degraded and other, misbehaviour seems less out of place."

This, remember, was 1989 not 1889.

The report memorably referred to "a prevailing stench of stewed onions" from mobile carts and shoddy sheds with fans having to eat hamburgers and chips outside in all weathers. "There is no reason why clean and attractive fast food outlets cannot be provided."

In short, said Taylor, most spectators experienced conditions which were "in stark contrast to the different world, only yards away, in the boardroom and lucrative executive boxes."

Looking back it is a wonder that so many football followers put up with this state of affairs for as long as they did. The truth is that by the early Eighties spectators were deserting the game in large numbers. Seasonal aggregate attendances dropped from their post-War peak of 41.2 million in 1948/49 to 16.4 million in 1985/86. By 1989 gates had begun to recover, but were still 10 million below the 29.5 million of 2006/07.

Hooliganism rather than bad toilets and dodgy hotdogs was the principal reason why people, and in particular those with young families, stayed away. The trouble had started more than 20 years before Hillsborough as younger fans, better able to afford admission prices, took over the terraces and turned harmless, raucous support into declarations of tribal warfare backed up by violence inside and outside the grounds.

The clubs tended to blame society and exaggeration by the media, content to take the money and hope for the best. Fans were segregated by steel fences and prevented from invading the pitch by what Taylor described as "fearsome high structures with florid arrangements of spikes, redolent of medieval weaponry. They look more suited to a prison than a sports ground."

Visiting supporters were often marched to grounds under police escort reminiscent, said Taylor, "of a column of prisoners of war." In a sense this is precisely what they were.

Hillsborough was the result of police negligence on the day but the mindset which, for a few fateful minutes, mistook a safety problem for a security problem was the result of the years of crowd violence which had preceded it. After Taylor, terraces gave way to seats and the perimeter fences came down. Not that hooliganism was banished, it was simply priced away from football grounds.

The Football Association's Blueprint For Football, published in 1991, was derided for its naive assumption that sanctioning a breakaway Premier League would produce a more successful England team, but it was right to point out that "the levels of comfort and sophistication of our football grounds are inadequate to the requirements of a population who are more discerning than they have been in the past and who confront a range of leisure opportunities that vastly exceeds the range available to their predecessors."

In short, people now had more to do. Football, the FA concluded, had to move upmarket to follow the affluent middle class. Present-day prices reflect this trend.

People can now watch football matches confident they will enjoy decent facilities and not be killed. No sane person would wish for a return to the days of packed, swaying terrace crowds only a crush barrier away from catastrophe.

Yet something has been lost from the atmosphere of the average match which is not easy to define.

Perhaps it is that air of freedom and spontaneity which used to go with an afternoon on the terraces. Before crowds became violent and rival fans had to be forcibly kept apart it was possible to go a ground like Stamford Bridge much as a stroller in the park would stop off at the bandstand for a bit of pomp and circumstance. The casual fan could saunter in five minutes before kick-off and find a decent viewing point amid a crowd of 50,000-plus. The only way of doing this now would be a buy a ticket off a tout and even then there would be no way of moving around.

Crowds do not roar in the old way. In advocating all-seat stadia Taylor did not think the atmosphere would suffer. "I am not convinced that the cherished culture of the terraces is wholly lost when fans are seated," he said. "Watching the more boisterous and demonstrative sections at all-seated grounds I have noticed no absence of concerted singing, chanting ,clapping or gesticulation in unison."

Maybe so, but standing up and gesticulating in unison will get fans thrown out on more than a few grounds now.

Even at the largest stadia, such as Old Trafford and the Emirates, the crowds, while they manage a decent shout, do not roar as they did. The Hampden Roar came from the bowels of the Scottish soul, but modern fans merely exercise their lungs. Perhaps the all-pervasive influence of television has produced a breed of spectator that waits upon events instead of willing them along.

Hard to believe that in the early 1950s the Football League banned live radio broadcasts of matches because, as the then president Arthur Drewry pointed out: "We are a little afraid that on wet Saturdays there is every encouragement to indulge in listening to rather than watching football." Now fans can plug in an earpiece and do both.

Do the characters in crowds still abound? Fifty years ago grounds like Millwall's old Den were full of them. A small, wizened man wearing an old army greatcoat and clutching a battered toy lion used to sit within earshot of the Millwall directors box and hurl abuse at its occupants until, inevitably, he was thrown out. But he was always there next time.

Being a football fan used to be about being slightly absurd for a couple of hours. Fans still may be as daft as ever, but they do not seem to have so much fun. Maybe the problem is that it is no longer a matter of "a shilling fair thrawn away" as much as 50 quid or more down the drain.

David Lacey suffered the decline and fall of Brighton and Hove Albion for the Evening Argus and covered 10 World Cups for the Guardian before retiring in 2002. He is now a columnist.

__Favourite player:__ Jimmy Langley (Brighton and later Fulham). A hard-tackling full-back who rarely committed a foul even when challenging from behind. Was also a long-throw specialist.

__Favourite match:__ An FA Cup quarter-final at the City Ground in 1967 when Johnny Carey's Nottingham Forest came from behind to beat Harry Catterick's Everton 3-2 in the closing minutes as Ian Storey-Moore completed a hat-trick.

CHARADES CLINCHED ARSENAL JOB FOR WENGER

Arsene went on to transform attitudes in English football

By Amy Lawrence

IT IS A shame that the general public's perception of Arsene Wenger is based on the dreaded post-match television interview. It is not the easiest stage to be yourself – straight into a lens, immediately after you have spent 90 minutes of purgatory in a state of unimaginable stress on the sidelines. At best people see a straight faced analyst. At worst they see a very bad loser. But as the man himself has often said: "Show me a good loser and I will show you a bad winner."

It is odd that his TV persona is quite charmless because away from the cameras Wenger is particularly engaging company. When he first arrived in England, Sir Alex Ferguson struck the first of many verbal blows by sniping: "What does he know about English football, coming from Japan?"

The answer, as it turned out, is that he knows an awful lot. Not just about the minutiae of football and coaching, but also about economics and social politics – without that knowledge he may not have cracked an environment that is mistrustful, and sometimes downright disrespectful, about foreigners. He certainly wouldn't have been able to form a strategy that enabled his club to consistently punch above its financial weight, while constructing a super stadium and futuristic training complex. In the early years, it was common to come away from one of his press briefings feeling that you learned something, or that you were encouraged to think about things in a different way.

Wenger has become such a landmark on the English footballing landscape it is easy to forget how much resistance there was to his appointment at Arsenal in 1996. David Dein is the man credited with convincing his fellow board members that he knew of a man capable of redrawing the ambitions of a club that was in a rut at the time. Dein had known Wenger socially for a few years. While Wenger was coaching Monaco, Arsenal's then vice-chairman had a boat moored in the South of France and as football people whose paths crossed they always enjoyed a chat. Wenger once visited London and Dein invited him to dinner after a match at Highbury.

It was during a post-meal game of charades that Dein made a mental note about his guest's personal qualities, recognising how much effort Wenger took to join in, even though he was not as proficient in English as he is now. He ticked enough human as well as football boxes to be a bold choice for Arsenal manager one day, Dein reckoned. It was still a very experimental choice. A coach from overseas? At one of England's most traditional football institutions?

Even from within the club, Wenger's arrival was regarded as an enormous gamble. And in some cases a joke. The captain Tony Adams winced, wondering: "What does this Frenchman know about football? He's not going to be as good as George [Graham]. Does he even speak English properly?"

Ray Parlour did impressions of Inspector Clouseau. But these two players, and many of their team-mates, were quickly converted. The man's methods might have caused a few shockwaves – notably when he had the players practising muscle-honing poses in the hotel ballroom as preparation for his first match. Stretching routines, and nutrition, are just two of the staples which he believes gives players the optimum chance to be in the best physical shape. Even if it makes one per cent of difference, he reasons, that percentage point could be the difference between winning and losing.

His attention to detail is legendary, and obsessive. A social life comes a poor third behind studying games, and then studying more games. It seems strange today, now that training ground meals at most professional clubs are more nutritionally balanced than eggs and chips followed by jam roly poly and custard, and players tend not to spend spare afternoons at the pub. But Wenger's ideas were initially perceived as radical.

It yielded some outstanding results. He inspired a league and FA Cup double in his first full season, a feat his evolving team repeated four years later. It was then that he was asked about the possibility of going the whole of the following season undefeated.

"It's not impossible," he replied. "I know it will be difficult for us to go through the season unbeaten. But if we keep the right attitude it's possible we can do it."

About a month later, a lad called Wayne Rooney lashed a last minute winner for Everton against Arsenal at Goodison Park. Then Arsenal lost to Blackburn. And Southampton. And Manchester United. All before Christmas.

Wenger spent much of the campaign being mocked for boasting that his team would produce an unbeaten season. But his prediction that it could be done was only one year out. In 2003/04, Arsenal emulated the achievement of Preston North End's Invicibles in 1889. Nobody thought it could be done in the modern game. What made it even more impressive was the style with which it was achieved. Arsenal fans called it "Wengerball" in reference to a flowing game that was marvellously easy on the eye.

There are not many finer sights than Wengerball in full flow. Then again, there are not many more excruciating sights than Wengerball on a bad day. It is arguably the most frustrating style of football ever created. There is some truth in Alan Hansen's well worn critique that Arsenal have no plan B, and that they don't like it up 'em. Without such a stubborn commitment to an aesthetic passing game – one which means scarce time at the training ground put aside for organising the defence or practicing corner routines – Wenger might have had more trophies on his CV.

Bizarrely, Arsenal under Wenger have simultaneously been one of the most admired and criticised teams in Europe. One crucial thing his single-minded approach does promote is a strong relationship with his players. So what is it about Wenger that strikes such a chord with his charges? Essentially he tries to treat them like adults and respects that players are entitled to their own minds too. Without that, it is unlikely individuals as headstrong as Patrick Vieira and Thierry Henry would have stayed in England as long as they did, when both were regularly prized at higher-paying global superclubs. These two giants of the Premiership era – his best buys ever as Arsenal manager – embody everything about Wenger's ideal for a footballer.

Gifted ball players, supremely athletic, and dedicated, strong personalites. If only signing players was always that easy. Wenger has fared remarkably well in the transfer market, even though he tends not to be a major spender. In fact he is notoriously frugal compared to his direct rivals at Manchester United, Liverpool and of course Chelsea. His spending habits demonstrate not only an eye for a bargain, but also a preference to create and mould a great player than buy one ready made. Henry was a winger in a rut at Juventus, and Vieira, Kolo Toure and Cesc Fabregas were complete unknowns in England. All became established world class performers.

His critics quibble that Arsenal is no longer an "English" team, given the scarcity of true Anglo-Saxon accents in the dressing room. In general, the English players he has bought in the past – a catalogue of disappointment headed by the incomparably ineffective Francis Jeffers – have not worked out as well as his imports. But the more pertinent point for Wenger is a fundamental belief in good players, rather than nationalities.

"We represent a football club which is about values and not passports," is his maxim. So deeply has he imprinted his personality on Arsenal, it is hard to imagine how the club would function without him.

When that time does come, which Wenger will we remember? Will it be the shameless football romantic, whose philosophy of beautiful football at all costs graced the Premiership with probably the prettiest, most stylish passing game of recent memory?

Or will it be the sore loser, whose long face in times of trouble often preceded petty complaints that less skilled opponents were nothing more than spoilers?

Above all we should remember that Wenger has transformed attitudes in English football. "I remember reading in my first full season that a foreign manager can never win the league in England," Wenger once recalled. "I feel I opened the door for foreign managers, because I proved that you could be successful even if you are not from here. I believe I contributed somewhere to open people's minds to think differently."

Amy Lawrence has covered football for the Observer since a terrifying ordeal at Selhurst Park in 1996 where her first match report – a gentle affair including seven goals, penalties, red cards and a late winner – inspired a timely bout of writer's block. Fortunately, she recovered enough to enjoy writing about what Pele so perfectly described as "God's game" for seasons to come.

Favourite player: Zinedine Zidane. All the greats have that magical capacity to entrance everybody on the pitch and in the stadium. In the modern game, nobody had it as purely as Zizou.

Most memorable match: Liverpool 0 Arsenal 2, 26 May 1989. Sport with the kind of dramatic and emotional kick that doesn't come along very often in anyone's lifetime.

THE PRIVATE WORLD OF ROY KEANE

Becoming close is mission impossible – and always look at him when talking

By Matt Lawton

THE FIRST meeting with Roy Keane did not go terribly well. It was in a hotel at Dublin Airport and the then Manchester United captain was walking out of the breakfast room. He was alone and I thought it a good time to ask him if there was any chance of a chat after he had finished training with his Irish international colleagues. I'm not entirely sure what happened next, but amid the expletives came a lecture about bad manners. I had invaded his personal space, which I thought took some doing in a public area, but I stood there calmly while he continued his tirade and simply marked him down as a lunatic who was best avoided in the future.

Then, however, the following day arrived and Keane spotted me in the hotel reception area. "What was it you wanted to talk about?" he said, and after a brief explanation we sat down for what was a fascinating interview.

When I saw him again in a post-match mixed zone after a Champions League game at Old Trafford, he was only too happy to stop and talk. Until, that is, my manners let me down for a second time. Distracted by the sight of Dwight Yorke clowning around behind him, I dared divert my gaze away from the Irishman and towards his jubilant team-mate. It was only for a split second, but long enough to send Keane into a rage. "If you're not going to look at me I'm not going to answer your f****** questions," he said. And that was pretty much that.

When my then sports editor asked me to approach Keane's lawyer Michael Kennedy, who doubled as his agent, and offer him the opportunity to "write" a column for the newspaper, I didn't expect to get a positive response. I could imagine what Keane would say. Like the idea, and don't even mind the paper (the Daily Telegraph at that time), but the bloke's an idiot.

I felt like an idiot midway through the negotiations that then followed. Keane, to my delight, was interested, and not even remotely offended by what amounted to a derisory financial offer. Some newspapers pay footballers in excess of £20,000 for a single ghosted article. The money on the table on this occasion was 10 per cent of that. His lawyer was as pleasantly surprised as I was that he was not insulted.

Then, however, something really rather embarrassing happened. My sports editor informed me that I had in fact offered a good deal more than he was prepared to pay. To my horror, twice as much. Time to confirm what Keane had long suspected.

The telephone call to his lawyer was not an easy one. "I think you've probably blown it, but I will talk to him anyway," said the respected Michael Kennedy. "Ring me tomorrow."

I did, but only because it would have been bad manners not to have done so. "Well I can't believe it, but he's still prepared to do the column," said Kennedy. Extraordinary.

We met up to discuss arrangements during a Manchester United tour of the Far East. A room was set aside at the team hotel in Bangkok. I arrived about an hour early and never took my eyes off him during the entire conversation. I can't be sure but I might have even broken the world blinking record that day.

When the start of the season arrived, everything appeared to be fine. He called me and we arranged to meet at a hotel near his home for what would be the first column. Again I arrived early and so did he. He clearly does take the whole manners thing pretty damn seriously, I thought. He would not accept a drink. Not even a glass of water. But we sat there for an hour for what, I have to say, was one of the most interesting conversations I have ever had. The column was a cracker.

Sir Alex Ferguson had just sold Jaap Stam to Lazio and the Irishman said he was as stunned as anyone. He was not the slightest bit concerned if his words offended his manager or the club he served with such distinction. Stam, he said, had been treated like "a piece of meat" and he was hugely sympathetic.

Two weeks later and it was time for column number two. Same place, same time. Again he was early and again he declined the offer of a drink. We sat there for an hour or so and discussed the issues for what was another terrific column. Behind that dark, sometimes slightly sinister glare, I thought, is an intelligent man with incredible self-confidence. I recall trying to enter into a discussion about formations and tactics. "It's got nothing to do with that," he snarled. "It's about players, and getting the best players on the pitch."

Between the second and third columns, the combustible Keane was sent-off at Newcastle. He was furious with himself for allowing Alan Shearer to get the better of him, and he expressed as much in the column that then followed. But plans for the fourth column were cancelled, with an apologetic Kennedy suggesting the red card had affected his client profoundly. Keane would later reveal in his auto-biography that the incident had in fact left him considering retirement.

That fourth column was never written and it was not until Keane walked out of the Republic of Ireland camp shortly before the 2002 World Cup that we came into contact again. A bidding war had broken out between rival newspaper groups for the first Keane interview on his return to Manchester and my employers at Associated Newspapers were prepared to make what they hoped would be a competitive offer. Bidding on behalf of the group's Sunday titles in Ireland and England, as well as the Daily Mail, I managed to use a combination of the company cheque-book and our past association to seal the deal. The interviews followed, first for my colleagues on the Sundays and then for the Daily Mail. I was in Japan with the England team and the time difference made it a very late night. But the interview took place over the phone and the copy followed.

Typically of Keane, it was terrific and I remember being struck by what seemed to be a genuine lack of regret. No matter that he had just denied himself the opportunity to play in the World Cup when he was at the peak of his powers. No matter that he had divided the opinion of a country. What also registered with me more personally was the fact that he had given me his home telephone number. Never had he surrendered it during my brief time as his ghost-writer. Rarely did he even pass it on to team-mates. But I now had it and when a story broke the very next day that suggested he was about to fly back to Ireland's pre-World Cup base on the island of Saipan I had the perfect way of checking it out. I did think twice about using the number for a second time and I was relieved when he resisted any temptation he might have had to scream down the phone. He very calmly informed me that he would not be going back and I then apologised for having used his number again so soon after being given it. "I won't make a habit of it," I said as a bit of a joke.

"Don't worry," he said. "I wouldn't have given it to you if I wasn't already planning to change it. Getting a new number tomorrow."

A further interview would follow a year later, days after Keane had celebrated a seventh Premier League title in a decade of success at Old Trafford. We met at the same hotel as before and this time sat there for two hours.

"I'm buying you a drink this time," I said. "You don't have to drink it, but I'm not sitting in this bar again without at least ordering something."

He still had no regrets about the World Cup. No regrets about his book and those hugely controversial comments about Alf Inge Haaland. He even seemed that much more relaxed about being sent-off. It had happened that season at Sunderland. "Jason McAteer would annoy anyone," he said, rather amusingly, in justifying his behaviour.

What he never mentioned, during that time as a columnist or indeed in any of the interviews, were the kind of things he would quietly do while captain of United.

Phil Townsend, the club's director of communications, revealed to me not so long ago how Keane would borrow a club minibus and take a dozen youth team players on visits to young offenders' institutions and other such places. It was a regular thing. His way of educating the club's young players while also giving something back to the Manchester community. A loyal family man, there is clearly another side to the fierce competitor we saw on the pitch and now observe in the dug-out at Sunderland.

Prompted by that, I tried to get in touch with Keane again for yet another interview. I wrote to him at Sunderland and hoped our previous encounters would greatly enhance my chances of securing another meeting. Eventually, I received a call from a press officer at the club. The message, which he said had come from Keane, was to the point. I was back at Dublin Airport, at the back of the queue.

Matt Lawton is football correspondent of the Daily Mail. Prior to that he spent seven years in Manchester as a football reporter, first for the Daily Express and then the Daily Telegraph.

Favourite player: So hard to identify one, but I don't think a player has ever excited me more than Paul Gascoigne did during the 1990 World Cup. I only hope he finds some kind of peace, and that football does all it can to help him.

Most memorable match: Brentford v Notts County, 12 April 1993. My 23rd birthday and my first live match report. After filing my copy to the Daily Express, I called the office and checked that everything was ok. "No," said then news editor, Charles Sale. "It's shit. Do it again." I was so traumatised my career almost ended before it had even begun.

POOLS ARE THE HART AND SOUL OF FOOTBALL

Super Cooper obeyed Fergie's "champagne" orders

By Samantha Lee

'AS THE sun set over the shipyards, a war-weary Hartlepool United battled the North Sea winds at their ramshackle Victoria Park home to lay gallant claim to three valiant points.'

Here we go, another old boy from the broadsheets makes his bi-decade pilgrimage to the North East, intro already penned as he steps off the train at Church Street station.

Writing one match report on Hartlepool United every 20 years didn't seem to inspire originality from some quarters of the press. The now home to many a million pound yacht was still the 'shipyards,' the award-winning and studiously tendered ground was still 'ramshackle' and the North Sea was still throwing up biting gales in the middle of a mild April.

They want to try a 9,000-word week working on the Hartlepool Mail, fulfilling the punters' thirst for insight and pub-fodder, while combing every word for an argument to have with the local reporter come next Saturday afternoon. That being me for six seasons between 1999 and 2005.

But while I wasn't poring over the international squad announcements, preparing for cup finals or even taking note of anything beyond the second round draw at times, there was always something to write about covering a lower league club. Yes, I did occasionally glance over in envy at my national colleagues, booking flights to Greece, the Nou Camp or even planning jaunts to Wembley. There were times when they also glanced enviously in my direction.

What I enjoyed over many of them was good old-fashioned contact reporting. If I wanted to speak to a player I picked up the phone and talked to him. In the current climate of agents, press officers and media spokespeople, trying to find out why David Beckham has been handed a transfer or ask for an explanation as to why Michael Owen seems to have lost his scoring boots requires a covert operation the SAS would be proud of.

It worked both ways, though. They had my number too and I received one or two ear-bashings from players less than happy with under-average marks out of 10. All of which were sorted out by the time the phone was put down, agreeing to disagree at times and once printing an apology when an outstanding defensive performance from Mark Robinson saw him awarded a 0 thanks to a slight typo which the sub was, of course, duly blamed for.

Premier League clubs now have video play-back in the press box and three-course meals waiting for the scribes before kick-off. I'll stick with shouting down to the press boys "who got the last touch?" and standing bang outside the dressing room getting an insight into the manager's true feelings any day.

People complain there's too much money in the Premier League these days. Players' wages are too high, tickets cost too much and is there really any need for a third and fourth strip? Take all of that away and what have you got? The good old football leagues.

In my time covering Pools I hitched rides on the team bus when trains home from Plymouth on a Saturday evening were non-existent. I joined the lads for a pint on their day off during pre-season trips to Norway and Holland, notebook and pen back at the hotel so they could talk freely without reprise.

I also struck up a few good friendships. One of which was with former manager Neale Cooper, a genuine heart-on-his sleeve Scotsman, whose departure from Hartlepool was very much shrouded in mystery.

Neale cut his teeth in football under the then just plain Alex Ferguson at Aberdeen and was part of the 1983 Cup Winners' Cup team that included the likes of Alex McLeish, Willie Miller, Jim Leighton and Gordon Strachan, who saw off Real Madrid in Gothenburg. The young dressing room clown and probably the last person to attempt a Fergie impersonation within ear-shot of the most fearsome gaffer in football turned to management like many of his former Pittodrie team-mates.

Neale will be remembered by many for his rather rash challenge on Charlie Nicholas three seconds into an early '80s Celtic-Aberdeen clash. But far from it being a moment of madness from a young teenager out to impress it was very much planned, albeit not quite the way it turned out.

Neale recalled that day with his trademark cheeky grin and how Ferguson had called him to one side on Monday morning and told him he was in the team the following weekend.

"They have this guy there," Neale regaled in his best Fergie voice. "Charlie. Champagne f****** Charlie they call him. I want him stopped and you will be the man to do it. For the next week I want you to think about nothing else but Charlie f****** Nicholas, you got that?"

Two days later after another heavy training session, Ferguson called over his young midfielder.

"What you doing son?"

"I'm just off for a shower boss," was Neale's reply.

"No you're not, you're thinking of Charlie f****** Nicholas, now get out of my sight."

And so it went on each day. By the time Saturday afternoon came Neale said he'd spent every waking and many a sleeping minute sticking to Fergie's orders.

"I was that wound up, the whistle blew, the ball went out to Nicholas and the next thing I know we're both lying on the deck and I'm surrounded. The Celtic players are screaming blue (well green) murder at me, the ref is on his way over and I have several thousand people in the stadium wanting my blood.

"I look over to the Celtic bench, they're all out of their seats, red faced and wanting to kill me too. I then looked over to our bench and in the midst of all of the fury I see Fergie, a content smile on his face and a knowing nod in my direction, at least I'd kept one person happy."

Neale took over at Hartlepool after the unexplained sacking of Mike Newell, who had taken Hartlepool into League One as runners-up following predecessor Chris Turner's good ground work.

The now bald-headed Scotsman took them straight into the League One play-off semi finals the first year and was heading there once again when his untimely sacking came days before the last game of a season which was to take them to their first ever play-off final. The reason behind Neale's sacking was never made public by chairman Ken Hodcroft, a businessman in the oil industry by trade and looking after the club for his employers, Increased Oil Recovery. I spent a very long day and night trying to prise some sort of explanation out of him but the best I could get from someone late to the game of football was hints that Neale was homesick for his children, who were back home in Aberdeen with his ex-wife. But this had always been the case and Neale was just another man who worked away from his children and looked forward to snatched trips home and summer holidays with his daughter and son Lewis, who is now a promising member of Liverpool's youth academy.

Of course when football fans don't get straight answers, the analogies from the pub boardroom come out as fact. So I called a still tearful Neale and offered to buy him a pint. I also put the many conspiracy theories to him, no matter how scurrilous they sounded.

"You had a fight with the chairman?"

"No, but I wouldn't mind going toe-to-toe with him now."

"You have some sort of drug problem?"

"Drugs, Sam. I'm daft enough without any of that stuff."

"Women?"

"Women?" he repeated. "I'm a single man with my own personal life, and I don't bring it into the dressing room or onto the training ground."

And so it was the story that eluded me, and by the sounds of it, Neale Cooper too. But as I said, never a quiet moment covering a lower league team.

Samantha Lee started her career in sports journalism at the age of 16 shadowing sports reporters at her local paper, the Hartlepool Mail. She cut her teeth with her first full-time job at 19 as sports editor of weekly broadsheet the Carluke and Lanark Gazette. She joined the Mirror before becoming chief sports writer at the Hartlepool Mail. She now runs the North East PR firm Publicity Seekers.

Favourite player: *Brian Honour, a name that will mean little outside of the North East, but the grittiest most determined little winger I've ever seen.*

Most memorable match: *Hartlepool United 6 Manchester United 0, 1988. It might have only been a pre-season friendly, but it's one to stick up the [Manchester] United fans isn't it?*

FAB BUT NOT YET A GREAT

The Arsenal midfielder is a class act ready for the next step

By John Ley

JUST TYPING the name of Fàbregas into an internet search engine tells its own story. "1-10 of about 3,220,000" pages are immediately traced. It may not be on a par with the 12.3 million offered for David Beckham or the 13.5 million that Pelé commands, but it tells a story of the remarkable popularity of a player who, let's face it, is still a baby.

Further proof of Cesc's elevation can be found in the index of Brian Glanville's excellent Arsenal Stadium History. Printed in 2006, when Fàbregas was still only 18, there are seven references to the youngster, yet just five for the great George Eastham, a veritable bastion of 60's Highbury history.

Francesc Fàbregas Soler was born on 4 May 1987 in Arenys de Mar in Catalonia, Spain. The fact that questions are being asked as to whether Arsenal's coveted star, one who at the age of 20 was being tipped as the next captain at the Emirates Stadium, can become one of the game's most complete midfielder, says much for the Spaniard's elevation to a status enjoyed by very few players of his tender age.

A chance meeting with Fàbregas at Arsenal's swanky training headquarters in leafy Hertfordshire told me all I needed to know about Fàbregas the human being. Manager Arsene Wenger's weekly press conferences are held in a block separate from the main building, but adorned with memories of the club's success, from George Graham to Charlie George, from Eddie Hapgood to Thierry Henry. Sepia prints stare down from high walls, memories of a bygone age when flat caps and Woodbines were a necessary commodity to follow the Highbury greats. Nowadays, a red and white shirt with a number four on the back is all that Arsenal's disciples need to confirm their adoration for their Golden Boy.

Yet, despite those reminders on every wall, around each corner, Fàbregas remains modest, a youngster brimming with humility. Seeing me coming down the stairs, he steps politely to one side, offering that handsome smile that turns young girls to a quivering jelly and proffering a hand. He does not know me, but a young man schooled in politeness and modesty, both at home in Spain and in the Arsenal 'family' would do nothing else. He seems genuinely grateful that I offer a good luck message ahead of the following day's game.

So, we have ascertained his character. But good guys don't always make champions. Can he be great? As one who lives, eats and sleeps football statistics – no, really, I do, it's quite sad – let's get to the facts. Fàbregas made his Arsenal debut on 23 October 2003, in a League Cup tie at home to Rotherham United, becoming Arsenal's youngest ever first-team player, aged just 16 years and 177 days. He then became the youngest goalscorer in Arsenal's history in a later round of the League Cup, scoring in a 5–1 win against Wolves.

And in the Champions League, Fàbregas became the second-youngest goalscorer in the competition's history after scoring the third goal against Rosenborg in a 5–1 win. And the records extend to international level: when Spain's successful Euro 2008 coach Luis Aragones fielded him against the Ivory Coast, Fàbregas became the youngest player capped for Spain in 70 years.

So, those are the facts, proof that Fàbregas is special, a footballing genius in waiting. But how special? And how can he improve on his already massive leap from fresh-faced Spaniard to coveted star? And if he continues to burgeon, what can Arsenal do to keep hold of their jewel, the man who could sparkle more than any others in the crown of English football?

The 2007/08 campaign, particularly the first half, offered evidence enough of Fàbregas's capabilities. Comparisons in football are, variously, easy and impossible. Different eras produce different standards. Is he the next Liam Brady? Or a Spanish Michel Platini? Or, comparing him with 21st century contemporaries, is he on a par with Barcelona prodigy Lionel Messi, or a rival for Manchester United's Cristiano Ronaldo?

What marks him out, at his best, is his individual flair, his finesse and flamboyance, his aptitude to delight, his ability to shine, his determination to entertain. With the stylishness of a modern day Zico, he has the ability to drop a shoulder, the speed of a George Best to leave defenders so quickly that rumours persist have to check their diaries to see if they have missed a day.

It could have been different. Had he decided to stay with Barcelona, he could now be starring alongside Messi. As a 'volante', a defensive midfielder, in Barcelona's youth team, he sparkled. Schooled at Barca's youth headquarters at La Masia – the farmhouse – he became a rival with Messi on the Playstation, but decided greater challenges lie abroad, rather than at home, and Wenger was able to persuade the 16-year-old to swap Catalan for London.

In Hertfordshire he roomed with Philippe Senderos, a player more at home with the works of Jean-Paul Sartre than a DVD of Jean-Alain Boumsong, and his sensible approach to life as a foreign youngster at Arsenal was to prove invaluable for Fàbregas.

Now jealousy guarded, Fàbregas is wrapped up in the equivalent of footballing cotton wool – a contract, signed in 2006, that demands he remains in North London until 2014 when he will be 27. That has not prevented speculation of a move back to Spain, with rumours emanating from Real Madrid, rather than Barcelona, that the world could be offered to entice him home.

But as long as Wenger remains at the Emirates Stadium, Fàbregas should be retained. Wenger's bond with the Spaniard is, according to the player's first agent Joseba Diaz, "like a father and son relationship." That relationship proved invaluable in the summer of 2007 when Real Madrid came courting. With Thierry Henry leaving for Barcelona, Fàbregas's refreshing loyalty said much for his love for the club. "I have a great responsibility this season and I can't wait to get started," said Fàbregas. "It made me very excited that a club as big as Madrid were interested and that made it very difficult. It's a chance that doesn't come around very often, but I'm only 20 and have to keep improving, and I want to do that at Arsenal."

And referring again to the father figure that is "professor" Wenger, Diaz added: "Cesc is never going to let down the person who showed confidence in him."

Fàbregas had a good relationship with Henry, and when the pair were interviewed together after a game against Liverpool in the last season at Highbury, the Spaniard was asked if he felt he had been fouled for the visitors' goal. "Say yes," whispered Henry into Fàbregas's right ear. "Of course," he said under instruction.

And the young man does have a petulant side. Arsenal's frustration after drawing a blank in their FA Cup fifth-round tie with Blackburn, their first goalless domestic game at their new Emirates Stadium, provoked an extraordinary verbal attack by Fàbregas on the then Rovers manager Mark Hughes. The pair could be seen exchanging angry words after the final whistle, after which Hughes said: "When we shook hands at the end, the young man asked me a question which I thought was disrespectful. He asked me if I had played for Barcelona and when I said yes, he shook his head as if in disbelief. Then he said, 'Well, that wasn't Barcelona football.'"

Fàbregas later aplogised and now he must continue to grow. He is far from the complete article and football history is littered with players who failed to achieve full greatness. Fàbregas has the ability to improve, but whether it is with Arsenal remains to be seen.

Wenger's unerring belief in his youngsters, while admired by many, has come at a cost, with no silverware for three seasons to 2007/08 and without a League title for four. Fàbregas is hungry; can he be patient? He is some way from the finished article. In FIFA's 2007 list of nominees for World Player of the Year, he failed to find his way into a list of 30 names. He did make the 50-player shortlist for the 2007 Ballon D'Or, to find the best player in Europe. It is when he starts claiming such accolades, and more than once, that he can lay claim to the belief many have, that Arsenal have truly nurtured something special.

A cautionary voice amid the worship was raised by Sir Alex Ferguson, the envious Manchester United manager, who suggested Fàbregas and other equally outstanding youngsters cannot be regarded as great players, because they have not yet got the medals. "Yeah, he's right," says Fàbregas. "I 100 per cent agree with him. I can't say I'm a great player." Although Fabregas does now have a Euro 2008 medal in his collection.

Modesty, diffidence and humility. Add a technical brilliance, a determination to improve and the backing of Wenger and offer time for the concoction to develop and we may just witness one of the truly great players.

John Ley is the longest-serving football reporter at the Daily Telegraph, in his 21st year, and contributing both to the newspaper and the website, where he features on a weekly television show. Previously he spent six years at the Oxford Mail, covering the rise of the club to the top division and League Cup success.

Favourite player: Denis Law. The King was clever, resilient, brilliant on the pitch and a gentleman off it. A true maestro. George Best was great – but Law was a genius.

Most memorable match: Tottenham 0 Arsenal 1, May 1971. Being in the stand, sitting in front of Eusebio, and seeing my team win the title at White Hart Lane. Bliss.

2018 WORLD CUP COULD BE WON BY NUMBER 10

(and not Wayne Rooney)

By Martin Lipton

WHEN GORDON BROWN met French President Nicolas Sarkozy in London for a bi-lateral summit in March 2008 there was only one perfect venue. The "Entente Amicale" required a neutral meeting point, where French and English cultures mixed, where the two main protagonists would have common ground, where they could share the star-dust. So it was no wonder that the conference took place not in one of the grand committee rooms of Westminster or one of the grace and favour government residences that dot the south east. Instead, it was the Emirates Stadium, home of Arsenal, France's enclave in Albion. English money, French talent and intelligence.

The important stuff came first, too, with Brown and Sarkozy waiting until they had gone through the serious business of meeting Arsene Wenger for a kick-about before they got down to the tittle-tattle of discussing Iraq, Afghanistan and the Common Agricultural Policy.

Ludicrous? More than slightly. And if any incidents to cause an international stir had taken place, we all know Wenger wouldn't have seen them.

But if anybody truly doubted the seamless and apparently intractable fusion of football and politics, their ignorance was surely ended by that meeting in north London. Brown, the Raith Rovers – and, it seems, England, Scotland, Manchester United and Tottenham – supporter, getting the chance once again to boast his sporting credentials, having promised everything in his power to help bring the World Cup back to this country in 2018. It is a role the Scot – and, possibly, his successor – will need to play all the way to D-day in 2011. Make no mistake, if all the talk is just for show, we can kiss goodbye to the idea of seeing the World Cup here again in the next 20 years.

So far, at least, it seems Brown is genuine. After all, actively and financially supporting Raith is hardly glory-hunting, although you do wonder if, unlike Geordie Munro's "wee lassie", he might choose Idaho over Kirkcaldy.

But the present occupant of 10 Downing Street is not the first, and certainly will not be the last, politician to talk up his affinity with football. Over the years, plenty of his predecessors – and their opposite numbers abroad – have used the game as part of their appeal to the working man, to make them appear more "normal".

Benito Mussolini praised Italy's 1934 World Cup winning team as "soldiers", while the success of AC Milan fuelled Silvio Berlusconi's bid for power in that country's Parliament, employing the likes of Franco Baresi to canvass for his Forza Italia party.

And the prime British example of that Prime Ministerial approach came from the only man to win four General Elections for Labour, Harold Wilson. Wilson was a fraud in many ways, an Oxford Don who in private smoked large cigars rather than the pipe he waved around, and while declaring a life-long yearning for home town club Huddersfield, he saw football as a stick with which to beat the patrician outlook of his political foes. The Yorkshireman was the fan from the Leeds Road terraces, in stark contrast to the aristocratic Tory Alec Douglas-Home, who seemed far more at home on the grouse moors of Scotland.

Wilson's "man of the people" act worked in 1964 and while the next General Election two years later would probably have been won anyway, events at Wembley on July 30 were to play their part in the campaign which followed a few months later.

"Have you noticed," mused Wilson, "how we only win the World Cup under a Labour Government?"

Four years later, the link was even more firmly fixed in Wilson's mind. Defending their trophy, England met West Germany again, in the heat of Leon, Mexico, on June 14, throwing away a two goal lead. Wilson had been expected to retain power in the general election shortly after the quarter-final, but that defeat plunged the country into a black mood. A poor set of trade figures the next day added to the feeling of gloom and within 96 hours of the game the removal fans were arriving in Downing Street to help install Ted Heath as Premier. Wilson always blamed Peter Bonetti!

Of course, politicians have not always sought to embrace the beautiful game. Many cite Margaret Thatcher's treatment when, as opposition leader, she was roundly booed attending a Scottish Cup Final, as the moment the Iron Lady began her personal grudge against both the biggest sport in the country – and Scotland as a whole. In 1980, Thatcher – who had named "the No. 10, Whymark" as the man of the match in the previous year's Cup Final, even though he was not actually playing for Ipswich – was famously kissed on the steps of No. 10 by Kevin Keegan and Emlyn Hughes as England headed off to the European Championship.

Within five years, however, hooliganism brought to its ultimate nadir by the riot during Millwall's game at Luton and the horrors of Heysel saw Downing Street and the FA in open conflict. FA secretary Ted Croker was summoned to a meeting, to be ordered by Thatcher: "'What are you going to do about your hooliganism?"

Croker replied: "Not our hooligans, Prime Minister, but yours. The products of your society."

Croker, not surprisingly, became the first holder of his office not to receive a knighthood upon his retirement.

Thatcher's identity cards scheme was defeated and as the modern media age altered perceptions of society, she became the exception, rather than the rule. Successor John Major preferred cricket to football, but was compelled to declare his allegiance for Chelsea, although it was the man who was to turf Major out of office who really exploited the link. Tony Blair used football as a metaphor for his "young, fresh" image, playing keepy-up with Keegan, although he never actually claimed to have watched Jackie Milburn play for Newcastle from his seat on the Gallowgate as many detractors would have you believe he did.

But Blair is the only Prime Minister to effectively sack an England manager, using the pulpit of the Richard and Judy sofa to demand Glenn Hoddle's head for his maladroit musings on the disabled in 1999. He also appeared on Football Focus too, naming Arjan De Zeeuw as one of his favourite players. Real knowledge or good briefing? You choose.

What is unquestioned is that politicians will always seek to use something which has wide appeal, and few pastimes cut through the social classes and the focus of the nation quite like football. And while there will be sneering in the game over politicians claiming affinity to bask in any reflected glory – David Cameron is, apparently, an Aston Villa fan, while his preceding Tory party leaders Iain Duncan-Smith and Michael Howard supported Spurs and Liverpool respectively – it can work the other way too.

After all, Sir Alex Ferguson – who has called Steve Bruce a "class traitor" for his voting habits – has been one of Labour's biggest backers, despite run-ins with Sports Minister Gerry Sutcliffe.

And if England are to host the World Cup in 2018, then the FA bid will not need just the tacit support of Gordon Brown and any Government in office during the bidding period, but genuine, enthusiastic and energetic involvement, from Day One. That was lacking when England bid for the 2006 tournament, despite the passion the late Tony Banks brought to his role.

Blair felt burned by association as Manchester United ducked out of defending the FA Cup in 2000 to play in the inaugural World Club Championship in Brazil after Banks brought political pressure to bear on Lancaster Gate (as it then was). Subsequently, Blair kept his hands off, not even bothering to attend the final vote in Zurich, in stark contrast to his vital role in bringing the 2012 Olympics to London with a show-stealing appearance alongside David Beckham in Singapore.

Brown, having already pitched the merits of England to FIFA chief Sepp Blatter on two occasions, will have to bring the same determination to the 2018 cause that he has throughout his life to the Labour Party. If there is any sense that the Government is not wholeheartedly behind the bid, then it will have no chance of success. Brown needs to make Blatter feel loved, too, because with just 24 voters, and a casting ballot of his own, the FIFA President is the key to everything.

Like it or not, the battle for 2018 will be won more by the Whitehall mandarins and men in suits then by Beckham, Steven Gerrard or Wayne Rooney. Giving Blatter a bit of what he wants – like support for his quota policy, devised to ensure young homegrown talent is developed by major clubs the world over – will help too. But Brown, like his hero and friend 'Slim Jim' Baxter, the former Rangers, Nottingham Forest and Scotland legend of the 1960s and '70s, will have to do the showboating when it matters.

Politics and football? Two sides of the same coin, I'm afraid.

Martin Lipton has been chief football writer of the Daily Mirror since 2002, having held similar roles at the Press Association and the Daily Mail.

Favourite player: I grew up believing Glenn Hoddle was the incarnation of the deity. But then I saw Thierry Henry play.

Most memorable match(es): So many to choose from. For sheer pleasure, despite the nightmare for deadlines, Liverpool v Alaves in the 2000 UEFA Cup Final in my favourite ground, Dortmund's Westfalen Stadium. Every substitution changed the game.

For excitement, Argentina 2 England 2, St Etienne, World Cup 2nd round 1998.

For sheer disbelief, Germany 1 England 5 in Munich, September 2001.

CELTIC COULD REPEAT FEAT OF 1967

FC Porto showed size does not necessarily matter

By Kevin McCarra

THE CELTIC side of 1967 is always described as the first British club to win the European Cup. They were, but that is not really how I think of them. My memories are personal.

I recall the excited disbelief in my great aunt's house as we watched the black and white television pictures of a bunch of guys, who had all been born within a 30-mile radius of Glasgow, coming from behind to beat Internazionale 2-1 in Lisbon.

For a nine-year-old, I had been backward in developing an interest in football but that cured my arrested development. Decades later, I co-wrote a book about the side.

In my experience, there is no truth to the gloomy advice that you should never meet your heroes. They proved to be warm people whose lack of pretension was ingrained. The midfielder Bobby Murdoch had, by common consent, been the best player in the team. After we had been for lunch in a restaurant one day late in the 1980s, I moved to flag down a taxi, only for Bobby, aghast at this extravagance, to insist that I must get a bus back into the town centre. Nor were these down-to-earth men transformed into pompous bores when asked about their exploits. The winger Jimmy Johnstone was more concerned with his social life than his place in history, but I never anticipated that I would have to stand on the fireside rug in his house and attempt to recreate the move in which he set up one of Celtic's goals in the 1967 Scottish Cup final victory over Aberdeen. My impersonation can't have been up to much. Jimmy still didn't remember anything about it.

It was all so very long ago. Of that line-up, Jimmy, Bobby and the goalkeeper Ronnie Simpson are dead now. Their fame sprang from an era when Scottish football was flush with talent to a degree that is no longer conceivable. Rangers played in the Cup-Winners' Cup final the week after Celtic took the European Cup and had the ill-luck to be facing Bayern Munich in Nuremberg. Even then they only went down in extra-time.

Still, Celtic's story is unique. Nine of the Lisbon team had come through the club's youth system. That potential could have gone untapped because Celtic were moribund. The chairman Robert Kelly meddled in team affairs that were very far from being under the control of Jimmy McGrory, who had been one of the most prolific centre-forwards in football history, scoring 398 goals for Celtic in the League alone.

Management for the pipe-puffing McGrory seemed to consist of observing that "It's a good day for shooting" as his team left the dressing room. He was a great Celtic figure marooned in the wrong post. The chairman, to his credit, ultimately accepted that and replaced him in 1965 with the Hibernian manager Jock Stein, who insisted on absolute control. He had been a successful captain and centre-half at Celtic in the 1950s, but his genius was for management. Stein's curiosity about football was as profound as his understanding of it would become. The craving for knowledge led, early in the 1960s, to a trip to see how the Argentinian Helenio Herrera ran Internazionale. Stein learned fast. Herrera was the losing manager in Lisbon.

There was vast scope for modernising Celtic. Training before Stein entailed much lapping of the track at the stadium and, during evening sessions for youngsters who were part-timers, some would hop over the wall of the enclosure for a fag. Legend has it that the little dots of light from the cigarettes could be made out in the winter darkness.

Stein held absolute power in an age when players had no automatic right to move to other clubs even when their contracts had expired. Since the manager, an ex-miner, had a great suspicion of fashion the photographs of his 1967 line-up contain no clue that this was the summer of love. The short back and sides was the sole haircut tolerated. Nonetheless, Stein could show great warmth when the moment was right and he was not humourless. Stein had already retained the British Manager of the Year award before the European Cup final and, killing time in Lisbon, picked up a small hat and announced that it would have fitted him the previous season.

Celtic were made deadly by their very innocence. They played in a fast, attacking manner off-set by touches of shrewdness in Stein's tactics. It would have been folly to ask Jimmy Johnstone to do anything other than express himself when the jinking winger could be so uncontainable. He may have been at his most inspired in the first leg of a European Cup tie with Red Star Belgrade in 1968. The diminutive Johnstone was a brave man who could never be intimidated by barbarous full-backs, but he did dread air travel. That came to Stein's mind when

Celtic were drawing 1-1 at half-time. Unbeknownst to the rest of the side, the manager told Johnstone that he would be excused the trip to Belgrade so long as Celtic won by four goals. The winger made two and scored two as Red Star were swamped 5-1. Following the last goal he baffled team-mates as he kept on yelling, "I'm no going."

Memorable as the anecdotes are, it is a mistake to suppose the 1960s were always a light-hearted escapade for Celtic. Many of the players had suffered constant angst and disappointment before Stein's arrival, but he had the answers to all of that. His impact was the sum total of countless wise decisions and nothing escaped his notice. A snooker table at which the squad used to while away the time before kick-off was, for instance, removed and the players then had to occupy themselves with table tennis, which kept them on the move and hone their reflexes. There was, above all, a rethink of the side. Murdoch, who had no pace, was given a deeper role, while the streetwise Bertie Auld was converted from winger to schemer.

On and on the process went. Attacking full-backs became part of Stein's answer to packed defences that had to be stretched to breaking point. The lightning quick Bobby Lennox, once classified as a winger, honed his knack for getting away an accurate finish early, before a goalkeeper had quite set himself. Such were Celtic's standards that they got to the Lisbon final without much trouble. The tightest scrape came in the quarter-final, when the resilient Yugoslav team Vojvodina were overcome with a header by the centre-half and captain Billy McNeill from a corner kick. He had a penchant for that sort of thing and scored in three Scottish Cup finals.

A clash with Internazionale, however, was a test of a wholly different order. The opposition were, all the same, an ageing team on the verge of disintegration and their faith in defensive tactics was entirely inappropriate. They took the lead in the final with a penalty, but that egged on a tireless Celtic team who might have won by a thumping margin.

Two goals were enough. The equaliser was an encapsulation of the side's adventurousness as the right-back Jim Craig squared for the left-back Tommy Gemmell to finish with a drive of typical boldness from the edge of the penalty area.

Celtic's winner was characteristic, too, with Stevie Chalmers, onside by a fraction, sharp to turn home a ball that Murdoch had hit left-footed towards goal. Murdoch had hurt his preferred right foot early in the final. It says everything about his excellence that, decades later, it came as a surprise to some team-mates to learn that he had been injured.

Celtic barely appreciated the scale of their accomplishment until the difficulties of repeating it sank in. The same was true of fans who, in many cases, had never been abroad until they set out for Lisbon, often by car or train. In this modern era, supporters hop on to budget airlines and follow the club around the continent almost as easily as they might go to, say, an away fixture with Aberdeen. All the same, as sophistication has risen the prospect of clubs such as Celtic appearing in another European Cup final has declined.

Everyone knows now how television income allows the clubs in Italy, Spain and, particularly, England to afford a calibre of cosmopolitan squad that is unimaginable elsewhere. None the less, the Champions League is a knock-out competition from the last 16 onwards. If a club uncovers two or three outstanding footballers and can cling to them for a little time while blending them with some solid performers then they might upset the odds. Porto, victors in 2004, are no wealthier than Celtic and their example gave hope to everyone among the relatively disadvantaged.

Celtic are better off and better run than they were in the mid-1960s when flakes of rust would drift down from the roof of the Jungle, as the enclosure was known. So all it needs now is contemporary equivalents of Jock Stein, Jimmy Johnstone and the rest of the folk heroes.

Give it time, lots of time.

Kevin McCarra is football correspondent of the Guardian, Prior to that he worked for the Times, the Sunday Times and Scotland on Sunday.

__Favourite player:__ Henrik Larsson. A superb, single-minded striker with Sweden and, mostly, Celtic. His prompting as Barcelona substitute turned a 1-0 lead for Arsenal into a 2-1 defeat in the 2006 Champions League final.

__Most memorable match:__ Scotland's 1973 win over Czechoslovakia to reach the World Cup finals for the first time in 16 years. The whole country was delirious with pride and joy.

VINNIE WAS THE CRAZIEST OF THE CRAZY GANG

And his bite was as bad as his bark

By Paul McCarthy

"OI, McCarthy, you f****** w*****!"

Not exactly what you expect to hear when you're strolling down Regent Street, minding your own business. A quick glance to establish whether there were any other McCarthys in the immediate vicinity. No? Thought not.

As I turned round, there he was. Hollywood tan, diamond in his ear, trademark grin, head stuck out of the passenger window of a giant black Mercedes parked in a bus lane. Of course.

Vincent Peter Jones. It was good to see him.

❂❂❂

BY THE time I joined the South London Press in 1988, the Jones Boy's infamy was well established. The clenched fist. The tram-lined crew cut. Gazza's nuts in his hand, the FA Cup Final tackle which started at Steve McMahon's neck and ended up just a yard or so south.

So for a kid who'd spent his early journalistic career on the Basingstoke Gazette covering nothing more controversial than somebody not wearing the correct shoes at a bowls match, to work on a daily basis with Wimbledon's Crazy Gang was a fairly daunting experience.

Thankfully, Bobby Gould was a godsend. On my first day at the training ground, he took me into the first team dressing room, stood me in front of all the players and said: "This young man is here to do a job of work. As long he treats you honestly and fairly, I expect you do the same."

I can't pretend I wasn't absolutely petrified but Bob's words broke the ice and I was accepted. Unfortunately, that meant the usual ceremony of ritual humiliation to see if you had big enough balls to work with Wimbledon.

My car tyres were let down at least four times, I was soaked with water from an upstairs changing dressing room and was constantly wound up by a group of players who tested everybody, no matter how minute or massive their reputations.

And Vinnie was the leader, no doubt about that. He'd bought into the Crazy Gang ethos absolutely. The halcyon days of their anarchy under Dave Bassett might have passed, original Gang members like Wally Downes and Steve Galliers were on the way out and there was a slight mellowing, but as Vinnie explained: "If you'd whined or grassed or copped the hump, you'd have been finished with the lads. We'd have done for you."

At times, it felt like that. I also wrote the Wimbledon matchday programme and made a joke at Vinnie's expense. An hour before the game, he tracked me down in the secretary's office, literally lifted me off my feet by my throat and threatened merciless retribution.

His anger lasted all of two hours and afterwards I found him with a pint and a Hamlet, celebrating a Wimbledon win and only too happy to tell me how he'd "bossed the f***** game."

There was no escaping his presence. In a club of the steeliest characters – Lawrie Sanchez, Dennis Wise, Dave Beasant – Vinnie stood out as a leader.

Sanchez had little or no time for the ridiculous cartoon posturing of somebody like John Fashanu, who talked about himself constantly in the third person and was never fully accepted in the Dons dressing room.

But Vinnie? Vinnie was the heartbeat of the cause as far as Sanch was concerned and while the pointless excesses and violence sometimes frustrated and bemused Sanchez, he knew Wimbledon were a better team for Vinnie's presence … and that's the only thing that mattered.

I really got to know Vinnie when I left the SLP to join the News of the World. It also heralded my darkest moment of my journalistic career and possibly Vinnie's life.

The editor, Piers Morgan, wanted a new columnist and somebody, only half seriously, mentioned Vinnie's name. Piers loved the idea, embraced it with a zeal and I, as the only reporter on the paper who truly knew him, was deputed to be Vinnie's "ghost."

For a season or so, it was a fantastic gig. Vinnie was everything you'd want in a columnist; controversial, outspoken, funny and with a willingness to speak his mind which readers loved.

More importantly, Vinnie loved it. So much so, that he actually volunteered for "assignments," including a trip to down to Cardiff after he was called up by Wales where we spent the three-hour train journey learning the Welsh national anthem and where he was mobbed in a working man's club we popped into for a, ahem, quiet drink.

Sadly, this delight in being "on the scene" led to his downfall. I persuaded my sports editor that it would be a great idea for Vinnie, his agent and myself to go to Dublin to see England play the Republic of Ireland, write the column from the banks of the Liffey and have a bit of a night out at the same time.

All good in theory. Except that I was called away on another job and didn't fly to Dublin, English fans rioted and forced the game to be abandoned after less than 30 minutes ... and Vinnie bit the nose of a Daily Mirror news reporter.

It was a party piece I had seen Vinnie perform on unwitting pals and never once did he draw blood or even leave a mark. This time, cold drink had been taken and poor Ted Oliver had a lump taken out of his hooter.

Given the violence that had taken place in the stadium just hours before, this was beyond the pale and it was my job to make Vinnie realise the seriousness of it all. No excuses, no alibis, only a full cough and a hands up would save him from the sack. So I told him. And he gave the most emotional interview I've ever known from a footballer. Utterly shamed and remorseful, he talked about how he went for a walk in the woods near his Hertfordshire home with a shotgun and how it was only the thought of how his beloved wife, Tanz, would have to identify his body which stopped him from pulling the trigger.

He'd done what was asked but it wasn't enough for Piers. On the Sunday after Dublin, the News of the World ran with a front page that read "We Sack Vinnie" and a scathing editorial alongside his emotional confession.

I could see why the paper had done it, the public outcry was too strong for any editor to withstand. But it didn't stop me from feeling sick for a man I'd grown to like and, in a perverse way, admire. If I was a manager, I'd want Vinnie with me. If I was a player, I'd rather have him alongside than against me.

We spoke intermittently but the relationship was, frankly, screwed. He phoned to thank me when he retired and I wrote how he was a loss to the game. But by that time, Hollywood beckoned, 'Lock, Stock...' was on the horizon and Vinnie was rubbing shoulders with the likes of Robert de Niro rather than Robbie Earle. The Jones Boy had moved on.

❂❂❂

"'OW YOU doing, you old toss-pot? Still writing s***?"

"Yes, mate, it's on a par with some of those films you're in!"

"F***off! Anyway, got to go, meeting up with some mates for a couple of drinks before I go back to LA."

"Ok, Vin, take care."

"Yeah, I will do. I'll give you a shout next time I'm over."

And then he was off, still in the bus lane. From Rickmansworth to Regent Street to Rodeo Drive, simple as. He never did call but, then again, if it was a choice between Madonna and me, no contest.

Paul McCarthy is sports editor of the News of the World. Previously: chief sports columnist of the People; football correspondent of the Express; chief football writer of the News of the World

Favourite player: Michel Platini. He did the kind of things that inspired every kid in the playground to try. Classy, elegant and with the sort of swagger that made you hate the French but fall in love with their football.

Most memorable match: England v Argentina, World Cup 1998. Owen's goal. Beckham's red card. England's bravery. Batty's penalty. And the knowledge Glenn Hoddle had built a team that should have won the World Cup. Not sure how many more times I'll ever be able to say that.

BECKS APPEAL

United dressing room felt there was more style than substance to David Beckham

By David Meek

CELEBRITY POSER or one of the all-time great players? Still the arguments rage about David Beckham's place in the football pantheon of stars.

Opinion is probably fairly evenly split. You know the two camps: His admirers point out that he was a key man in one of Manchester United's greatest sides, the team that won the unique Treble, and he has won 100 caps for England as well as captaining them with distinction.

Ordinary players don't have that kind of record. Who could forget his masterly free kick and goal that took England through to the World Cup in Japan and South Korea, a gem in a truly inspirational performance that saw him cover every inch of Old Trafford? Who could not fail to be impressed by his inspired performances playing in the centre of midfield that saw United win the FA Cup against Newcastle United in 1999 and then complete the Treble by beating Bayern Munich in Barcelona? Will we ever forget him scoring from the half-way line against Wimbledon at Selhurst Park on the opening day of the 1996/97 season?

His whole career, for both club and country, is studded with outstanding displays, his ability to cross from the right wing and his amazing goals from free-kicks that bent and swerved to pave the way for Cristiano Ronaldo's dynamic dippers.

But the Beckham critics will tell you that he never went past a man – like Ronaldo, say – because he didn[1]t have the pace and he was never an artful dribbler. There was also the gathering distraction involved in the show business lifestyle he shared with his wife as the Posh part of the Spice Girls, and his fall-out with his manager and mentor, Sir Alex Ferguson.

It's complicated any accurate assessment of David Beckham's place in the football firmament, as I was reminded when I wrote a book entitled 'The Perfect 10' in which I chose my 10 best, or favourite, Manchester United players. With a club like United it's a job to whittle the list down to 10, even though I did limit it to the players I had reported on and interviewed in my 37 years as the Manchester Evening News reporter covering the Old Trafford club.

It didn't save me from a frank exchange with Rio Ferdinand, though, when we met one day at the Carrington training ground but Ryan Giggs said the book was fine because he was in it. Rio, though, said he was surprised there was no Roy Keane in my selection and I explained that when it came down to a choice between Keane and Bryan Robson, they were both fantastic captains but that Robson won the day because he scored more goals than Roy.

Rio's reply was to point out that there was no Paul Scholes. I admitted I felt guilty about that but said that it was all very well suggesting who should be included but not so easy to decide who should be left out to make way. "Who would you have left out?" I challenged.

Straight away came the reply: "David Beckham."

I asked how could I overlook a player who had provided me with more copy than anyone since George Best, and possibly Eric Cantona.

Rio said: "So, it's not so much a team of 10 perfect footballers as a Celebrity XI then." Ouch!

Even among the experts in the dressing room there is clearly a feeling that there was perhaps more style than substance to David Beckham. Maybe we shouldn't be too surprised at that. After all, Steve McClaren clearly had mixed feelings about the boy when he was appointed manager of England and dropped him and as a member of his squad after the disappointing World Cup campaign of 2006 in Germany only to reinstate him for a friendly against Brazil and then play him in a 2008 European Championship qualifier against Estonia.

England manager, Fabio Capello, also seemed to be in two minds about the player when he took charge mid-way through 2007/08. When he was manager of Real Madrid he dropped David and described him as "half an actor" and turned his back on him after the announcement that the player was going to join Los Angeles Galaxy in the United States.

"We cannot count on him. You can't pretend to have the same enthusiasm when your head is elsewhere," he declared.

It looked to be the end of the road in Spain, but no, Capello returned him to the team and was rewarded by a Beckham inspired revival that saw Real Madrid come from behind to win the Spanish Championship.

Now Capello had a different hymn sheet with comments after one game like: "Yet again, the Englishman was the decisive player. He was a titan, he gave us a festival of measured passing. At times it seemed he would win the game on his own."

Everyone assumed that when Capello gave him his 100th cap in the friendly against France that it would signal the end of his international career, but no, the manager hinted that Beckham could play a part in the World Cup qualifying campaign for South Africa in 2010.

"It's still open. He did well against France and I sometimes go to see him in Los Angeles. It all depends. There are players who at 33 or 34 take good care of themselves," he said.

There has in fact never been any doubt about David's fitness and stamina. He had very few injuries with Manchester United and he had a durable resilience to match. Not every player could have bounced back so successfully when he was made a scapegoat and pilloried following his World Cup dismissal in France in 1998. It couldn't have been very pleasant for him when West Ham fans burned an effigy of him on his first away trip the following season.

But from quite an early point in his career, David has had to put up with being mocked. A favourite target for comedians and impressionists, they have made him out to be thick and gullible, and manipulated by a shrewish wife. He has had to endure some terrible obscene chanting, some of it involving his wife, which must have been very upsetting. But rarely has he lost his temper or hit back, certainly not in public.

I once needled him when there was speculation about him leaving Manchester United and he kept quiet until finally coming out with a declaration that he would after all be staying. I said on one of the club's television chat shows that he should have made the position clear a lot sooner, unless he was letting the suspense build until he could come out with a major highly-paid newspaper article.

It was perhaps a bit unfair and it certainly got to him because he asked to see me. We met at the training ground with Gary Neville appearing in support and in fact doing most of the talking. But that's David Beckham, a self-effacing, relatively shy boy who, considering the fame and fortune that has come his way, has changed very little. If it hadn't been for Gary I suspect he wouldn't have bothered to make an issue of it. We shook hands and that was it, and he went back to his beloved football.

Under the apparent laid-back manner, there has always been steel, both mentally and physically. How else could he have gone so quickly from villain to hero and shake off the terrible World Cup slagging to share in the Treble of 1999? Including internationals, David made nearly 60 appearances that season and was one of the few players who avoided United's rotation system.

Ferguson said: "I rested most of the players at some stage of the season but not David Beckham. He has the best stamina of any player at the club. He has had fantastic energy since being a boy, and despite everything he has been through, I have never doubted him."

So why did it all go wrong at Old Trafford with Ferguson making little effort to keep him once he knew that David's agents were courting Real Madrid? Basically the United manager felt that the youngster he had played father to after bringing him to Manchester from London had lost some of his commitment and that's something Fergie can't abide. He also felt that the celebrity part of Beckham was beginning to irk some of his team-mates and that the time for parting had come.

Sir Alex had considerably modified his old fashioned tendencies to accommodate the constantly changing hair styles.

"Who is the prat in the plait?" said one headline. The sarongs, the Alice bands, David's fascination with his wife's show business world ... but I will never forget Ferguson muttering to me one day: "You should have seen what David wore to training today, a sparkly track suit that made him look like Gary Glitter."

So off he went to Real Madrid to become a Galactico and then join LA Galaxy to play Major League Soccer in the States and combine the best of both his worlds – football and showbiz.

Sir Bobby Charlton, a star similarly admired, and now a director of United, was the man who first set David on his way after noting his skills at one of his summer schoolboy coaching camps, and he is another who doesn't seem too sure about his protégé as celebrity or great player:

He said: "In terms of image he is number one, with people wanting to know what he is wearing and what he is saying, but he is also a very good player. He is perhaps not great in the Pele sense, but he was a very good player. He didn't like losing and you would always want him in your team."

Both David Beckham and Sir Alex Ferguson found the parting of the ways difficult but they probably best summed up their feelings when David returned to Old Trafford last year for UEFA's exhibition match to mark United's 50 years participation in European competition. David, referring to his former manager, told the Old Trafford crowd: "We had our ups and downs, but I owe almost everything to him."

Fergie was equally gracious in reply: "He had great years here. He was a great player."

As kiss and make up tales go, there wasn't a dry eye in the house.

As to whether he was a great player or a celebrity – I believe he was both.

David Meek was the Manchester United correspondent for the Manchester Evening News for 37 years, taking over immediately after the Munich air crash in 1958. Since his retirement in 1995 he has written a number of books, including The Unique Treble with Sir Alex Ferguson, as well as collaborating with the manager for his match day programme notes. David also contributes to the club's radio and television stations.

Favourite player: George Best because he introduced a new concept to football with his magical and mesmerising skills. Others have since come close like Eric Cantona and now Cristiano Ronaldo but George lit up the game, such balance, such daring, such courage.

Most memorable match: The European Cup quarter-final second leg against Benfica in Lisbon in season 1965/66 when George Best ignored Sir Matt Busby's cautious tactical plan and cut loose to score twice in the first 12 minutes on the way to a 5-1 victory. With Benfica destroyed on the night, George came home christened El Beatle and on his way to stardom.

LITTLE BRITAIN

Influx of foreign managers and players a double-edged sword

By David Miller

AT THE end of April 2008, as another league season climbed towards its climax, there was euphoria at White Hart Lane when it was announced that Tottenham Hotspur had signed Luka Modric, the Croatian midfielder from Dinamo Zagreb for £15 million. Spurs had run through another frustrating season of chequered fortunes, the highlight having been a victory in the Carling Cup over Chelsea. It was 47 years since the club last won the league title, and the arrival of Modric was viewed as the key to opening the door to new glories.

Yet was this truly a moment of delight at one of England's best-loved clubs? Times change, and the game in England, and to a lesser extent in Scotland, has become so dominated by foreign imports that it can no longer strictly be called English at all, or even British. I believe the signing of Modric, outstanding player though he is known to be from his part in helping to eliminate England from the 2008 European Championship finals in the autumn of 2007, when outplayed by Croatia at Wembley, was as much a matter for anxiety as for celebration.

How long can the status of the British game, in relation to the rest of the world, most notably in England but no less so in Scotland, Wales and Northern Ireland, be sustained in the face of the double threat: the suppression of home talent by resort to the employment of a flood of foreigners, alongside the equally damaging decline of social and sporting activities, by which young boys who once upon a time acquired the fundamentals of balance and control between the ages of eight and 12 – when playing from dawn to dusk throughout the parks and side-streets of the land – are increasingly preoccupied with electronic games and other diverting activities? How far Britain has descended from that glorious occasion in 1958 when all four Home associations reached the World Cup finals in Sweden, to the point now where even England, with the once mighty power of four fully professional divisions, struggles to defeat the likes of Macedonia and Norway.

The illusion of English influence is increased by events in the so-called Champions League, in which for two successive seasons (2006/07 and 2007/08) there were three clubs from the Premier League: Chelsea, Liverpool and Manchester United, who dominated the semi-finals, with a fourth, Arsenal, in the quarter-final stage.

Yet if we look at the squads of those clubs in the semis, no fewer than 33 of the 45 players were foreign. Their prominence may momentarily be exciting, but the underlying reasons behind it can only in the long term be damaging for the survival of the British game – and indeed is additionally a matter of anxiety for UEFA, because of the way that the money pouring into the leading English clubs from the fount of television is corrupting the structure of competition, both national and international.

I can recall Bill Nicholson, legendary manager of Spurs over 30 years ago, already complaining as he scoured Britain for fresh young talent: "There aren't the players around any more."

That has become increasingly so. In the era between the two world wars, and even into the Fifties, it used to be said that a football manager only needed to go to the pit-head and call down the mine-shaft and up would come a dozen footballers worth a place in the First Division.

There were two reasons justifying this anecdote: the fact that football was the preoccupation of almost every able-bodied boy, and that the life of a professional player offered an escape from the drudgery of either the coal face or the factory floor.

Hunger and poverty are a motivational force in generating footballers, and boxers, as has been witnessed over a century with the stream of exceptional performers from the great cities such as Madrid, Milan, Manchester, Tokyo, New York and elsewhere. Hunger generates drive and ambition, and in almost every sport today a lack of drive can be identified, in what unquestionably amounts to a social malaise that has not yet overtaken Latin America, Africa and much of Asia.

The consequence of lack of British players goes beyond the import of foreigners by avaricious clubs. It has been accompanied by the import of foreign coaches, and the equation veers ever downwards. If there are fewer exceptional players in Britain, it is likely that there will in turn be fewer exceptional coaches, already embarrassingly apparent with the appointment of successive foreigners to manage the England national team, Sven-Goran Eriksson succeeded, after a brief and lamentable interval with Steve McClaren, by Fabio Capello, who could barely speak the language of those he must inspire.

Where now are the eminent home-bred coaches who command authority in the world game? Rafael Benitez, Arsene Wenger and now Luiz Felipe Scolari have the reins at Liverpool, Arsenal and Chelsea respectively at the start of 2008/09, only Sir Alex Ferguson among the big four's top men heralding from within our own isles.

Go back 50 years and British coaches ranked among the world's best, led by George Raynor, who from humble beginnings in Rotherham emerged as an inspiring organiser during war-time service in the Middle East, and guided Sweden to the final of their own World Cup in 1958.

Arthur Rowe, creator of Tottenham's ascent towards the summit in the Fifties, had learned his art in Hungary. His assistant Vic Buckingham famously moved to West Bromwich and thence to Holland and Spain. Bobby Robson, after guiding rural Ipswich to domestic heights was likewise later acclaimed in Holland, Spain and Portugal, Howard Kendall also making his mark with Athletic Bilbao. Terry Venables was the last English coach to earn distinction abroad when leading Barcelona to triumphs in the mid-Eighties.

And, of course, here at home there has been an unending stream of visionary manager-coaches post-war: in England, Matt Busby (Manchester United), Scot Simon (Preston), Leslie McDowall (Manchester City), Stan Cullis (Wolves), Alf Ramsey (Ipswich and England), Ron Greenwood (West Ham and England), Malcolm Allison (Manchester City), Nicholson, Matt Gillies (Leicester), Brian Clough (Derby and Nottingham Forest), Bob Paisley (Liverpool), Jack Charlton (Sheffield Wednesday, Middlesbrough and Republic of Ireland) and latterly Ferguson.

From Scotland came Jock Stein, Andy Beattie, Andy Roxburgh and Craig Brown; from Wales, Dave Bowen and Mike Smith; from Northern Ireland Peter Doherty and Billy Bingham; with the Republic, Jack Charlton.

Where now are those home-bred with a reputation that extends beyond Dover? Maybe Martin O'Neill, candidate for the England post in 2007, will emulate with Aston Villa his former mentor Clough. Steve Coppell, Gareth Southgate and Alan Curbishley have been confined, by lack of imagination among greedy chairmen at other bigger clubs, to respective limited financial scope with Reading, Middlesbrough and West Ham, and there is no clamour as yet for their services abroad. Roy Keane with Sunderland and Mark Hughes with Blackburn and now Manchester City might conceivably make the break-through into the big league. Yet the more English players are repressed from the highest levels, the less likely it is that they will emerge as coaches to guide the future of the game in Britain.

How far events have turned in a century from the time when the four Home associations effectively led the world. Although the Football Association – so named without a country title because, upon its formation in 1863, there was no other association – was not among the seven founding members of FIFA in 1904, the FA joined the following year, and subsequently the other Brits; though all withdrew after the first world war because of disputes on amateurism, and were absentees from the first three World Cup tournaments 1930-38, only re-joining the stage from 1950 onwards.

Yet having won the Olympic Games in 1908 (London) and 1912 (Stockholm), defeating Denmark both times in the final, the English were held in the highest esteem among foreign nations, witness the fact that Arthur Drewry and Stanley Rous were successive FIFA presidents, 1956-61 and 1962-74 respectively.

Throughout the second half of the twentieth century respect for English clubs, essentially British-orientated until the mid nineteen-nineties, remained at the highest level on the broadest front, from which almost any of 16 or more clubs from the major cities were likely to be represented in one of the three European competitions. Throughout this time these clubs produced a profusion of players, born within, and then representing, the four Home associations.

For England, there would be a shoal of international players, the more so as football became more tactically structured from the Sixties onwards – prior to which selection of the England team by an unworldly FA committee largely opted for the individual man-of-the-moment from any particular club. With the methodology led by Busby, Nicholson and Ramsey, and then Don Revie with Leeds, the controversies for an England manager were never so much who to put in as who to leave out.

While Manchester United in the Sixties offered Bobby Charlton, Nobby Stiles and Alex Stepney, Leeds and Liverpool had seven and six candidates respectively: Cooper, Madeley, Reaney, Jack Charlton, Hunter, Clarke and Jones for Leeds, Clemence, Neal, Thompson, Ray Kennedy, Callaghan and Keegan from Liverpool.

From Forest with Clough there were Shilton, Anderson, Woodcock and Birtles. And so it went on, through to Arsenal in the Nineties, with Seaman, Adams, Keown, Dixon and Ian Wright.

Today, if the top players from the big three – Ferdinand, Hargreaves, Rooney and Carrick for Manchester United, Terry, Lampard, Joe Cole and Ashley Cole from Chelsea, Gerrard and Carragher from Liverpool – are injured, then Capello is scouring lesser clubs for lesser players. It is a sorry plight in the land of the founders.

Worse might follow if the British Olympic Association persist with their wish for fielding a British team for the Olympic Games of London 2012 – a move vigorously resisted by the Scots, Welsh and Irish. Were a British team to appear, including such players as Rooney and Gerrard, there would be an inevitable demand from sections of Africa, Asia and Latin America that, if Britain could field a single team for the Olympic Games, then why indeed should they not do so for the World Cup: never mind that FIFA has given assurances that a combined Olympic team would not jeopardise the historic individual membership of the four.

Loss of separate status for Scotland, Wales and Northern Ireland would hasten their decline as fountains of the game, England's unique position as founders of the game would disappear, and standards throughout Britain would continue their downward spiral in both playing and coaching. Lord Moynihan, chairman of the BOA, is adamant that a British team for 2012 must be entered.

His defence of the Olympic ethic, "in the interest of all young eligible competitors" may be a noble short-term ambition, but it holds perilous dangers for the future of English, and British, football.

David Miller has worked for over 50 years in sports journalism and is the author of more than 20 books including biographies of Stanley Matthews and Sebastian Coe.

Favourite player: *More than even immortals such as Di Stefano, Pele and Maradona, Stanley Matthews could take the ball closer to an opponent and then disappear like a ghost. For 30 years he was arguably the best-known Englishman abroad other than Winston Churchill.*

Most memorable match: *Blackpool's 4-3 victory over Bolton in injury time in the 1953 FA Cup Final surpassed fiction. In his third final appearance, Matthews destroyed wavering Bolton, who had led 3-1, casting a magical spell across Wembley.*

ALLY'S BARMY

No national manager was more out of touch with reality than Ally MacLeod

By Alex Montgomery

ALLY MACLEOD was far too ridiculously confident, too carried away with blind self belief about the true quality of his Scotland team to realise he had dug a hole for himself so deep he would never be able to clamber out.

It was MacLeod who forecast Scotland would bring back a medal from the 1978 World Cup finals in Argentina, though he cheerily conceded, with a nudge and a wink, he didn't know what it would be, gold, silver or bronze, but a medal for sure. MacLeod spoke with such certainty a country which had good reason to be sceptical over forecasts about the fortunes of the national side swallowed his outrageous optimism.

Some 25,000 who weren't already on the march south with Ally's Army, turned up at Hampden to wish bon voyage to the squad. The emotion of the afternoon filtered through to the press box high above the old stand though even then there were those who felt Scotland were deluded and suffering from a worrying case of what our neighbours south of the border call 'premature ejockulation'.

The convoy of players and media to Prestwick Airport from Hampden confirmed concerns that the whole circus was out of control. The route was lined by thousands of flag waving Scots, whole families, who felt it was no less than their duty to add support to the men they had been led to believe were capable of being champions of the world or at worst good enough to make a considerable impact on the world stage.

It was on the British Caledonian DC10 flight en route to Buenos Aires that the grumbling signs of discontent materialised. First there were rumours quickly confirmed that the players were flying into battle when the Scottish Football Association still hadn't agreed the bonus payments to be made. It would be a significant payment too if MacLeod was correct in his long range forecast; and yet days before the first match against Peru the players were forced to demand a meeting to finalise the details.

There was a more dangerous outside influence awaiting, though it might not have been blatantly obvious at the time. But as the campaign progressed and the Scottish camp reeled from the Argentine media's printed assaults, the root of the animosity can be traced to MacLeod's blustering manner which would be construed by those who didn't know him as arrogance.

We had stopped first at Recife, then flew on to Rio before making the final sweep over the River Plate to BA. The Argentines had reporters stationed to greet and talk to the managers, coaches and if possible the players. All that was needed was a quick hello, and a pleasant "it is great to be here" message. Simple, but instead of being pleasant MacLeod brusquely dismissed the reporters and told them they would have to wait until his first press conference from the team's hotel in Alta Gracia.

It was a monumental mistake. He had left them with nothing.

There is nobody more motivated to inflict pain on an opponent than a reporter scorned, especially a foreign reporter now alerted to pick up morsels juicy enough to manufacture a scandal.

Thanks to MacLeod, Scotland were to be the target country of the Argentine media. It wasn't mere coincidence that nothing went right for Scotland from that moment. It opened a wound that would be proved fatal as events contrived from every angle to destroy MacLeod and his boasts. It is difficult to believe there has ever been a national manager more out of touch with reality than MacLeod as he led Scotland to the slaughter.

To have been there, to have witnessed the humiliation is to carry the scars; to be a Scotland player was to be ridiculed, to be a member of the Tartan Army was to be laughed at. It was a truly unpleasant experience.

It didn't help that a number of the officials who travelled with Scotland wore tracksuits when they walked about Alta Gracia. It made them easy to be photographed and wrongly identified as players boozing it up in the local bars. The Argentine media revelled in these stories they said were the hard drinking Scottish footballers and not what they were, naïve members of the official SFA party.

It certainly didn't help Scotland's cause when a group of players were caught trying to climb back into their hotel, a base they despised to a man. They had spent a lot of time and thought earlier in the evening trying to get out of what Lou Macari, a teetotaller, described as a prison. A senior official leaked the story not out of anger or mischief but because he thought it was funny. The world's media including our own didn't. It was another stick to bash the Scots before the tournament had started.

Scotland might have been able to maintain their credibility had the performances in the opening matches against Peru and Iran been respectable.

The 3-1 defeat against the Peruvians had their national coach Calderon saying afterwards without a hint of humour "I would like to thank Scotland for the team they presented us with." Thanks indeed.

MacLeod had not done his homework on the South Americans. He didn't tell his defenders that the winger Munante was as fast as the wind; he didn't prepare his players to properly counter the brilliance of the veteran Cubillas who turned the Scots inside out on the day. These two errors alone represent a dereliction of duty which cannot be forgotten.

Morale was so low among the players after the trauma of defeat it all but disappeared when Willie Johnston of West Bromwich Albion was sent home having failed a drug test. The banned substance Fencamfamin was part of the medication he had taken in tablet form to reduce the effects of hay fever before the tie.

The SFA could have fought his case on the grounds the charge was a medical nonsense, but didn't. Johnston was flown home like a criminal to the delight of the Argentine press, being shepherded onto the plane at gunpoint. He never played for Scotland again.

Scotland went on to drew 1-1 against the Iranians which is the equivalent of Manchester United drawing say with a League One team, and lucky to get away with a draw.

With the shock results came more stories of unrest, set up in Argentina but filtered back home where the players' families were becoming increasingly concerned about the state of mind of their sons, husbands and boyfriends. It was a pressure which added to the turmoil in the camp.

By the time the final group match was to be played against Holland in Mendoza MacLeod was a man utterly deflated, a sad figure looking only for some comforting words or action. These would come only from his family though he thought he had a friend in his final press conference before the flight to Mendoza for the final group match, the tie against Holland.

The media had turned up to taunt the losers and record whatever attempts he would make at justifying the two previous results.

MacLeod faced us sitting on a wobbly looking chair on the lawn at the back of the hotel which the players had earlier nicknamed "Stalag Luft." He looked nervous, as he should have been.

But then he spotted his 'friend' a big silly submissive dog its tail wagging and obviously more used to a kick than the hand of friendship.

"He's my only friend," said MacLeod. The cameras clicked, only MacLeod talked. And as he tried to entice the dog nearer it turned and brushed against his hand. He was not bitten but he was embarrassed, we all were. The dog it seems was wary of him too.

There is a belief among within football that reporters love to see teams not just beaten but torn part; that somehow we revel in the despair of managers, players and clubs or in the case of international football whole countries. For the record it is easier to deal with a winning group of players than one not just losing but doing so disgracefully.

Scottish reporters are renowned as supporters with typewriters, but the performances plunged to such extreme depths in Argentina they couldn't be disguised by even the most patriotic press box fan. Scotland's form stank and MacLeod and his players were ostracised by their own media including one whose intro read: "Is the man mad?"

On the eve of Scotland's last match against the Dutch I received a call from a prominent player in the squad. He told me he had had enough, he was going home and I should meet him at Buenos Aires international airport.

I asked him about the match and he agreed that would come first. I then asked what he would do if Scotland were to win by the three clear goals they needed to qualify. He told me I would find out if I was at the airport and that not only would he be there but I may be surprised at some of the other well known faces in departures. His attitude highlighted all that was wrong with this campaign: poor planning resulted in desperately unhappy players plus the wrong team selection.

It was typical that Scotland should win their last match 3-2 against the Dutch, the eventual finalists, with the introduction of Graeme Souness and Archie Gemmill, who scored the goal of the tournament.

Did non-qualification stop a walk out by a number of players that would have been the unmatched scandal of '78? I will never know. We had all by some degree been sucked in by MacLeod's appealing rhetoric. It was entertaining, it was what the Scots wanted to hear, but surely only if it was possible to realise.

Ally, always up front, often interesting simply judged it wrongly as did others who should have known better and didn't question the madness early enough to dilute the expectations. Too many listened and reported without considering the truth of the situation. They left their criticism of MacLeod and his humiliation until it was all over and he was officially Scotland's Public Enemy Number One.

Ally, is no longer with us. He died on 1 February 2004 after a battle against Alzheimer's. He was 72.

Alex Montgomery is a former chairman of the Football Writers' Association. He was chief football writer of the Sun, chief football news reporter at Today and chief football writer at the News of the World. Currently contracted to Mail on Sunday. He has written books with and about Terry Venables, Charlie George, John Hartson and Martin O'Neill.

Favourite player: Alfredo Di Stefano – statuesque, controlled, supremely skilful, a master footballer. Only one? Johan Cruyff and George Best, plus Jim Baxter, Willie Henderson, Denis Law and Jimmy Johnstone were supreme entertainers.

Most memorable match: Real Madrid v Eintracht Frankfurt, Hampden Park, Glasgow, 1960. The brilliance of Real Madrid entranced a record crowd of 135,000 who stayed to salute a 7-3 victory remembered as the greatest of finals.

Behind Paul Gascoigne's manic mask there was always a fragile, flawed yet kind character.

Now we know why Arsene Wenger never sees anything.

Jamie Redknapp was the modern football icon until his crumbling knees forced premature retirement.

David Ginola rescues Neil Silver, his biographer, because he thought he was worth it – there were three more chapters of the book to write.

"Look at my medals...I've got loadsa silverware." Vinnie Jones with his 1988 FA Cup winners' medal after Wimbledon defeated Liverpool – or as John Motson put it, the Crazy Gang beat the Culture Club.

Mark Hughes is a poodle turned rottweiller which the Manchester City manager "can understand but not explain."

Barry Fry celebrating Barnet's promotion to the Football League in 1991. The pantomime season ran for 12 months at Underhill with Fry and chairman Stan Flashman the stars.

Among Lennie Lawrence's worries as Charlton manager were winning matches, which stadium the club would play at and a rubber shipment from the Far East.

Roy Keane demands 100 per cent effort from his players and 100 per cent eye-contact from everyone who speaks to him. Those who glance away rarely forget the moment.

An emotional Pele after helping Brazil to win the World Cup in 1958.

The most powerful man in world football – Sepp Blatter, the president of FIFA and slave master.

Brian Clough – one of the best and most imitated managers of all-time.

Mido decided it was a good idea to take off his shirt after scoring for Tottenham. This earned him a yellow card.

David Beckham has managed to be both a great player and a celebrity.

Dennis Bergkamp tries to make referee Graham Barber change his mind but fails.

Martin O'Neill has the gift of the gab and the gift of the job.

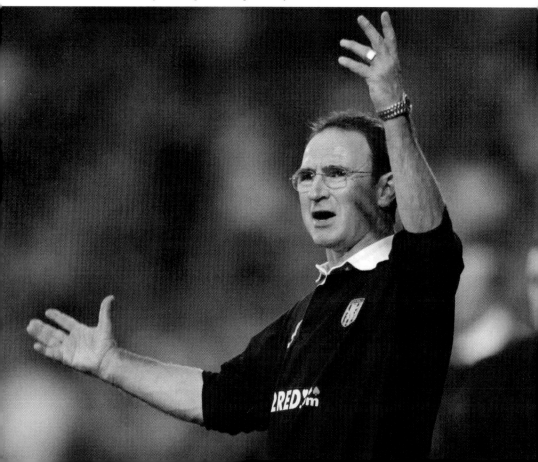

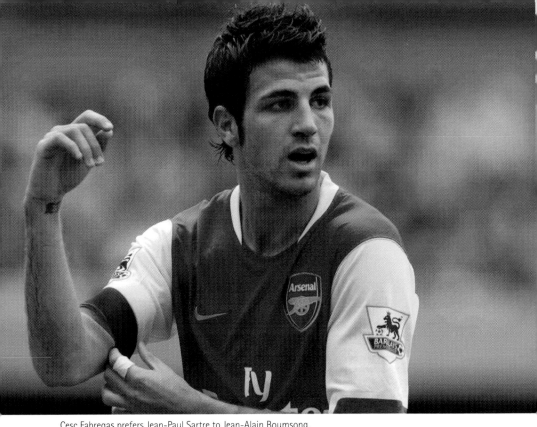

Cesc Fabregas prefers Jean-Paul Sartre to Jean-Alain Boumsong.

No manager has had greater control over a club than Manchester United's Sir Alex Ferguson.

Before his first England cap: new boy Alan Hodgkinson (second left, standing) and the other England players (minus late arrival Stanley Matthews) are addressed by manager Walter Winterbottom (left of picture). Back row (l to r): Jack Marshall (coach), Hodgkinson, 12th man Ray Barlow, Roger Byrne, Derek Kevan, Colin Grainger, Duncan Edwards. Front row: Billy Wright, Ron Clayton, Tom Finney, Jeff Hall, Tommy Thompson. Imagine the outcry if a current England player was photographed with a bottle of beer as Roger Byrne was.

Alan Hodgkinson aged 72, gloved up and ready for action.

After 27 knee operations and leukaemia treatment Geoff Thomas's specialist said: "At this stage most people go swimming." Thomas completed the Tour de France instead.

Ivory Coast's Didier Drogba is one of many leading players to come out of Africa and grace the European stage.

Neale Cooper was banned from having a shower. Instead the Aberdeen defender had to think of Charlie Nicholas.

Peter Osgood – "Why does he act like a clown?" asked Sir Alf Ramsey.

Stanley Matthews with the FA Cup he helped Blackpool win in 1953.

Former Scotland manager Ally MacLeod had an Elm Street (aka nightmare) at Argentina 1978.

Arjan De Zeeuw's cv includes voted Wigan's best player of all time, being spat upon by El Hadji Diouf and receiving praise from Tony Blair – surely a unique hat-trick?

The changing face – or rather head – of football. Aston Villa fans of the 1920's – was it mandatory to wear a cap in those days?

At USA 94 the chemist's friend Diego Maradona gave Gerry Cox his greatest scoop.

FRANZ BECKENBAUER WAS MY CHAUFFEUR

And I told the Queen Mother not to give up her day job

By Ken Montgomery

FIFTY YEARS in football journalism were inspired, for me, by a bizarre, almost unbelievable goal. The ball ricocheted sensationally from a Rangers defender's goal-line clearance and into his own net – off wee Willie Jack's backside.

Scottish football had never known such an upset. First Division giants Rangers 0 Second Division no-hopers Kilmarnock 1. David had mugged Goliath.

Willie was a diminutive striker who played for my home-town team Kilmarnock – Killie as they are known throughout Scotland – back in the 1950s. His sensationally freakish Hampden Park goal in the Scottish League Cup semi-final ensured him of a permanent place in Kilmarnock's football folklore. And I was in a packed Hampden to see the miracle unfold.

My dad had taken me to Hampden as a starry-eyed 12-year-old schoolboy along with what seemed to be the town's entire 42,000 population. Everyone feared the worst. But the Ibrox giants were felled, and the newspapers next day had a birthday. "Bottoms up for Killie ... Rangers are rock bottom," and, inevitably "Jack the giant killer" were just some of the headlines I still remember.

From that moment, I was hooked. I had only one aim, and that was to be a football writer. Thanks to my local paper, the Kilmarnock Standard, the Yorkshire Evening Post and finally, for 30 years as chief football writer of the Sunday Mirror, my dream was fulfilled.

Football has taken me to well over 100 countries, and allowed me to meet some amazing people. Yet as we set out for Hampden that day back in 1953, the Kilmarnock Academy kid had career visions of becoming a Primary School teacher. That was before wee Willie Jack's rump intervened.

Killie are not a big club, doing well to survive in the Premiership on home attendances that struggle around the 6,000 mark, unless Rangers or Celtic are the visitors. They have won the Scottish League Championship only once and the Scottish Cup three times in their history.

Nor is Kilmarnock a big town. But it is the birthplace of one of Scotland's great historical heroes, William Wallace, it's the home of Johnnie Walker whisky while our National Bard, good old Rabbie Burns, once lived just 10 miles down the road in Alloway.

It's a long way from Kilmarnock to Kuala Lumpur, from Ayrshire to Auckland in New Zealand or to America and Australia. Because of football writing, I've been lucky to see them all.

But the game to me has not just been about going to far away places with strange-sounding names. It has also been about meeting and mingling with dozens of famous faces over the years, some serene, some charming, many incredibly amusing, and some who were absolutely formidable.

Into that latter category I have no hesitation in placing Margaret, now Baroness Lady Thatcher. The Iron Lady invited me, along with a handful of Fleet Street colleagues, to 10 Downing Street to discuss the horrendous afternoon of the Hillsborough disaster.

That black afternoon, when an FA Cup semi-final between Nottingham Forest and Liverpool was tragically ravaged by the deaths of almost 100 fans. It is a day I will remember with immense sadness for the rest of my life.

The Prime Minister probed us, over coffee and biscuits, into the cause of the tragedy, but we had to explain that our Press Box seats were in the main stand overlooking the centre-circle, so we were more than half the length of the pitch from the Leppings Lane terrace where tragedy struck.

Even when the game was abandoned after eight minutes, it was hours afterwards that we were to learn the full extent of the crowd crush. I'm afraid we could offer Mrs Thatcher no more help than we could to the relatives and friends of those crushed to death so horrendously.

In much happier circumstances, it was wonderful to meet the late, great Queen Elizabeth the Queen Mother. Indeed, it was even more enjoyable to play a few shots of snooker against the great lady in London's Gough Square Press Club. The Queen Mum loved her sport, especially National Hunt horseracing. The lady oozed charm, warmth and elegance, and was gracious enough to admit : "I'm not very good at this, am I, young man ?"

She smiled that warm smile when I replied: "With respect, Ma'am, I wouldn't give up the day job."

Another compelling and indeed commanding figure I met on my football travels was Lt. Colonel Aslanides of the Greek Paras. He was a key figure in the Military Coup in Greece in the late 1960s.

Journalists travelling with an England Under-21 side on a close-season tour were invited to dine with the Greek military top brass at the exclusive Royal Athens Yacht club. And when the Lt. Colonel took a real shine to my cigarette lighter, I gave it to him as a gift.

Imagine my surprise, delight and amazement when he turned up at our hotel the following morning and presented me with a two-foot-high Greek doll, dressed in beautiful National costume. Who said football writers would never earn employment with the Diplomatic Corps?

The late Alan Ball, one of England's World Cup-winning heroes, could never have been described as a diplomat. But with Ballie, bless him, what you saw was what you got.

I was in Arsenal's team bus after the Gunners had played Dundee in a pre-season friendly game. I heard Alan plead with his manager, Bertie Mee: "Boss, you've got to sign that little ginger-headed kid who played against us. He's going to be a star."

Arsenal didn't take Alan's advice. Everyone now knows what a fabulous career Gordon Strachan enjoyed as a player, with Aberdeen and Manchester United.

Football writers have also been known to be chauffeur driven by football legends. In my case, Sir Stanley Matthews drove me all over Malta when he had retired to the island and I was there to cover a Wales international match.

Franz Beckenbauer, the Kaiser himself, picked me up at Munich airport one day when I went to West Germany to interview him. I had been told by German Football Federation secretary Wilfried Gerhardt that he had arranged for a car to meet me. What he didn't say was the Kaiser would be driving it. Now that really was travelling in and with style.

Much has been made of today's pampered players and their sky-high wage packets, yet in my capacity as executive secretary of the Football Writers' Association, I have found many of football's biggest names to be genuine, approachable guys. I have helped to organise dinners to honour Cristiano Ronaldo, David Beckham, Thierry Henry, Eric Cantona, Frank Lampard, Sir Bobby Charlton, Sir Alex Ferguson and Sir Bobby Robson. It was a pleasure meeting them all.

Even David Beckham said he loved it when I introduced him to a Tribute Night audience as: "A man after my own heart. He's sent the missus out to work while he's out enjoying himself here at the Royal Lancaster Hotel." Victoria, that night, was in concert with the Spice Girls.

Great games. Great games. I have been lucky enough to enjoy more than my fair share of both. But I think the most astonishing sight I've seen – apart from Willie Jack's rump-assisted goal (Killie lost the final to Dundee) involved the late, great Bobby Moore. I was ghost-writing a column with Bobby soon after he left West Ham to join Fulham. He arranged to pick me up one morning on the way to Craven Cottage, so we could do the column in his car.

Typically, the unflappable, immaculate England icon arrived a good 15 minutes early. My wife asked England's World Cup-winning idol if he'd keep an eye on our three-year-old daughter while she went upstairs to hurry me along. Imagine our amazement, our astonishment, when Pat and I got to our sitting room door and saw Leanne perched gleefully on Bobby's back as he crawled on hands and knees over the carpet, treating our daughter to a piggy-back ride.

I swear Bobby's blushes were as red as a Manchester United shirt as he realised we had watched him entertain Leanne. What a great guy he was behind that so-cool exterior.

My wife still smiles when she recalls Bobby Moore crawling on her carpet, or the great big kiss on the cheek she received from David Beckham.

The game has changed dramatically since I started in sports writing and I have been lucky enough to meet, interview and report on so many of them. It has indeed been a long way from Kilmarnock to K.L., and from Ayrshire to Australia, but it been well worth the experience.

Ken Montgomery is executive secretary of the FWA, after spending his career with the Kilmarnock Standard, the Yorkshire Evening Post and, for 30 years, the Sunday Mirror as chief football writer.

__Favourite player:__ Triple dead-heat between England's Tom Finney, a true gent; John Charles of Wales, a real gentle giant; and Dave Mackay of Scotland, football's original Braveheart.

__Most memorable match:__ Real Madrid 7, Eintracht Frankfurt 3 in the 1960 European Cup Final watched by 135,000 at Hampden.

I DO LIKE CRICKET

Football could benefit from cricket's closer contact between players and media

By Glenn Moore

D AVID LACEY, who appears elsewhere in these pages, tells a tale dating back to the 1980 European Championship. A few journalists are having a drink in a bar near the England team hotel when Ray Kennedy, the Liverpool midfielder later tragically afflicted with Parkinson's Disease, walks in. The hacks offer to buy Kennedy a drink.

"No, let me buy you one. You blokes do a lot for us," is the gist of the reply.

Such an exchange is inconceivable now, three decades on. It is not just that few modern players would share Kennedy's sentiment, the likelihood of a player walking into a bar occupied by journalists is slim indeed. There are a few individual friendships between players and newspapermen but, collectively, England players are kept very much in seclusion. Players and press used to share a plane to away fixtures, as is still often the case with Premier League clubs engaged in European competition. Glenn Hoddle put a stop to that when he became national manager in 1996.

Two years later, as England prepared for the World Cup with a tournament in Morocco, he even engineered a situation where the team and media were in separate continents, the press being left in Africa while the team returned, between matches, to Spain. Even prior to Hoddle the team hotel was strictly off-limits with security guards keeping press and public away. The Football Association do ensure there are plenty of interview opportunities, but they are formal occasions, conducted in marquees in the hotel grounds, or at the training base, not in the hotel itself. Intriguingly there was a thawing in relations during the 2006 World Cup because players' families found themselves sharing the media hotel in Baden-Baden. The families were warned in advance to be careful who they spoke to because of this unfortunate juxtaposition. In fact in such close proximity barriers dropped and rapprochements were made. While there were a few disagreements the parents found most of the media were not the ogres their children had made them out to be. On the flip side some journalists realised there was more to the players than the one-dimensional caricature many are cast as.

While England remains an extreme example clubs increasingly seek to keep the media at a distance too. Training grounds, especially the shiny new ones springing up from Cobham (Chelsea) to Carrington (Manchester United and City) have guardhouses and barriers securing the entrances with journalists only allowed in by invitation. It is a long way from the days when reporters could walk in and watch training, as remains the case at, for example, Barcelona, or simply ring up the players' lounge at the training ground – always a risk when it came to calling Melwood, Liverpool's base, as John Aldridge would answer and attempt to impersonate whoever you were asking for.

There are some sound reasons for this. Such is the profile of the Premier League there are genuine security issues surrounding players. The media interest is now huge, with so many journalists covering football, from papers, news agencies, TV, radio and websites, some form of control is necessary. It must also be admitted that we, in the media, have not helped ourselves at times with the coverage of players' personal lives, and "top-spinning" of quotes. Some loss of trust is inevitable. Both sides pay a price however.

A journalist is more likely to write favourably of a player with whom he has a personal relationship. It is human nature. Had Hoddle been less contemptuous of the press he might not have encountered such fierce criticism following his comments about disabled people, and he may have survived. Contact between players and press also helps each understand one another better. The struggling midfield maestro can point out, in confidence, that he has been labouring under a chronic ankle injury, or his baby is seriously ill, or that the flash little winger may look good but he is always losing the ball in the wrong place leaving the midfielder out of position. The journalist, meanwhile, could apologise for mis-reading the player's performance the previous week, and giving him four out of 10, but let the player try judging 22 people at once, and write a fat paragraph about them, all before the final whistle.

There was a time when such exchanges happened, but not any more.

Cricket is different. My Lacey moment came in Guyana in the early 1990s when I was covering Australia's tour of the West Indies. I walked into a restaurant and looked around for a friendly face. There were no journalists present, but an arm waved me over.

"I'm Mark," said Mark Taylor, Australia's opening bat, unnecessarily. He then introduced Steve Waugh and Ian Healy. We were not friends but they knew I was part of the travelling press corps. As the tour wore on players and press would often share a drink. That is less common now as Test cricketers either drink less, or avoid doing so in public. Like footballers they also have agents and an interview may well be arranged through a kit sponsor, or energy drink manufacturer, rather than casually fixed up after training. But on tour cricket writers are still often billeted in the same hotel as the players and meet them over breakfast, in the lobby, or the gym (just as players now drink less, hacks now exercise more, up to a point). Journalists will still go out for dinner with players and I vividly remember having a drink with England celebrating cricketers after they had won the Trent Bridge Test in the 2005 Ashes series.

My re-introduction into the cricket circle was aided then by the presence of the Independent's cricket correspondent, Angus Fraser, a former Test player much respected by the current team. That so many ex-pros are in cricket's written media (aside from Alan Smith, the Daily Telegraph's ex-Arsenal striker, most football ex-pros are in broadcast media) helps maintain friendly communication between the two groups.

So does the fact that the media spotlight is less intensive, and less intrusive, than in football. High-profile individuals like Ian Botham and Freddie Flintoff make the news pages, but few others do and many welcome some press interest. Thus it is still possible to ring the dressing room at many county grounds and speak to a player waiting to bat.

Is there is any difference once you finally sit down with a player, microphone in hand, having negotiated the agent and the press officer? Not as much as might be expected. There is a common perception that footballers are thick and cricketers are intelligent. It would be more accurate to say cricketers are better-educated than footballers, in part because the sport's structure enables them to remain in education past 16. Footballers can be equally good interviewees, amiable and happy to talk, especially foreign players (who tend to come from an environment where the media is closer to players), or those with a few years' experience.

Young athletes, in any sport, tend not to have too much to say as they know little of life beyond the confines of the training pitch and young footballers, in particular, can be wary having been warned off the media by a jaundiced senior pro. Increasingly clubs, or agents, seek copy approval but this is infrequently given and in this respect the situation is nowhere near as bad as in Hollywood, yet.

The game will never return to the days when journalists would carouse late into the night with the Spurs team in the Bell & Hare after matches. We hacks cannot afford the bar bill in China Whites to start with. There is, however, scope for improving relations if clubs, and journalists, have the will. It would benefit all sides but cannot be considered likely. Clubs, in many cases, are more paranoid about the press than players. They cannot see the argument, advanced several years ago by Bayern Munich, and common in golf, motor racing and tennis, that if you give journalists an easy life, providing them with plenty of access, few will look for something different. But if you do not, the space between the advertisements still has to be filled, and the hack will look to agents and disaffected players to fill it.

The crux is that football's dominance has changed the sport's relationship with the press for good. Cricket, which even gets squeezed for space in July these days, now needs the media more than the media needs cricket. Football, being generously bankrolled by the television companies, appears to believe the print industry is a beast it needs to tame, not befriend.

Glenn Moore is football editor of the Independent, having been football correspondent 1994-2004. Between 1990-1994 he covered cricket, primarily for Reuters, and still some cricket reporting.

Favourite player: It is a privilege to watch players like Eric Cantona, Ruud Gullit, Cristiano Ronaldo, Cesc Fabregas, Zinedine Zidane, but I stopped having favourite players when I started working in the game.

Most memorable match: Personally, Gillingham defeating Wigan in the Division Two play-off final, 2000; professionally England v Argentina in St Etienne, World Cup 98. Both matches had everything.

I LOVED THIERRY TAKING THE MERC

He talked about "Eye-berry" like a lover

By Sue Mott

TALKING TO footballers is a dodgy business that does not necessarily result in illumination. Some possess the wit and repartee of comedians, while others only boast the conversation of a goldfish mouthing clichés like bubbles in a tank.

"The ball just come over and I hit it." Or "We're just taking it one game at a time." Or "I done it for the lads." All of them bubbling to the surface of the great goldfish bowl of sport to lapped up as gems falling from the lips of the gods.

But so great is football's grip on modern culture, it has become essential to speak to footballers anyway, whether they like it or not, and with all the complications involved in the transaction.

In the old days it was a case of paper and pencil in the car park and a race to see if your quarry could drive over your foot in a Ford Cortina before you'd cornered him for a quote about his latest defensive lapse. These days an industry has been constructed around so-called player access, a slight misnomer given that the access can be fleeting, halted, indecipherable, unwillingly pursued by both parties and subject to sudden interruption.

"I am sorry. I am going now," said Jens Lehmann, the Arsenal goalkeeper, leaping to his feet and marching from the room. Thirty minutes had elapsed since the start of the conversation which he had been told would last half-an-hour. One could only admire his immaculate time-keeping, and wish that such perfection had extended to his goalkeeping.

Then there was the Roy Keane debacle. A phone call from a sports editor to pass on the news that you have an exclusive one hour interview with the then Manchester United legend is enough to cause heart murmurs in anyone. But when you are about 300 miles away, on holiday in some obscure rural idyll of Devon, beyond all reach of civilised transportation links, the issue becomes rather pressing.

Bad things happened, of which the worst (apart from the twin prop plane from Truro, or some such unlikely spot, to Gatwick and a plane change to Manchester) was discovering the road to Plymouth unarguably blocked at 5am by a stream of cows embarking on their morning's ramble to pasture and that by standing on the gate shouting for help, the interviewer's white trousers were now covered in cow dung – and, more to the point, would be so for the rest of the day.

Panic, imprecations, dabbing with a wet sponge and several hours later, Roy Keane hailed into view, clutching a slightly menacing dog, and one feared for one's job, life and trousers, not necessarily in that order. But if memory serves, he was charming. He even bought me a prawn sandwich for lunch, which might have been an ironic statement given his views on corporate hospitality at Old Trafford, but was, in fact, an act of pity. Good bloke.

So was Brian Clough. As a University newspaper novice at the time, I could not have expected any cooperation from the man on the brink of not one, but two, successive European Cups with unglamorous Nottingham Forest. But above all else, he was mischievous. He seemed to take great delight in banning the BBC for some perceived slight and devoting time to an awe-struck learner instead. "Oi, young lady, you with the teeth," he used to call in the hearing of my professional counterparts and I'd be invited into his office to transcribe his wisdom into pitifully-poor swathes of shorthand.

He once told me how much he would have loved to be a teacher. "Imagine passing on education to all those little girls and boys," he said with genuine sincerity. Shorthand permitting, I wrote up the story and the Daily Mail nicked it without paying me. But the compensation was meeting a man whose iconic status as a manager remains to this day. I might be able to claim I glimpsed the vocational zeal in Clough that made him such an effective mentor to the unstarry all-sorts that played for the Forest. That and his swearing.

The F word and football interviews are rarely parted, or rather they *were* rarely parted in those days before foreign-taught English and manners were imported into the domestic game. An interview with Charlie George, my Arsenal all-time hero, was an exercise in expunging all permutations of Anglo-Saxon in our ensuring conversation which did not lend itself to a lengthy draft.

However, there are moments in life that are magical and waiting outside Iceland, the frozen food store, on the Caledonian Road, as instructed, for my rendezvous with Charlie remains one of the highlights of my professional career. It was never precisely clear why we had to meet like renegade spies from the Eastern bloc, but judging by his slightly peripatetic lifestyle, there might have been people whose acquaintance he was keen not to rekindle.

It was a wonderful lunch we spent together. He spilt gravy down his tie, insisted that scoring a goal was better than sex and betrayed his on-going love of Arsenal with every word. At the time he was giving guided tours round Highbury, in the last days before the developers wrecking ball moved in, and it remained a lottery whether he ever remembered to dispense with the F-words when there were children present. Probably not, but there were no complaints.

From Arsenal hero circa 1971 to the London club's greatest striker. Thierry Henry. What a smoothie. It was the season before he left for Barcelona, the one truncated by injuries and frustrations for both player and club alike, but he still arrived like a conquering hero, dressed in black from head to foot, except startlingly white trainers. The first inkling I had of his arrival was the sighing to a half of a £250,000 Mercedes sports car whose doors opened upwards like some sort of space shuttle, followed by the emergence of that famous smoothly shaven head.

He talked about "Eye-berry" like a lover. "What I love about Highbury is when we play on a Saturday and I arrive early to walk alongside the pitch alone. It's just me, the pitch and the stadium. No-one is there. Sometimes I 'ear the fans. You know, from previous games, from previous goals I score. Great moments come back to me like an echo."

You are simply not going to get that kind of romance from talking to old-timers like Tommy Smith whose reputation for being handy with the hatchet is part of football's folklore. That is what I thought anyway, on my train journey to Blundell Sands. I was wrong. It was deeply romantic, but in a different way.

There is a quote about Smith handed down to posterity from the great Liverpool manager, Bill Shankly. "Take that bandage off! And what do you mean *your* knee. It's Liverpool Football Club's knee!"

That's how it was in those days. You served, you sacrificed. In 18 years at Liverpool, Smith suffered injuries that would eventually require two knee, one hip and an elbow replacement, not to mention sufficient metal rods in his body to fully justify his old nickname 'Anfield Iron.'

I asked him about that. Was it worth it? Sunk into his armchair, only able to walk short distances these days, he looked at me as though I was mad. "'Course it was," he said, blazing with sincerity, "for the camaraderie, the fans, for the success we had. I felt lost when I left Liverpool."

It took a while. He made 632 appearances for the club, won four First Division medals, two FA Cups, two European Cups, two UEFA Cups and a set of scars of which he was inordinately proud. He is a throwback to the years when a local lad could dig Mr Shankly's garden, paint the Anfield terraces and go on to become a hero to the masses on the Kop. How could you not love the man who used to give Jimmy Greaves, the mercurial Tottenham striker, a copy of the menu at the Liverpool Infirmary whenever he arrived at Anfield for a match?

Some opponents, however, were trickier than others. No footballer, no interviewer, could ask for greater a challenge than George Best. Not because he was in any way unhelpful to the questing journalist, but because there were so few words to convey the sorrow of his transformation.

The last time I saw George it was the year of his death, 2005. He was living in a health spa, of all places, buzzing with half-naked women convinced that a well-oiled aromatherapy massage would right all the wrongs of their existence. If only it had been as easy to fix one of the on-going tragedy that was the story of his own life.

He looked tired, the once-lush Beatles hair-do now brittle and grey, lines and creases round those mesmeric eyes. But the wit and intelligence that defined one of the greatest football careers of all time was still there. He was only 58. He would die six months short of his 60th birthday, a ravaged alcoholic, yet a deeply-mourned and treasured personality. His goals were replayed a thousand times over, but I prefer to remember his last words to me.

I wanted a contact number just in case there were any follow-up questions. "You can have my mobile if you like," he said and read out his number to me. I am a child of the Sixties when George Best was simply the most beautiful, talented, charismatic creature on God's earth. I looked at the number I'd just written down and gasped.

"George, do you realise, half the women in the world would kill for this number."

He smiled at me and winked.

"Half the women in the world have got it," he said.

Sue Mott is a freelance sports writer, formerly tennis and football correspondent of the Sunday Times before going on to become feature writer, columnist and interviewer for the Daily Telegraph.

__Favourite player:__ The afore-mentioned Charlie George whose goal in the 1971 Cup Final against Liverpool sealed Arsenal's double and his fate as my immutable hero.

__Most memorable match:__ Italy v Brazil in the 1982 World Cup when I was given a ticket for the match by Brazil fans in Barcelona and mourned with them a 2-3 defeat to Paolo Rossi.

A TALE OF ONE CITY

Everton can overtake Liverpool as Merseyside's top club

By Mike Parry

IT'S A grim prospect for a middle-aged Evertonian.

To think that I might spend the rest of my life with Liverpool being recognised as the bigger of the two Premier League clubs on Merseyside is hard to bear. Not a day goes by without me thinking at some point about the relative strengths of the clubs and how Liverpool have moved away over the last couple of decades to become, unassailably, the top club in the city.

It hurts to write that and it will hurt many who read it.

But I take comfort because as grim as it may seem now, I am quietly confident that there will be a restoration of the balance of power in the city over the next five years.

The present position begs two questions. Firstly how did the position of Liverpool dominance come about after a century and more during which Everton were often the top club? And, perhaps more importantly, if Everton are going to catch up with their neighbours, how are they going to do it?

Let's trace the more recent history of these two great clubs. Perhaps the moment when they were most evenly matched in the post-War years was the opening game of the 1966/67 season.

It was the Charity Shield. Everton were the FA Cup winners and Liverpool had won their second League Championship under Bill Shankly. The trophies were paraded around Goodison Park along with the World Cup, carried by the two men who had played in the victorious England team, Ray Wilson and Roger Hunt. A third World Cup winner, Alan Ball, would soon make his debut for Everton, having been signed from Blackpool for £110,000, then a British transfer fee. The stadium that day was the citadel of English football power. Everton were the more established club, having been the traditionalists in the game since their conception in 1878. They had the superior stadium with Goodison Park being chosen over Anfield as a World Cup venue.

The Toffees were known then as the Merseyside Millionaires. They enjoyed the personal patronage of Littlewoods Pools and shopping tycoon, John Moores. They were the aristocrats to Liverpool's rough and readiness. But they had a secret weapon that Everton did not have. Something that shaped their destiny to this day.

It was Bill Shankly.

The fiery Scotsman was recruited from Huddersfield in 1959 to try to haul Liverpool out of the Second Division where they had been in the doldrums for eight years. By 1962 Liverpool were back in the First Division which they won for the first time since 1946 two years later. They succeeded Everton who had won the title in 1963 under Harry Catterick.

Catterick and Shankly were side-by-side with success but as individual men they were miles apart.

The Liverpool manager was more like a fan. He often wore a red and white scarf, he encouraged fans to visit Melwood, Liverpool's training ground and he was fantastic with one-line quips when addressing huge celebratory crowds during his era of success, the most famous one being that "football is more important than life or death."

His players believed he was fonder of the fans than he was of them, telling his team on the coach to away matches: "Look at all these people who follow us. You owe them all a victory." He gave tickets away to supporters outside the ground and one time he gave a fan a fiver after discovering he had no money to get home.

Catterick came over as an altogether more conservative man to the point of being reserved and rather dour.

Each was the most successful manager for their clubs to that point in post-War Britain.

But Shankly instilled a spirit in his club that didn't exist anywhere else. I think he was a recruiting sergeant then for the grown-up Liverpol fans of today. He was particularly popular with young fans who warmed to his rascally charm.

And when he surprisingly stood down after winning the FA Cup for the second time in 1974 he was succeeded by his assistant Bob Paisley who steered the club through its greatest ever year.

Not only did Shankly take care of Liverpool during his own reign, he was looking after their future. He assembled the famous boot-room team, from where Paisley came, that looked after the club for another two decades.

Everton's succession following the departure of Catterick in 1973 was nothing like as successful.

There was a Shankly legacy at Anfield that did not exist on the other side of Stanley Park. While Liverpool built on Shankly's foundations Everton did not properly build on the achievements of Harry Catterick – two league titles, one FA Cup and beaten finalists in another.

For a decade and more Everton entered the wilderness. They became a mid-table team with an occasional cup run while Liverpool became kings of Europe. Undoubtedly this is the era in which the clubs started to move apart.

Howard Kendall brilliantly restored Everton's fortunes in the Eighties and remains the club's most successful ever manager but even then he was not able to see Liverpool off. They were, by then, too established as one of Europe's top clubs.

In 1985 Everton won the European Cup-Winners' Cup and were acknowledged as one of favourites to win the following year's European Cup, having secured the league title as well. That was the crucial moment when Everton should have acted, as they did when they won their previous title in 1970. Then they built the biggest tiered stand in the world to make Goodison a leading ground for a top club.

But no such activity took place off the field in the Eighties. The ground should have been redeveloped.

Heysel, of course, ended Everton's European ambitions – though that was an irrelevancy compared to the loss of the lives of 39 supporters in Brussels. What is more relevant is the fact that despite being banned from Europe for longer than the other English clubs – they were given three years extra exile – Liverpool did not let it interfere with their domestic game and they won three more titles in the next five years.

What is puzzling to all Evertonians is the question of the respective wealth of the two clubs. It's fair to assume that in the Eighties they were clubs with similar resources. Same sized grounds and income. Both could afford the top players in Europe. Gary Lineker, heading towards his peak, was recruited by the Blues.

But as Everton's period of success dwindled away so did the financial muscle that they had possessed from the Moores era. Sir John is thought to have become Britain's first self-made billionaire through his business acumen. He stepped down as chairman in the late Sixties but came back briefly in the early Seventies to try to revive the club. He still had a share-holding but he didn't fulfill the same role as he had under Harry Catterick when he underwrote the signings of all the top players.

The Moores' power and wealth seemed to transfer itself almost overnight to Liverpool. David Moores, the nephew of Sir John, from the modern generation of the family was a fanatical Liverpool fan and eventually became chairman of the club. Moores reportedly received over £80 million for his shareholding when the American businessmen, Tom Hicks and George Gillett took over Liverpool but that is virtually loose change for the Moores family.

In the 2008 Sunday Times Rich List, the family, headed up by matriarch, Lady Grantchester, the daughter of John Moores, appear as the 60th wealthiest people in the country with a fortune of £1.2 billion. That is just about the sort of money that could support a big-spending policy but it seems that the umbilical money cord between the family and the club has forever been severed.

Local businessman Peter Johnson became chairman of Everton in the Nineties after amassing a fortune in the food industry.

But he was never the sort of chairman who wanted to use his own millions in the way Jack Walker did at Blackburn. Today's chairman, Bill Kenwright, is a successful theatre impresario with a world-wide business. But he does not have a personal wealth running into billions which is what is needed these days to be able to buy success.

Liverpool built on their fantastic record in Europe. They became a world brand which brought them top revenues in sponsorships and endorsements. Recently, of course, they have had two American billionaires squabbling over their ownership but despite all this Everton CAN become the biggest club on Mersyside again.

I am absolutely astonished that, with the popularity of the Premier League around the world, a billionaire businessman has not already snapped up Everton. They could probably be bought for less than £100 million.

Kenwright's attachment to the club is because he is a life-long fan. He is the chairman so that the club remains in safe, caring hands while the search for a new investor goes on. He doesn't even draw a salary even though he deals with club affairs every day on top of running his theatre productions all around the globe.

Robert Earl of Planet Hollywood fame is a new director of Everton. His wealth is listed at £236 million in the Rich List and his business acumen is invaluable. Yet even his appointment to the board has not transformed Everton into a club that is going to sign £20 million-plus players.

However, a new era is definitely emerging for Everton. They are well advanced in their plans for a new 55,000-seat stadium. Part of that exercise involves a world-wide search for a naming rights partner which could raise up to £45 million in the first couple of years.

That might sound like small beer in the modern game but it will put Everton into the market-place and give them exposure in areas where they have never been before.

I am confident that will trigger a re-awakening of the club once there is a realisation of its full potential. In 2007/08 the club opened their new training centre, Finch Farm, a state-of-the-art development which will both attract and nurture new talent.

At the same time Liverpool seem to be running into uncharted waters. Stability has always been the key word at Anfield but these days it is a ship which is being tossed about in a rogue sea. The plans for the heralded 60,000 – and then 70,000 and then perhaps 60,000 again – capacity stadium are not as advanced as Everton's own project.

Their financial position is not at all transparent and at the time of writing the ownership question is in turmoil. Those who run Everton FC believe that they are entering a new era which will give them the ability again to challenge at the very top. Every fan believes in their own club, most of us blindly.

The facts show that having faith in Everton is not blind faith. During my lifetime every other club in the Premier League except Liverpool and Arsenal have spent seasons in a lower division. That includes European Champions Manchester United and Aston Villa and domestic champions like Chelsea. It's true of some of the very biggest clubs in the land: Newcastle, Leeds and Spurs. Other clubs have tasted glory, Nottingham Forest in particular plus Derby and Blackburn Rovers and then gone into eras of disintegration.

But though Everton have had depressing years, even decades, they have never suffered full-blown decline, although famously they came within 45 minutes of relegation in 1994.

In many respects a football club is an image of its fans. The Goodison faithful will never settle for the fact that we are the second club on Merseyside on more than a temporary basis. If you look at other two-club-cities – or regions, one club will always be dominant.

Manchester City will never overtake United. The Old Trafford mob have so consolidated their position it is impossible. The same is true of Newcastle and Sunderland and Villa and Birmingham. But in Liverpool that is not the case. The position could change around in just a couple of seasons. Manchester has become dynastical.

The city of Liverpool is cyclical. And the cycle of fortune will turn again in Everton's favour.

Mike Parry is a Breakfast Show presenter with TalkSPORT radio. A former head of communication at the Football Association, he was previously executive editor of the Sun and news editor of the Daily Express. Also author of books including There's An Awful Lot of Bubbly in Brazil.

Favourite player: Alan Ball. He was the spirit of Everton in the Sixties and Seventies when a truly great team was built around him. He left the club far too soon. His heart was as big as the entrance to the Mersey Tunnel and I cried when I heard he had died.

Most memorable match: Everton v Rapid Vienna, European Cup-Winners' Cup Final, Rotterdam, 15 May 1985. Everton won 3-1. They had already won the league title and were playing Manchester United in the FA Cup Final three days later on the Saturday. It was the greatest Everton display I ever saw. As we moved away from the ground in a coach I was in shock because I'd seen the team playing like a legendary Real Madrid side. We'd reached heights that I had never imagined. I believed there was no end to what that team could achieve.

CLOUGHIE CALLED ME A DISGRACE

And my love affair with Bristol City started

By Jonathan Pearce

IT WAS Saturday 14 September 1968. The Ashton Gate match programme described him as "one of the game's brightest new managers." With a diffident air he sat down two yards from us. A boy next to me hefting an impossibly huge red and white wooden rattle smashed it onto the roof of the dugout. The manager shot up and in a classic case of mistaken identity chastised me in that unmistakable drone.

"Young man. You're a disgrace!"

They were the only words Brian Clough ever spoke to me.

It was my first ever visit to Bristol City. On hearing Cloughie's lecture, my dad swore it would be my last. The other lad owned up. I was reprieved and a love affair was born that has lasted 40 years.

The game finished nil-nil. The first three matches I ever saw all did. I couldn't quite work out why I'd fallen for the game. Sometimes I still can't. But of all the thousands of matches I've seen, I'll never forget the day Gibson, Jacobs, Briggs, Wimshurst, Connor, Parr, Crowe, Garland, Galley, Kellard and Sharpe ran out in the all red strip in front of me.

Some were rotund. Others were toothless and fierce. The crowd sung that they'd "walk a million miles for one of your goals John Gaaaallleeeey." I drank it all in.

I still have the match programme with its Football League Review insert that used to carry articles on my idols of the day. Any snippet about Eddie Gray or Bobby Moore was gleefully read and Garland was worshipped with the best of them. He was the local lad, the golden boy with the flaxen curls who would lift City into the First Division. He never did. He had to be sold to fund the Dolman

Stand, a futuristic cantilever affair named after the avuncular and visionary club chairman.

Season ticket prices were advertised for the new stand on that day. £8 10/- for the most expensive seats. Those were the days we sat silently in the dark at home when the bailiffs came knocking. How could dad, a lecturer in electrical engineering who was the wisest man I've ever known and the most useless with money, ever afford it?

It was the best present ever when somehow he did. It was from the new seats that we watched manager Alan Dicks slowly piece together a team that was to consume my every waking moment.

"Uncle Alan" was a neighbour and family friend. He persuaded dad to work for him as club's education officer. I'll never forget being in the car when we picked up superstar new signing Bobby Gould from the railway station or when a 16-year-old Glaswegian with unruly hair and an impenetrable growl called Gerry Gow moved into the Dicks house on his arrival from Scotland.

He kicked the ball about in the streets with us kids and had us mesmerised when he broke into the first team weeks later. Even when he decked Gould during a game and was subbed in shame, I still worshipped him. The hair grew scruffier, that tackles bit harder and he was at the hub of an emerging young side built around local lads like Geoff Merrick at the back with his fair frizz, striker Keith Fear with his mercurial skills and more Scots like the gangling Tom Ritchie.

Dad pioneered the use of video-tape for game analysis and training purposes. At just 12, I was climbing onto gantries to film with him and travelling to matches on the team coach. In 1974 mighty Leeds, the other club of my boyhood dreams, came to town for an FA Cup fifth round tie. They'd been unbeaten in 29 league games. City had no chance.

But Fear scored a belter and instinctively I jumped forward. Unfortunately the leap took me clean off the gantry 100 feet above the stand. Only a grab by a quick thinking Match of the Day soundman saved me.

It was magical adventure at the Elland Road replay. No-one gave City a prayer. Donnie Gillies, a square-jawed striker from Glencoe poached the legendary goal and City hung on as Leeds laid siege. With moments to go the walrus-like Ernie Hunt screamed in agony and clutched a toothless mouth claiming Peter Lorimer had kicked him. Precious seconds were wasted while he had treatment. Leeds momentum was gone. We'd won.

Moments later in the delirious dressing room I asked Hunt how he felt. With teeth in place and a perfect smile he owned up. He'd conned the ref. Lorimer hadn't touched him. Shocked? Disgusted? I was ecstatic and learning lessons for the playing career that surely lay ahead of me now that I was training at the club on midweek evenings.

I tackled like my mentor Gerry Gow. I had the flashing brilliance of Fear and the courage of Ritchie. At least in my own head I did. In truth, I had the turning circle of a bull-elephant and the pace of an elephant seal on dry land.

It was still a shock though when the letter came that I was not to be offered an apprenticeship. I still have that too. How could I throw it away? I stared at it through the tears for two solid days after barricading myself into my bedroom.

Dad couldn't deal with it. His dreams as well as mine had been shattered. He got me trials at a couple of other clubs but knew my heart wasn't in it. I was hooked on City. Something was stirring. I wanted to be part of it.

Paul Cheesley, a prodigal son from the nearby village of Pill and initially a flop when he was brought home from Norwich, suddenly blossomed into a rampaging, goalscoring centre-forward. His relationship with the rangy Ritchie became talked about throughout the land.

"Ches" scored a hat trick in a thrilling 4-3 win at York, filmed by us from the roof of a toilet at Bootham Crescent. Ritchie hit three at home to York – 35 league goals between them that season. It was heady and glorious. In April 1976 Clive Whitehead who looked like something from The Hair Bear Bunch cartoon scored against Portsmouth at the Gate. City were promoted to the First Division for the first time in 65 years.

The stay was epic. On the first day of 1976/77 we were at Arsenal who paraded their £333,333 striker Malcolm Macdonald. He cost more than the whole City side that day. But attacking the Clock End, it was bargain basement buy Cheesley who rose the highest to head the only goal. It was the stuff of fantasy.

Three days later a point at home to Stoke took City joint top. But it was the day when an ice chip of utter desolation pierced my heart. Peter Shilton and Cheesley rose for a cross. They fell, crumpled and Paul's knee was wrecked. His career was over in a split second.

He would have been an England striker. City could have built a side capable of surviving for years around him. It was all gone. Icons arrived. Norman Hunter, Peter Cormack and the returning Garland were feted. On the final night at Coventry, with both sides fearing the drop, kick-off was "accidentally" delayed for five minutes. So when the news came in that rivals Sunderland had lost at Everton, Coventry and City played out a farcical 2-2 draw.

There was enormous pride at then seeing my primary school pal Kevin Mabbutt break through and score a hat trick at Old Trafford and quirky interest at the first foreigners drifting into the club. But brittle foundations were crumbling.

Seventh at Xmas 1978, the club didn't strengthen. Money, instead, was crassly spent on 10-year playing contracts. Hunter left the following summer. Relegation was inevitable and for me a major change was in the air.

Dicks persuaded BBC Radio Bristol City to give me a job. His letter thanking me for my work for the club is still my proudest possession. My first years behind the mike were gloomy, though. Dicks was sacked. Bobby Houghton with his ice-cold stare came in and sold Gow. They went down again.

Worse followed. Despite selling Mabbutt to stave off the banks, financial disaster loomed and in February 1982 with moments to spare before the club went bankrupt, the "Ashton Gate Eight," a fine group of men agreed to tear up their contracts to save BCFC.

I'd grown up with some of them. Through tears I had to interview them. Another relegation came and went. Dad lost his job. I lost my love for the club for a while. To this day I feel bitter towards the buffoons who let it happen.

In a ramshackle hut on a Kibbutz in Israel my ardour was rekindled. I couldn't help boasting to a group of fellow travellers from around the globe of the exploits of "the greatest football club in the world". On 19 September 1982 we found an old radio and tuned it into the BBC World Service. City were at Northampton. It would be a romp, I told them.

It was. Northampton Town 7 Bristol City 1. The world laughed at me. I felt homesick for the Gate and so I came home, just in time to pick up the microphone again at Rochdale, where a 1-0 defeat left my football club bottom of the league. Six years before I'd seen them sit on top of the lot. Now I'd watched them go 92nd.

It didn't matter. That wonderful old England left-back Terry Cooper was the manager and he wooed me back to Bristol City with his craggy old tales and heart warming humour. City fans have always had to learn to laugh. There would have been too many tears otherwise.

My support is now from afar but the memory is always near of the day that Cloughie opened his mouth and a door opened in my life to such rich, unforgettable experiences.

Jonathan Pearce has been a radio/TV commentator and presenter since 1980. He has presented and commentated on BBC 1, BBC 2, ITV, Channel 5, Sky, BBC radio 5Live and Capital Radio. Since 2004 he has been one of the leading commentators on Match of the Day

__Favourite player:__ Bobby Moore. He was as immaculate off the pitch as he was on it and became a great friend and work colleague before his untimely death.

__Most memorable match:__ The 1990 World Cup semi-final between England and West Germany. It was a surging, gripping drama. England came so close to the final. They've not looked doing so ever since.

WHY ENGLAND MUST HAVE AN ENGLISH MANAGER

No country has ever won the World Cup under a manager of another nationality

By Jeff Powell

WHEN SVEN The Impaler was appointed manager of England I chose to express my serious reservations in what was meant to be a humorous way, writing something along the lines of 'the mother country of football selling that birthright down the fjord to a land of skiers and javelin throwers who spend half their year in round-the-clock darkness'. 'Chauvinist' and 'xenophobe' were among the kinder words used to describe me by the knee-jerkers among my Fleet Street colleagues who fell over themselves to hail Mr Eriksson as the messiah come to save us from the hellfire and damnation of never winning the World Cup again. What they could not accuse me of was criticising with the benefit of hindsight.

That first of many articles about Sven-Goran's odyssey through England – many of this country's more nubile female residents included – was penned the very day the Football Association confirmed his coming. Not the day after that announcement; not the day after his first match; not the day after his quarter-final failures in either the 2002 World Cup or 2004 European Championship. And definitely not as belatedly as the day after England's last-eight exit from Germany 2006 – at the hands of his managerial nemesis Luiz Felipe Scolari for the third time running.

That was when the penny, the kroner and the escudo finally dropped for the last of his media defenders.

There were a number of reasons why I objected to Sven. To begin with, given my advanced middle age, we had bumped into each other down the years at all kinds of matches in many and various parts of Europe. Pleasant chap though he was – and is – it appeared that money was disproportionately important to him when compared with football. The FA, who foolishly kept increasing his multi-million pound salary every time he showed the real extent of his devotion to England by sloping off to talk turkey with the likes of Manchester United and Chelsea, got the message in the end.

Then there was his obsession with the opposite sex – Nancy, Ulrika, Faria to name but three – and whether wearing his trousers down around the platform-heeled shoes might be a bit of a handicap for the national head coach.

Nor – even though he alone has done the League and Cup double in three separate countries, namely Sweden, Portugal and Italy – did his record as a club manager stack up quite as well as it appeared on the surface. Gigantic spending in the transfer market had as much, if not more, to do with the more elevated of those successes as coaching ability, tactical acumen and man-management skills. Also, albeit through no knowledge or involvement on Eriksson's part, the winning of Italy's Serie A with Lazio which so impressed then FA chief executive Adam Crozier, was accompanied by raised eyebrows about the integrity of some of the final matches of that league season in a country not exactly unacquainted with suspicious result patterns.

Then, above all and let's make no bones about it, Eriksson was not English. That sentence should not in any way be construed as an admission that its author is a jingoist who relishes bashing Johnny Foreigner. As the proud and happy husband of a Latin American society beauty – no, England did not come home from Mexico 86 without a trophy – let me assure you I am no racist. However, I do believe that England should be managed by an Englishman, or at the very least by a native of the British Isles who is steeped in our domestic game. More than that, no nation which likes to think of itself as a major soccer power should have a foreigner as head coach.

Prejudice? No. Practical reality.

First the facts. No country has ever won the World Cup under a manager of another nationality. Not Uruguay, not Italy, not Brazil, not Germany, not Argentina, not France ... and most definitely not England. Think of it, who could have been more English than Alfred Ramsey, later 'Sir Alf', in 1966?

Nor have any of the others ever hired a foreign head coach. Yet England, in Mr Crozier's desperation to make the FA as trendy as the Saatchi and Saatchi advertising company by whom he was previously employed, took a leap into the unknown with Sven. Of itself, that was unwitting self-condemnation of the failure by Englis football's ruling body, with all its high-falutin' courses, to develop a single coach they deemed good enough to manage England.

Also, the FA failed to realise that not even such a self-proclaimed Anglophile as Eriksson can ever be possessed of such a naturally instinctive grasp of English culture as an Englishman, not even of our football culture. The national football team is part of the national identity. The English game is embedded in our soul, stitched onto the mores of our society, pumping through our veins and arteries. English football is not French, Brazilian, German or Italian football. . . nor Swedish football. Its high tempo and full-blooded commitment to the battle reflects the national character. We are historically a war-like people and that is the way we play our national game. The increasingly cosmopolitan make-up of the Premier League teams has made it easier for such prominent foreign coaches as Wenger, Benitez and Mourinho to succeed with our leading clubs but the England team, by its very definition, is restricted to English footballers. To control and inspire the beast, you have to feel its heat in your bones, in your heart, in every fibre of your being. This is no more possible for a foreigner than it is for a non-Englishman to sound the clarion call to patriotic arms if all else is failing on the pitch in, say, a World Cup quarter-final.

This is not an endorsement of the chest-thumping and flag-waving which was Kevin Keegan's interpretation of the demands of international football management during his unhappy spell in charge of England. But the moments of extremis do arise at this most rarefied level of the game when the cry for the team to give its last ounce for the country is all that is left, can a foreigner deliver that exhortation? Er, which country is he screaming about?

Every time I have written in this vein countless journalists among Eriksson's Swedish compatriots beat a path to my door with their sauna twigs. (Forgive me, boys and girls, but some of you asked for that!).

Time, modesty cannot quite forbid me from mentioning, has proved me right. Sven, for his part, never took it personally. Not as far as I could tell. Not judging from his courtesy when we bumped back into each other on such widely differing occasions as the Footballer of the Year Dinner in London and George Best's state funeral in Belfast. Maybe he understands the problem. His heart is in football, even if it is other parts of his body which the game cannot reach. He is Swedish, after all.

That proved no impediment to Sven doing a better job at Manchester City, subsequent to his England sacking, than he was given credit for by that club's inscrutable owner. But when it comes to England, cry God for St George ... and for somebody with a name like Harry.

Jeff Powell started in journalism as a 17-year-old with the weekly Walthamstow Guardian in native East London and became sports editor. Joined Daily Mail full time in 1966 as a sports sub-editor and moved to football writing in 1969. Promoted to chief football correspondent in 1971 and then chief sports feature writer, a position he still holds, in 1989. Has reported on all 11 World Cup Finals since 1966 as well as covering 39 European Cup/Champions League Final. Author of the the authorised biography of Bobby Moore.

Favourite player: Diego Maradona. Forget the Hand of God but remember the greatest World Cup goal of all which preceded it in that quarter final against England.

Most memorable match: The 1966 World Cup Final. Not just because this was England's solitary glory nor only because it planted the World Cup fully into the consciousness of football's mother country....but for seeing my much-loved and now much-missed friend Bobby Moore, the greatest defender of all time, lift the Jules Rimet Trophy.

A PUSSY CALLED PUSKAS

The great Hungarian played in the days when footballers were for the people

By Keir Radnedge

H IS NAME was Puskas. Solidly-built to say the least, he exuded self-confidence. Every hair was smoothed decisively into place. His eyes glinted with an air of both curiosity and suspicion. His persona was unique. He also had a great left paw. Hence the name: for this particular Puskas was a cat. Persian rather than Magyar, he was one of a succession of household pets down the years to bear a footballing identity.

The earliest had been a goldfish named Finney (after Preston's heroic Tom); corny maybe but I was very young and impressionable. Later came cats named after clubs and a dog improbably named after the Italia 90 World Cup. But then, travel broadens the mind even when it comes to small animals. And football travel broadens the mind in many other ways undreamed-of by Gabriel Hanot when the editor of L'Equipe conceived his great club competition in the mid-1950's.

A generation of baby boom schoolboys embraced geography at school, to the mystification of rugby-conditioned teachers, out of raging curiosity at the far-distant exotica thrown up by the vagaries of the next round of the European Cup. For that was what it was: "merely" the European Cup. A simple label which owed everything to its precise nature and nothing to the marketing men who later dreamed up the UEFA Champions League for a competition packed with, and usually won by, non-champions.

This was the international game I discovered. Information about players and their clubs and their countries was like gold dust. It took a lot of digging. So, dig we did – myself and a string of like-minded journalistic pioneers inspired by the doyen of them all, Brian Glanville. Geoffrey Green, in the Times, was one of the first national newspaper writers to delve down beyond the Johnny Foreigner stereotype which still held sway many years later.

A few years ago a bright-minded executive from a marketing company asked if I could recall which multi-national corporations had been assigned the sponsorship and television rights for the first European Cup Final back in the original old Parc des Princes in Paris in 1956? Patiently I explained that, in those far-off days, the tournament was about footballing glory not financial gain; that no-one had envisaged a time when a ball could not be kicked in anger or ambition without first signing the necessary commercial contracts. That is the ultra-obvious contradiction about football's rulers today. FIFA president Sepp Blatter sees nothing ridiculous in double-checking every legal dot and comma when he signs a multi-zillion-dollar contract for advert boards around the pitch ... yet he rails in baffled objection when the European commission insists that football respects the legal parameters dictated by the European Union over freedom of movement of labour.

The European Cup picked up steam courtesy of one of the other very greatest footballers I ever saw. Not Pele. Not Cruyff. Not Maradona. But Alfredo Di Stefano. The original total footballer; the man who won the first five European Cups and scored in every one of those finals; the man on whose achievements were founded the legend of the competition. Even a cursory glance at team photographs from way back then tells you that footballers of yesteryear could not have lived with today's athletes in terms of pace and physical fitness. But every great player was great in his own context and era. Think about how the genius of a Di Stefano or a Finney or a Ferenc Puskas might sparkle with the benefit of today's physical and dietary preparation.

The last time I saw Di Stefano and Puskas play was in the spring of 1965 when they lined up in a Rest of the World veterans' team for Sir Stanley Matthews' farewell testimonial game at Stoke. Matthews had returned to his original footballing home from Blackpool in 1961 to inspire a revival which brought Stoke back up into the First Division (equivalent of today's Premier League). The world stars who flew in to play tribute also included the Soviet goalkeeper Lev Yashin, the Czech World Cup runners-up half-back line of Pluskal, Popluhar and Masopust and the great Hungarian Ladislav Kubala, by then player-coach of Espanol Barcelona.

Even then, in the half-pace twilight of that slow-motion era, their talent was mesmeric.

The last time I saw Di Stefano and Puskas together was in a very different garb after the 1995 Cup-Winners' Cup Final in Paris, in the new Parc des Princes. UEFA had organised a 40th European club anniversary party and Di Stefano and Puskas were among the guests of honour before watching Arsenal lose in extra time to Zaragoza and "Nayim from the halfway line." I was heading down from the tribune to the press conferences when I saw the two of them in conversation, mingling with fans on their way down and out of the stadium. Totally anonymous. But that had been the way of it in their era, the days when footballers were for the people, of the people, among the people.

In their way, in their day, they had been privileged. When Real Madrid thrashed Eintracht Frankfurt 7-3 in Glasgow to win their fifth European Cup in a row – "on the bounce," as the current cliché has it – Di Stefano collected a £1,250 bonus for having been a five-times winner. Seemed a king's ransom in those days; but worth how much now by comparison?

Those were also days before the word "media" had been invented and before multi-platform publishing had bounced around the world off a network of satellites. Television was black and white and football was a smattering of highlights on a Saturday night or a rare international game in midweek; BBC television might occasionally show a prestige foreign national team game on a Sunday afternoon: sometimes Austria v Hungary, the oldest continental European rivalry, or one of Italy's European Championship qualifiers – including, notably, the tie in which the great Yashin saved a penalty from the young Sandro Mazzola.

Those were the days when teams did not worry about the viewing effect when blue shirts played against red and it was impossible to tell the difference on the miniscule grey-grain screen in the corner of the room. Those were also the days when a young reporter could trek down through France, taking in mighty Reims with Kopa and Fontaine, Barcelona with Suarez and Kubala, Kocsis and Czibor then Madrid with Di Stefano and Puskas as well as Paco Gento. Those were the days when the slow, stuffy overnight trains trundled back on up to the French border and then along the Riviera and across to Italy; first stop Turin (Juventus with Omar Sivori and John Charles) then on east to Milan (Inter with Angelillo, Milan with Altafini) and south to Florence (Hamrin and Seminario) then Roma (Schiaffino and Manfredini).

For Di Stefano and Puskas, read Raul and Van Nistelrooy now; for Kopa and Fontaine read Henry and Benzema; for Suarez and Kubala read Messi and Bojan; for Sivori and Charles it's Del Piero and Trezeguet; swap Angelillo for Ibrahimovic, Altafini for Kaka and so on. Those were the days.

Or so it seems, misleadingly no doubt. Football and life never stand still. My feline Puskas has long since padded off beyond the land of nine lives; the footballing Puskas died in November 2006. The curse of Alzheimer's meant he had been lost to himself years earlier; he had no recollection of having been captain of Hungary, of his 84 goals in 85 internationals, of his 358 goals in 349 games for the army club Honved, of masterminding a historic 6-3 win over England at Wembley and of thundering, for Real Madrid, a historic two European Cup final hat-tricks.

At least those of us of a certain age may remember and treasure picture-book proof of a unique talent which inspired a love of this game and captivated a footballing generation.

Keir Radnedge has been writing about international football for more than 40 years with a c.v. which has ranged from World Soccer to the Daily Mail and from Kicker of Germany to El Grafico of Argentina.

Favourite player: *Ferenc Puskas who proved that being one-footed is no bar to greatness.*

Most memorable match: *Bristol Rovers beating Shrewsbury in the 2007 promotion play-offs at Wembley and telling a steward, trying to hustle me out: "I've waited more than 50 years for something like this and I'm not going yet!"*

CALL SVEN SEXY BUT NOT SIXTY

The figure the Swede does not find attractive

By John Richardson

SVEN: SOPHISTICATED, suave, sexy they say, and always apparently at ease with the world.

A man so used to swimming with the piranhas that he always emerges without a blemish on his body. A crisis for Sven-Goran Eriksson, football manager and lothario is only when an unsuspecting journalist mentions his age.

You can accuse him of being a mercenary, being lifeless in the dug out and tarnishing the so called golden generation - the England team he presided over. Most scribes have dipped into their reserves of vitriol but like a boomerang the ice cold Swede always came back for more.

Few have ever seen him ruffled - until just a few weeks away from the end of 2007/08 before one of the least popular and poorly handled sackings of a Premier League manager. Manchester City's demanding owner Thaksin Shinawatra might have been on his case trying to set up transfer deals behind his back and insisting that he didn't have the time to wait for miracles.

"First half of season good, second half not so good," would have been his phlegmatic reply as the Eastlands heat increased. After all Sven doesn't do pressure.

But in the quiet of a compact room at Manchester City's training complex Sven's normal placid demeanour cracked for just a few seconds. He was asked whether having reached the age of 60 he would call it quits if Shinawatra sent him packing.

Disbelief quickly spread over Eriksson's face. "Am I finished with football at the age of 60?" he replied fixing the inquisitor with an incredulous look. "What a horrible thought. Do you think that I am old then?"

So that's it then. If anyone wants to ruffle Sven's feathers, don't lambast him for signing a dodgy Italian or getting his tactics horribly wrong. Just freak him out by suggesting he has acquired a few more wrinkles.

Undoubtedly, though, unlike some of his England predecessors Eriksson's time at Soho Square hasn't turned him into damaged goods. The leaving of his international post did cause plenty of consternation - despite the inevitable barbs which come the way it seems these days of every England manager.

He was hurt at having to call time on his five and a half year tenure.

He was hurt that accusations about his private life had also played a part in his eventual removal. But it didn't stop him politely shaking the hands and exchanging bon homie with football writers who had put the boot in. A bit like wishing the hangman a good day before the axe comes down but at least Sven has lived to tell the tale. And that's why he is popular with the media wherever he works.

Unfailingly polite and extremely good company for those who have shared the odd glass of wine with him. Following any bit of tittle tattle regarding Sven and his latest female conquest he would calmly show his hand and ask us: "Can you see a ring? No there is no ring. So what is the problem?"

Well only a fiery New York-Italian by the name of Nancy Dell'Olio as far as I can see Sven. The pair have had more break ups and reunions than Oasis and whether they are together right now in Mexico where he took over as national coach in the summer of 2008, your guess is as good as mine.

Anyway one thing that is certain is that Nancy was put in her place when it came to Sven's living arrangements in Manchester. The Swede was happily ensconced in a top hotel in the middle of the city.

A £900 a night suite seemed much more preferable to him than a des rez somewhere in Cheshire. In any case, he revealed to some of us, every time he went to view a mansion in the leafy suburbs a photographer from one of the top tabloids would mysteriously turn up.

The next day he would see extensive details of where Sven and Nancy were hoping to set up home. Obviously somebody was blowing the gaffe on their plans. The answer was right at Sven's side, the publicity-seeking Nancy. So bang went any ideas of a palatial residence out in the sticks.

Instead Sven opted for five star service at a hotel.

After all there was no need to cook and all Sven's other needs were catered for, including it seemed his sleeping arrangements. Safe to say a number of favoured females were wined and dined at the hotel. He liked his suite so much that he was even given permission to have it decorated to his own personal taste.

Sven never lost any sleep over his future as the noose tightened round his neck at City. One journalist may have thought that at the age of 60 Eriksson was about to be consigned to the scrap heap but he is now set to return to the World Cup stage in 2010 with Mexico.

In fact if it hadn't have been for some obviously ill fitting curtains at Chelsea chief executive Peter Kenyon's London home a few years ago then Sven could have been in charge at Stamford Bridge today. Eriksson was caught out through newspaper photographs discussing the Chelsea job with Kenyon while still in charge of England. The Swede has always claimed that he was planning for the future which was the right of any individual. But in true cool Eriksson style he came out of the so called Soho Square crisis with an improved England contract.

For those who don't really know Sven they might have felt that talking about England is a no go zone. Far from it, he still regards the time as England manager as one of the happiest points of his career.

As a boy in Sweden he grew up supporting Liverpool and Arrigo Saachi, an Italian coach he greatly admired, had once said to Sven before he retired that the only job that would have kept him working was the England one.

So when the approach came when Eriksson was in his fourth season at Lazio he was definitely interested. He even managed to smile at a quip made by Howard Wilkinson who as part of an FA delegation came over to Rome to talk to Sven.

Sven asked Wilko: "Do you think being manager of England is a good job?"

Wilkinson in true no nonsense Yorkshire style replied: "Yes, if you live in Paris."

But Eriksson loved the job and will tell you now that being forced to leave hurt him. And despite the accusations that he was like a pig in the proverbial receiving a large chunk of his FA salary for a further year, Eriksson tells it differently.

"I never want to go through that again. Taking money and not working. That is not me."he said.

Eriksson has always been popular with the players. Talk to them, as you do to try to sometimes dig up the dirt on the dressing room, and the Swede is rarely ever fingered. Inevitably there are the odd fall outs and disagreements but the majority of players who have served under Eriksson are gushing in their praise.

Not that he is anybody's fool. David Platt who knew Eriksson during their time together at Sampdoria insists that the Swede only does what he wants to do and won't be pushed around.

Those of us who got to know him better during his season at City than we did when he was at Soho Square were sad when he became Sven Going Eriksson.

Jokes about "bonus notches" on his Mexican bedpost may be inevitable. But if the football god is in good form we shall see England versus Mexico at the 2010 World Cup finals in South Africa.

Bring it on.

John Richardson is chief football correspondent of the Sunday Express. Before that Daily Mail twice, the Sun, Newcastle Journal, Birmingham Evening Mail, Brighton Evening Argus and Chester Chronicle.

Favourite player: Charlie Cooke. Although Chelsea have never been my team I loved the Stamford Bridge side of the late Sixties, early Seventies. A team of great entertainers with wing wizard Charlie at the fulcrum.

Most memorable match: QPR 5, Newcastle Utd 5. This was an incredible game on the artificial QPR surface in the early eighties featuring Newcastle talent like Peter Beardsley and Chris Waddle. Newcastle had been 4-0 up at half time. I told Newcastle manager Jack Charlton what a joy it was to watch only to be pinned against the wall with steam coming out of Big Jack's ears. He clearly didn't agree.

LIFE AFTER LOVE

I hoped Weymouth would lose – it was not a nice feeling

By Ian Ridley

HOW DO you describe the feeling? It's a bit like realising that you have done your best for your much-loved child but that it is time now for them to stand on their own two feet. This though you are worried about their headstrong, wayward and spendthrift ways; about the company they are keeping. You know that they are heading for trouble but nobody is going to listen to you, least of all them.

Yes, that's about how it felt after I resigned as chairman of Weymouth Football Club and returned full-time to the day job of writing about the game. Once you have crossed the line from covering football to being involved in it, you can go back but life and your attitude to this maddening sport will never be the same again.

Weymouth had been my club since, in that floodlit experience familiar to all who are captivated by the game, dear old Dad had taken me along to the rickety harbourside ground in the Southern League championship days of the mid-60s when Frank O'Farrell, later to be Manchester United's manager, was in charge.

Then, you could keep United and Liverpool, Arsenal and Tottenham, those mythical big clubs from regions remote to the coast of Dorset (actually, even 30-mile distant Bournemouth felt like a big and remote club). It would forever be my home-town club who would move me.

And exasperate me, to the point where, in my late 40s long after the halcyon days of the Conference when such names as Steve Claridge, Graham Roberts and Shaun Teale passed through the Wessex Stadium – concrete replacement on the edge of town for the ramshackle Recreation Ground – I could take it no longer. Now, after hauling ourselves back from the obscurity and ignominy of a regional division of the Southern League, we faced relegation back to it with gates having dropped to around 600.

I felt compelled to act. Armed with hopes, dreams, some time, energy, a few good contacts and a modicum of cash, I approached the board of directors offering to turn the club around. They refused, of course, but then came back to me a few months later when things hadn't improved. With a consortium of sympathetic souls, I took over the club and became its chairman.

First off, I sacked a dinosaur of a manager called Geoff Butler and installed as player-manager Steve Claridge, who took some persuading to give up his full-time professional career with Millwall when he still had plenty in his legs even though 37. We went back a long time, though, to his first spell as a young player at the club some 18 years earlier and he bought the vision of a five-year plan and the Football League.

The appointment set in train an astonishing year, all captured by BBC2's Football Diaries series, whom I had persuaded to follow us to bring some revenue into the club. Gates more than doubled to an average of 1,490, quite a figure for that level of the game. We recorded record income. On the field, we led the league for five heady months, beating our local rivals Dorchester Town 8-0 in front of 3,700 along the way. Claridge would score more than 30 goals but we faded in the final furlong to allow Crawley Town to claim the title and the one promotion place to the Conference.

That we didn't quite make it was due to an inability to invest in the squad in mid-winter. There were wrangles with certain board members who refused to buy the shares in the club they had promised. It became fractious behind the scenes.

Needing investment for the next season, I went along with other board members recruiting a local hotelier by the name of Martyn Harrison and he soon bought a controlling interest. I found him and his authoritarian ways hard to work with and quit a month into a new season.

So began the spending spree and the bitterness from which the club would struggle to recover.

Actually, the bitterness did not immediately kick in. Having decided to keep my counsel and consider the club's interests first, I bit only when Harrison sacked Claridge after a piffling FA Cup defeat. Unhappy that Claridge was the touchstone figure at the club and not he, Harrison had jettisoned the best thing to have happened to the club for years. I had retained a shareholding and spoke out angrily about Harrison's methods at the club's annual general meeting. We exchanged spiteful words via the club's internet forum, which put the mess in message board.

By now, though, the fans were largely besotted with Harrison, or rather the money he said he was pouring into the club. Garry Hill, the old Dagenham and Redbridge manager, took over on an enormous salary, was given a ridiculous playing budget more than double anyone else's at that level and duly steered the club to promotion to the Conference.

Knowing the finances involved, I confess to hoping that Harrison, and the club, would fail because it was all costing a fortune and the sooner the madcap joyride ended the better for the longer-term future.

Imagine that; hoping your team would lose. It was not a nice feeling.

Eventually Harrison pulled the plug, admitting to having built up debts of around £3 million accumulated in just two and half seasons. It was an astonishing sum at that level. Having first told us all that it was no-strings-attached money, now it turned out to be loans from his company, as I had warned all along. He had banked on getting a new stadium deal to reimburse himself but it had fallen through.

At first, he tried to get it back from new owners but none would bite. He offered it to me for £1, if I would take on the running costs of the club. But life had moved on; and once bitten, twice shy. Fans had not appreciated me speaking out and I did not want to go back into an unappreciative environment.

And so Harrison gave the club away to a local pop promoter called Mel Bush, who now installed his son-in-law Jason Tindall as manager. Within months, though, Bush had had enough, the club losing £10,000 a week, and passed it on to a property developer named Malcolm Curtis, who promptly sold himself the club-owned land around the stadium for a £500,000 investment into the club. Curtis sacked Tindall, replacing him with John Hollins, once of Chelsea and Arsenal, and the club just avoided relegation back down to Conference South.

You still following? Actually, it will probably all sound horribly familiar to many football fans who have seen their clubs bought and sold, become the playthings not of fans or locals but of egocentric businessmen or profiteering carpetbaggers. Are you watching Liverpool, Manchester United, Chelsea, West Ham, Manchester City... and a host of others, big and small?

I always have maintained that running Weymouth was little different to running a big club, despite the fewer staff and the fewer noughts on the cheques. You are still dealing with trying to maximise revenue and keep costs down, the biggest being players' wages. Above all, the politics are similar. Egos, expectation and human nature are the same from Newcastle in the North East to Weymouth in the South West.

It is why I now believe I have a better insight of what goes on within football clubs at all levels. You can sense whether the most important relationship within the club, that of chairman and manager, is healthy; how off-the-field matters are impacting on it. And the state of a team is directly linked to how well leadership from the top is filtering down.

My experience has taught me much, not all of it involving things I wanted to know. I am saddened by fans in the game whose heads are turned by the prospect of quick money that will always come back to haunt a club, and by their heightened expectations which mean that good husbandry and stewardship goes out of the window.

In these knee-jerk, quick-fix days, too many bray for a manager to go after just a few defeats, refusing to see the bigger picture of what the club is trying to achieve, both on and off the field. Realism, talking of their club's size and potential without getting carried away, can be the curse of a chairman when confronted by fans.

I still watch Weymouth from afar, go to the odd game here and there, but to be honest, it is hard work these days. Those naïve days of just following your team blissfully ignorant of boardroom power struggles are long gone. You know you could run the club better, attract a better manager who will assemble a better team. And you also know that you are better off out of it. At the very least you should have learned that lesson . . .

Ian Ridley is chief football writer of the Mail on Sunday, having previously written for the Guardian, Daily Telegraph, Independent on Sunday and Observer. He has also written seven books, including Addicted, the autobiography of Tony Adams.

__Favourite player:__ Johnny Hannigan, right-winger in the Weymouth team that won the Southern League title in 1965.

__Most memorable match:__ Weymouth 8, Dorchester Town 0, in which Steve Claridge scored a hat-trick on Boxing Day, 2003.

THE JOLLY COBBOLDS

Mr John and Patrick were the last of the Corinthians

By Brian Scovell

HERE'S AN interesting stat: nine out of the 20 Premier League clubs at the end of 2007/08 were owned by foreigners. Shameful! What about getting a quote from the Cobbold brothers, John and Patrick, the Old Etonian nephews of former Prime Minister Harold Macmillan who ran Ipswich Town FC from 1957 to 1990 and never took a penny out of the club and earlier in their reign, often paid the wages of the players when the club was hard up?

So let's try. Brr brr, brr brr – "Hello", someone with a posh voice answers at the 15th century Glemhall Hall, the Cobbolds' ancestral home near Woodbridge.

We tell him the startling news. "Good gracious," says the ghost of Mr John (as he was always called). "Tell them to f*** off."

Half-way through the 2007/08 season John Cobbold's beloved Ipswich were taken over by Marcus Evans, an obscure businessman who has nine houses including one in Bermuda. Evans has a reputation as the Howard Hughes of Ipswich football because hardly any of their supporters have seen him. He has attended one or two matches and an official said: "He seems a nice person. He's not really a football man. He's only in it as an investor, which is fair enough."

Mr John might well have sworn hard and long to hear the sad news but though he was a poor businessman himself when he and Patrick sold their brewery business for an under par sum, he probably would have accepted the inevitable because the club was in a desperate financial position after being put into administration.

He was so funny and so eccentric few people took exception to his extraordinary behaviour, forgiving (or ignoring) the fact that Mr John swore with every sentence. Each mid-summer the Cobbolds invited the whole staff to their party at Glemhall Hall and Mr John often came sliding down the bannisters in his pyjamas as his party act.

After a hard day's drinking, he would announce "I'm f****** off to bed – help yourself to Patrick's wine."

At one dinner to thank the junior squad for their efforts, he went up to the parents of one of the better players and said: "Get off to bed now and get cracking. We need you to produce another little Johnny in a few years time who can play as well as your lad."

I was at the Savoy for the dinner to celebrate Ipswich's first and only championship in 1961/62 when Alf Ramsey surprised everyone in the game by pipping Bill Nicholson's Double-winning team of the previous season. The Cobbolds invited some Bunnies from the Playboy Club, dressed in skimpy black and white outfits with tails. Unfortunately they took exception to Mr John's industrial language and, upset, the Bunnies fled.

Ramsey rose to speak and started droning on in a monotonous tone. A voice from behind kept interrupting: "C'mon Ramsey, stop boring everyone. That's enough, Alfie." This went on for some time until someone realised the man behind the curtain was Mr John.

He called Alf "Stoneface" and at one match he kept up his usual patter. Alf took no notice. "Why don't you say anything?" said Cobbold.

"It's a cold evening," said Ramsey.

Mr John snorted: "If that's all you can come up you better keep quiet."

Later he told the directors: "I've had to reprimand Alf for the first time since he's been here."

Ramsey believed his feat in winning the League Championship was better than winning the World Cup and no-one in Suffolk disagreed.

One of the chief guests sitting next to Mr John at the Savoy was his hated enemy Bob Lord, chairman of Burnley whom he called "Bollock Chops" because he was a butcher. Lord was reputed to have his own turnstile and was supposed to have kept the money for his own purposes.

The Cobbolds refused to sit in the Burnley directors' box and when Mr John heard Lord made a disparaging remark about the Jewish directors at Leeds, he reported the incident to the Football Association. When his letter arrived the man who opened it was Lord, the chairman of one of the committees.

"Throw that away," he ordered.

The next time Burnley played at Portman Road, Lord was driven by his chauffeur to the ground, got out and handed his business card to a member of the staff and asked him to take it to the Ipswich chairman. When the card was handed over, Cobbold tore it into pieces and said: "I hate racists. I won't have this man in."

Lord went back north without seeing the match.

Mr John wasn't too keen on John Smith, the Liverpool chairman, whom he thought was rather pompous. At one lunch in the Ipswich boardroom Mr John sat down and balanced on his head, like a wig, were some sausages. After a while the waiter came up to him and said, "Excuse me Mr John, there appears some sausages on your head."

"Oh are they?" said Mr John. "I must have forgotten to defrost them."

Everyone was convulsed with laughter, except for Smith. Asked about it later, Mr John said: "I thought I might get him going but he wouldn't move a muscle. He has halitosis, you know. Bad breath."

John Cavendish Cobbold was born in 1927 and Patrick Mark Cobbold, who was taller and dressed much better, came along three years later. Their father, Captain John Murray Cobbold, known as "Ivan" after Ivan the Terrible, took over Ipswich in 1936 and turned it into a professional club.

He was a friend of Winston Churchill and worked with him in the War Cabinet during WWII. His wife was Lady Blanche Cobbold, daughter of the 9th Duke of Devonshire, one of the Mitford sisters and brother in law to Harold Macmillan, later the Earl of Stockton.

The Cobbold boys were regular visitors to Chatsworth over Christmas and Mr John always had a ball at his feet running up and down the long corridors. "Actually he kept falling down," said Patrick. "He started drinking at a very young age." Both Cobbolds served briefly in the Guards and Patrick was accidentally shot in his leg by a fellow soldier and Harold Macmillan said: "He nearly died."

The most repeated stories of the Cobbold legend concerned Lady Blanche. No women were allowed into the boardroom at Portman Road because Mr John said: "You can't expect women to be jabbering away when I am telling dirty stories."

At the 1978 FA Cup Final – Ipswich beat Arsenal 1-0 – ladies were allowed in the Wembley equivalent and an official approached Lady Blanche, who was 80, and said: "Ma'am, would you like to meet the Prime Minister, James Callaghan?"

Lady Blanche looked sternly at him and said: "I would prefer a large gin and tonic."

As the kick-off loomed, she started going down the steps to her seat and Sir Bert Millichip, the FA chairman, told me: "To my astonishment I noticed that her knickers was slowly falling down her legs and ended up around her ankles. John Cobbold was coming behind and bent down and picked them up and put them in his pocket. She carried on as though nothing happened."

The Cobbolds called Lady Blanche "Mama" and behind her back they called her "The Old Grey Mare".

Captain Cobbold was blown up by a V1 doddlebug in the Guards Chapel in Whitehall in 1944 and Lady Blanche never remarried.

Major Andrew Napier, a close friend of Patrick, was in charge of the Coldstream Guards Band which played in the Cup Final and the Cobbolds arranged that 'The Old Grey Mare Ain't What She Used To Be' should be played when she appeared in the Royal Box. Only the Cobbold brothers laughed.

Around that time Lady Blanche had a puncture and changed it herself. Harold Smith, a long serving director of Ipswich, said: "Not many women of 80 would do that. She was a very tough nut."

The Cobbold brothers left it to the professionals to run Ipswich and Mr John would say: "Our job is to pour the drinks." They brought fun and laughter to the game and Bobby Robson told me: "They were wonderful people and they never interfered. When things were tough, they would invite Elsie and me out for dinner. Early on we were well beaten by some brilliance from George Best and the crowd barracked me. Next day Mr John called a board meeting. He apologised to me for the shocking way the fans behaved and said if it happens again 'I will resign.' What a chairman."

One of the Cobbold pranks concerned the lobster at a restaurant in Spain on a UEFA trip. "You ought to have the lobster," said Mr John.

"Oh all right," said Bobby.

When it arrived he started picking at it and Patrick asked: "How is it, Bobby?"

"Fine, yes, fine," said Bobby.

They had taken out the meat and replaced it with bread crumbs. They crumpled up with laughter.

John Cobbold died of cancer in 1983 at the age of 56 and Patrick, who'd succeeded him as chairman in 1976, died in his bath of a heart attack in 1990 at the age of 60. I spent many hours with them over the years and like everyone else, I was desperately sad to see them go at such a young age. They were the last of the Corinthians, the people who liked to enjoy good sport and played the game in the right spirit.

David Sheepshanks, the present chairman, thinks there won't be any more Cobbolds. I hope he is wrong. The game needs loveable characters like them who let the professionals get on with it. The newer ones are only in it for the money.

Brian Scovell is now a freelance after working 40 years for Associated Newspapers (Daily Sketch and Daily Mail).

***Favourite player:** Danny Blanchflower who was the brainiest and most inspirational captain who also wrote trenchant newspaper articles and if he was alive today, he would expose the corruption that still lingers on in the game.*

***Most memorable match:** Sitting in the rain and sun at Wembley when England won the World Cup in 1966.*

O 'NEILL MORE THAN A MANAGER

The "late" Martin is always in control

By Janine Self

T HE PHONE rang. It was close to midnight and a certain tabloid journalist was startled into sudden wakefulness at the alarm-bell screech. At the other end of the line an unmistakeable Irish voice heard the slurred hello and queried in a surprised tone: "Were you asleep? Sorry, I was just returning your call."

The multi-faceted Martin O'Neill had caught another member of the fourth estate napping. Again. For someone who appears not to need any kip, what better time to check voicemail than the wee small hours?

It makes perfect sense to a man whose thought processes appear to be in perpetual motion; honed on a passion for crime and conspiracy and enhanced by an encyclopaedic knowledge of most things musical and anything sporting. Just don't ask him to text.

To describe Martin as a football manager, full stop, is to do him an injustice. Here is someone who subscribes to the chaos theory in everyday life while being utterly driven when it comes to the matter of work. Never expect him to be punctual for anything – he operates on the meter reader principle of a few hours leeway the wrong side of any allotted appointment. He turns up late, switches on the charm, cracks a joke and, somehow, no-one ever minds; adjust your clocks to Martin O'Neill time.

Yet this is someone who can puncture an ego with a casual flourish of his rapier wit and is as caustic as paint-stripper if he feels he has been wronged. The good folk at the Football Association, who wooed then dumped him as their choice for England manager have, hopefully, discovered that.

Turn the spotlight a degree or two, on a different day, in a different light, on a different occasion, and see a different man. Like a 1970s disco ball, it depends what angle you are coming from.

Interestingly – and that, interestingly, is one of O'Neill's favourite words – the only people who have a bad word to say about him are those who have not been allowed a glimpse of the personality behind the thick specs.

Ask any footballer who played for Grantham, or Wycombe, or Leicester, or Celtic, or Aston Villa why they would happily have slapped cement on some bricks and then raced smack-bang into the wall and they will volunteer: "Well Martin asked us to."

In Glasgow, as O'Neill was winning all there was to win, he jetted some of his Wycombe old boys to Scotland for a night out at Parkhead; the office and admin staff at Leicester were given the same VIP treatment north of the border. More recently Steve Guppy, of Wycombe, Leicester and Celtic, needed somewhere to keep fit before heading to the States in search of a coaching job. No problem, Gupps; Villa's state-of-the-art training ground at your service.

Martin O'Neill does not forget his friends. That includes journalists fortunate enough to have known him before much of his bonhomie with the press was bombed out of him at Celtic. Imagine how an intensely private man felt when pictures of his wife and two daughters sunbathing on a family holiday were printed in the news and showbiz pages?

O'Neill was appalled and amazed in equal measure. As far as this very complex man is concerned, he belongs solely and individually to the sports section of the tabloids and has done so from the moment he quit his law degree and Kilrea to join Nottingham Forest at the age of 19.

In some ways O'Neill is the antithesis of Brian Clough. Cloughie liked nothing more than to see his forthright views emblazoned in capital letters across the back pages of the papers whereas his former midfielder visibly cringes at controversy. It was in Scotland where O'Neill became a master at answering questions with another question, or simply saying nothing at all but in really long, rambling sentences.

The supporters thought he could walk on water, however, after leading Celtic out of the doldrums and to League titles, Cup medals and a UEFA Cup Final before leaving to care for his good lady, Geraldine, through her cancer treatment. Leicester fans, similarly, were treated to Wembley Cup Finals and trips into Europe. Villa have great expectations too and are unlikely to be disappointed.

It was on one of those jaunts on the Continent with Leicester when O'Neill found himself in his hotel bedroom in the early hours emptying his mini-bar for the benefit of the travelling, and very thirsty, press pack. Imagine Arsene Wenger inviting Her Majesty's not-very-sober finest for a nightcap.

More recently, a few days after taking over at Villa, O'Neill was in Holland with the team for a couple of pre-season friendlies. On the first evening he glanced at the motley media crew who had trailed after him and announced: "Let's arrange dinner."

A recommended eaterie was duly discovered. O'Neill turned up – late, obviously – with loyal backroom staff and chain-smoking duo John Robertson and Steve Walford in tow. The wine flowed as smoothly as the conversation – from Cloughie anecdotes to the hits of Jethro Tull, with a pit-stop to consider the assassination of Jack Kennedy. Had anyone that night been foolish enough to venture a wager about the FA Cup, O'Neill would have happily pocketed the cash. Give him the year and he can reel off the finalists, the score and the winning team. Bet Geraldine still needs to write him out a shopping list though.

Two days later and the small press pack were due to interview O'Neill at the team hotel prior to motoring north for Villa's second fixture the following night. This time he was late for a very good reason; a quick dash back to the UK on business had seen him caught up in the airport security scare which grounded every British airport for hours.

The Irishman finally arrived in the evening, leaving us journalists with the choice of hitting the road through the night or finding somewhere to stay. Villa's base was in the middle of nowhere so we were running out of options. Would Martin mind very much if a bunch of national daily hacks booked into the team hotel?

Not at all, came the reply. At 3am the following morning insomniac guests at the Dutch hotel would have spotted the Villa management and coaching staff locked in earnest and serious debate with the journalists. Subject? The best five songs of all time.

O'Neill, whose indecision is always final, would have had proper reason to dither. From Bob Dylan and The Who to the Killers and Snow Patrol, his listening is as diverse as you would expect from a man with two grown-up daughters. So no exclusive there, then.

Martin can recognise a story; in fact he is as fascinated as he is horrified by the machinations of the journalistic world. Rather annoyingly he is also capable of penning an eloquent, considered article when required.

When Wolves and Northern Ireland striker Derek Dougan died, O'Neill was asked if he would be prepared to provide a foreword for a book on the legend. This generally means the author writing it on behalf of the celebrity following a general chat. Not this time. Admittedly Martin missed a couple of deadlines but he painstakingly wrote every word in longhand and agonised afterwards as to its worth. He didn't need to – the piece was perfection.

O'Neill continues to seek Nirvana in football. He played for a footballing genius in Brian Clough and, while he hates the obvious comparison, there is no getting away from the similarities, which go far beyond the tracksuit on match days. Cloughie could cajole, charm, inspire and frighten his players all at the same time. But he gave them a Championship and two European Cups and, for that, they forgave him everything.

O'Neill, another maverick, leaves a trail of silver in his wake too. He makes promises and he delivers, which is why footballers want to play for him and why he will continue to be linked to every major vacancy even if England is a definite no-no.

There is a school of thought that the chances of a top-four job have passed him by. How about turning Villa into a top-four club and saving himself the hassle? Martin is a managerial thoroughbred, similar in outlook to Sir Alex Ferguson or Arsene Wenger, which is why both will cut through a crowded room to shake his hand.

They have built dynasties from the foundations up and that is what O'Neill has the opportunity to do at Villa. Not for him the European model of a Liverpool or Chelsea where the coach is drowned in cash but does not sit in on contract talks with players.

Like Clough, O'Neill wants to be in charge of everything from paperclips to multi-million pound transfers. Unlike Clough, he is unbelievably modest. He was a mainstay of the Forest midfield for years and he captained Northern Ireland at the 1982 World Cup, where they famously beat hosts Spain.

Yet listen to him speak and he was just a clod-kicking oik from over the water who, by an amazing fluke, happened to find himself on the same pitch as winger Robertson. O'Neill continues to be as self-effacing and when he is seriously embarrassed has a disarming habit of taking off his glasses so that his audience can disappear in the myopic haze.

Do not be fooled. O'Neill knows exactly what he is doing and why he is doing it. He also happens to be a thoroughly decent man who returns phone calls from pestering journalists. As long as you don't mind being woken up at midnight.

Janine Self has been a sports reporter on the Sun since 1995, starting in Manchester before moving to the Midlands in 1999. Before that she worked as a freelance for a host of national newspapers having become an unwilling victim of Robert Maxwell's decision to cull the Daily Mirror's Manchester office in 1988.

__Favourite player:__ Eric Cantona, but not Le Sulk of Manchester United. Instead all hail to the ooh-aah Cantona whose stunning cameo contributed to Leeds winning the title in 1992.

__Most memorable match:__ West Bromwich 2, Portsmouth 0 on Survival Sunday 15 May 2005. The Baggies became the first side in history to be bottom at Christmas and survive. The hinges nearly came off at the Hawthorns as Southampton, Norwich and Crystal Palace all failed to win and drop instead.

A MAN FOR ALL SEASONS

Hodgy told Ferguson that Schmeichel would win United the title

By Phil Shaw

"**T**HWACK." From South Yorkshire to South America, via Manchester, Moscow and myriad muddy pitches in between, the crisp, clean sound of Alan Hodgkinson's boot meeting the ball on the half-volley has been a feature of specialist coaching for goalkeepers longer than he cares to remember.

Young keepers, working for the first time with the man universally known as "Hodgy," see a thick-set, grey-haired man in his 70s. They are not prepared for the blur of the ball before it ripples the rigging. Even when forewarned, they are often powerless to prevent it.

That, however, is Hodgkinson to a tee. His undemonstrative, meticulous yet visionary contribution to football, which now stretches back 56 years, was one of Britain's best-kept sporting secrets until he received the MBE in the 2008 New Year's Honours.

Although he never won the Footballer of the Year trophy, he played alongside and against many who did. Then came a second career as Britain's first and foremost goalkeeping coach. Despite his age, Hodgy is still at the goalface every day, testing a new generation with his 25-yard half-volley. If ever the modern game produced a man for all seasons, it is Hodgkinson.

Behind the modest title of goalkeeping coach to Oxford United, now of the Blue Square Premier Division, there is a walking, talking, living history of post-War professional football. If he ever hangs up his gloves, he will write his memoirs. "It would be called From Pig's Bladder to Buckingham Palace," he smiles, adding, "with a sub-title of 'Via Wembley & Hampden.'"

But right now, it's a big "if."

Hodgy played 576 League games for his only club, Sheffield United, missing 14 matches in 16 years. He made his England debut at 20 – in a side containing Stanley Matthews, Duncan Edwards, Billy Wright and Tom Finney – while still a Second Division player.

A miner's son, he started the Sixties as a PFA activist who stood alongside chairman Jimmy Hill during the threatened strike by the players' union over the feudal maximum-wage system.

That fight won, he was soon plunging at the feet of George Best and clawing aside bicycle kicks by Denis Law, whom he rates his most dangerous opponent. Once he denied Manchester United victory at Old Trafford by saving a last-minute penalty by Bobby Charlton.

Later, as an unsung revolutionary espousing the "continental" concept of technique in a trade where recklessness and eccentricity were badges of honour, he was instrumental in launching the England career of David Seaman and bringing Peter Schmeichel to Manchester United. And as Scotland's goalkeeping coach for 16 years, he played the pre-eminent role in shedding the joke image of the country's keepers.

Hodgkinson was 16 when Sheffield United spotted him. In 1953 he travelled to Wembley with other young Blades and experienced an epiphany as Hungary trounced England 6-3. "That was the birth of modern football," he recalls. "It was all about fitness, flexibility and, above all, technique – the goalie [Gyula Grosics] included."

There were no goalkeeping coaches then. "We were self-taught. Being relatively small at 5ft 10in, I'd realised I needed super agility and did gymnastics at school. I learned about angles by cutting out pictures from the papers and studying them.

"At a game, I'd focus on the goalie. I played truant to go to Bramall Lane to watch Bert Williams, the Wolves and England goalie."

Hodgy had just turned 18 when he made a winning debut at Newcastle, against Jackie Milburn et al. In 1957, he was met off the United bus at Port Vale by a reporter who asked how he felt about being picked to play for England against Scotland at Wembley.

"I knew nothing about it," he remembers with a chuckle. "We celebrated by winning 6-0."

At Wembley, with 98,000 watching, the game was barely 60 seconds old when a pass intended for Matthews was intercepted. Tommy Ring scored for the Scots and Hodgkinson's first touch was to fish the ball from the net.

"I thought, 'Oh my goodness', but I couldn't let it get me down. I've watched the video and if I'd known then what I know now, I would've saved it."

England won 2-1 after Matthews set up Edwards for a 25-yard winner. The nervous, raw, Brylcreemed keeper won four more caps and in the 1962 World Cup in Chile provided back-up to Ron Springett from Sheffield Wednesday.

The advent of another No. 1 from the area, Gordon Banks, limited his international chances, but Hodgkinson remained a model of stability and consistency before retiring as a player in 1971.

For six years he was assistant manager to Gerry Summers at Gillingham. When that ended, he still had a family to feed and bills to pay, so he offered his services teaching the craft he knew best.

"There weren't enough hours in the day to satisfy the demand," he says, reeling off his employers: England Under-21s, Manchester United, Everton, Watford (where David James was a pupil), Aston Villa and Rangers. Helping Dave Sexton with the England Under-21 squad, he was asked to nominate a replacement when two keepers pulled out. Hodgkinson recommended Seaman, then with Peterborough, and stood firm when Bobby Robson questioned the wisdom of using a Third Division player.

"David was very laid back but even then he was an excellent keeper," Hodgkinson says. "Birmingham soon bought him." The rest is history.

When Alex Ferguson was looking for a commanding presence between the sticks, he asked Hodgkinson to check out the keepers United's scouts had identified. Returning from Denmark, his report concluded: "This goalie will win you the championship."

Schmeichel did not betray his judgement, although there was a rough patch when he let in five at Newcastle and six at Southampton.

"Fergie called me in. I knew he was displeased because when he is, he has an affliction where he keeps clearing his throat.," says Hodgkinson. "He said: 'Hodgy. The goalie. I blame him for 10 of the 11. The only one I don't hold him responsible for was David Ginola's curler.'

"I said: 'To be honest boss, I thought he could've done better with that one.' Fergie leapt up and said: 'So he was at fault for all 11! Tell him he's out against Sturm Graz.' I passed on the news to Peter, but I'd also told Fergie to let me work on him and monitor his attitude. He trained brilliantly, so I went back and pleaded for him to stay in.

"In the end Fergie said: 'If he messes up, I'll sack you.' Anyway, early on Peter made a wonder save, like Banks's from Pele in 1970. United won and went on to win the European Cup. Next time I saw Fergie, he laughed and said: 'Get out, you. You know everything!'"

Life as an Englishman in the Scotland camp began in 1986 after manager Andy Roxburgh invited him to lead a coaching course. It ended in 2002, following a difference of opinion with Berti Vogts, but took in two trips to the World Cup finals and two to the European Championship.

"Jimmy Greaves used to poke fun at Scottish goalies on TV. I thought it was unfair. I had a lot of time for Alan Rough and I worked with some smashing keepers with Scotland. The best, by some distance, was Andy Goram."

Hodgkinson first encountered Goram when coaching under Joe Royle at Oldham. "Joe kept raving about Andy and asking me to work with him. I first saw him on his comeback from injury at Coventry. Joe nudged me, saying: 'He's sensational, you'll see.'

"He conceded eight goals, and seven and a half were his fault. Joe leaned over and said: 'He's not normally like this, honest.'"

Hard work saw the surly youngster's flaws ironed out and the technique blossom. "I love seeing players improve when you work on them. The big guys, the ones who are 6ft 5in, need sharpness, mobility. The smaller ones need spring and to learn how to exude presence. I devise different programmes for both types."

Things came full circle in 2007/08 when Goram began coaching the keepers at Clyde. He calls Hodgkinson "my guru" and regularly calls him for advice.

So when, if ever, is Hodgy going to stop? Even quadruple by-pass heart surgery couldn't stop for long a fetish for clean sheets befitting the laundry at the Savoy; five weeks later he was out working Scotland's keepers on a frozen surface in Russia.

"My life in football has been a fantastic journey. I'm proud of the part I've played, not just as a player and coach but also in helping the PFA get players the pay we deserved. Yes, I've got great memories of Matthews, Law, John Charles and the rest. But I also live for the modern era. Football is a drug and I'm still addicted."

Six decades on, with that autobiography brewing inside and an MBE he hails as "for the whole goalkeeping industry", it's still about the thwack of boot on ball. "The day I can't beat my keepers from 25 yards," grins Alan Hodgkinson, "I'll pack it in."

Phil Shaw has written for the Guardian, Observer, Independent, Daily Telegraph, Scotland on Sunday and Time Out over the past 30 years, as well as editing The Book of Football Quotations.

Favourite player: Jimmy Greaves, the gaunt, crew-cut teenage striker, rather than the reactionary TV buffoon, was my first football hero at primary school – in Yorkshire! – and I've yet to see a finer finisher.

Most memorable match: Strangely for a Leeds fan, a 3-2 defeat at Stoke in 1974 remains vivid; Hudson outwitted Bremner, we lost a 2-0 lead and 29-game unbeaten start, but as JB Priestley described football, this was 'conflict and art.'

HOW I SAVED GAZZA FROM ITALIA 90 AXE

Gascoigne almost talked himself out of World Cup squad

By Rob Shepherd

BOBBY MOORE lifting the Jules Rimet trophy apart, one of the most iconic images of English football is that of Paul Gascoigne in tears at the 1990 World Cup finals. Then the nation empathised with his sadness. Such has been Gascoigne's grotesque decline and fall that few feel like sharing a tear with him anymore. With so many of his wounds self inflicted even his most fervent fans have found it hard to feel really sorry for him.

A couple of weeks shy of his 41st birthday Paul Gascoigne's tortured soul staggered towards the abyss. The player who gave English football the kiss of life ended up on being put on suicide watch consumed by addiction. It is to be hoped he is not beyond help because whatever his shortcomings, the English game and the mega rich generation of players from around the globe who ply their trade in the Premier League, owe Gascoigne a debt of gratitude for the impact he made in 1990 and the implications of the Italia 90 adventure.

Yet Gascoigne was perilously close on at least a couple of occasions of not making the journey.

It was early December back in 1989. England had just qualified for the World Cup final. The countdown to make the squad for Italia 90 had begun. Paul Gascoigne was out in the cold. A year after making his senior debut Gascoigne had failed to convince Bobby Robson he was worthy of a permanent place in the senior squad. So while the first team were preparing for a Wednesday Wembley friendly against Yugoslavia at their Bisham Abbey headquarters, Gascoigne was slumming it in south-east London with the B team who were playing the night before at Millwall's old Den.

Robson had re-instated B internationals to spread the net as wide possible to give fringe players the chance to impress. Earlier in the year Gascoigne had relished the opportunity on a summer B tour. In Switzerland he had scored a stunning individual goal followed by another impressive display in Iceland. I was one of only four newspaper reporters covering the tour and there was no TV or radio interest. David Platt, Paul Parker and Steve Bull all showed signs they could make the step up but it was clear Gascoigne was on a different plane.

Robson, though, was wary. Since his record breaking £2 million move from Newcastle to Tottenham in the 1988 close season Gascoigne had been sufficiently erratic on and off the pitch for Robson to brand him "daft as a brush."

Gascoigne started the new season in similar mode. Breathtaking one minute, baffling the next. Robson remained cautious. Neil Webb, Steve McMahon and Platt were ahead of him as potential central midfield partners to Bryan Robson. Gascoigne was becoming increasingly frustrated.

On the eve of the B international against the Yugoslavs I arranged to meet him for an interview in a snooker hall in Bexleyheath close to the hotel where the squad was staying, manager Dave Sexton having given the players a free afternoon. Since he'd come down from the north-east I had struck up a decent rapport with Gascoigne. Behind the manic mask there was a fragile, flawed yet kind character. Even when he did something stupid to get attention it was hard to dislike him. He wanted to be loved.

That Robson had left him in the B team again was hurting Gascoigne and he could no longer hide it.

The idea of the interview was merely for Gascoigne to come out and say how much he wanted to impress and force his way into the World Cup squad. But, with tape recorder running, he told me that he was fed up waiting to show what he could do in the first team. He had lost patience with Robson. He reasoned that after the World Cup finals a new manager would come in any way so he would wait for the new man.

Gascoigne was resigned to not making the World Cup squad and indicted he didn't really want to play for Robson anymore. In hindsight the suicidal streak was in him even then. It certainly would have been a bombshell at the time.

Like so many football writers I started out working for the Hayters sports reporting agency. The late great Reg, whose business was also a form of sports journalism academy, always stressed the importance of keeping your contacts. Sometimes Reg would tell us young hacks the mark of a good reporter was not always what stories they filed but the ones they didn't. Trust, Reg, would point out was the key to keeping contacts. So I told Gascoigne to calm down and think again. He did. He recognised a potential crossroads and took the right route. Back then he might have been daft at times but he hadn't lost his marbles. Had the sports editor of the now defunct Today newspaper known at the time that effectively I had 'airbrushed' the interview I would have been in trouble no doubt. But sometimes you have to go with your instinct. Play the long game.

Quite apart from all that, I was amongst those who passionately believed Gascoigne was the player who could make a difference for England. Robson would have dumped him for saying all the wrong things in a newspaper, but why run the risk I thought to myself?

The following morning a straightforward exclusive: "I'll prove I should go to World Cup" spread appeared in the paper. That night Gascoigne was outstanding in a 2-1 win. Come the spring, Robson did select Gascoigne for the full friendly against Czechoslovakia. It was billed as a make or break game for Gascoigne. In a 4-2 win at Wembley his display was quite breathtaking and he booked his place in the World Cup squad. A few days later when I asked Gascoigne's manager at Tottenham, Terry Venables, to put the player in context he suggested that he was a sort of combination between Dave Mackay and Maradona.

There remained many who were sceptical not just of Gascoigne's ability but his temperament. In a way, by Robson keeping him hanging on a string it kept the player in line – or as in line as Gascoigne ever would be. By then Gascoigne was rapidly earning a reputation for off the field excesses which invariably involved excessive amounts of alcohol. The combination of brilliant ball skills and bar room booze spills threw up the inevitable comparison with George Best. One reporter, John Roberts of the Independent, witheringly suggested that Gascoigne was not fit to lace Best's drinks. Wrong. We know now that Gascoigne was indeed in the same league as Best at the bar.

In terms of pure football ability? Even now he's gone I suspect most would still vote for Best's boots. But that summer I believe Gascoigne achieved more than Best in terms of a legacy to the English game. Let's put what would unfold during that summer at Italia 90 into perspective. At the time English clubs were still banned from European competition as a consequence of the Heysel disaster in 1985. A year had just passed since 96 fans lost their lives at Hillsborough. English football was on its knees. The Taylor Report was about to demand all-seat stadia and general refurbishment of facilities. The hooligan menace still loomed large. England went to Italy with a genuine fear that just one more eruption of major crowd trouble would see a ban imposed on the national team. With a general decline in attendances over the previous two decades more trouble, certainly international isolation would drive away the few sponsors who were prepared to invest in the game and leave it heading for bankruptcy. England's opening match of the finals against the Republic of Ireland in Cagliari did little to raise spirits.

A dreadful 1-1 draw with Ireland played out in driving rain prompted one Italian sports paper to pronounce that England were dragging the game back into the dark ages. Gascoigne could not make any real impact. Holland were next up.

Defeat against a side who two years earlier had humiliated England on their way to the European Championship finals would have put England in danger at the group stage. It looked like it was going to head for disaster when the hybrid sweeper system Robson had introduced wobbled at first, then captain Bryan Robson hobbled off with an Achilles tendon injury.

At the heart of the England team, up against a Dutch side featuring Ruud Gullit, Frank Rijkaard and Marco van Basten, were substitute David Platt and Gascoigne with just a handful of caps between them. Suddenly something magical happened. Gascoigne, cast as midfield main man, seized the moment. He teased and tormented the Dutch. He dribbled and beat opponents but timed his release of the ball so as not to get caught in possession. He did stepovers. He dinked balls into space. He sent over crosses and hit a couple of dangerous shots. The game ended 0-0 but England, with Gascoigne the inspiration, had been more than a match for the technically gifted Dutch. They looked a force. Rarely can such a warm glow have surrounded a goalless draw.

Such was the relief that Robson gave the entire squad the day off to let their hair down. While some opted to join then Tranmere chairman Peter Johnson and Villa supremo Doug Ellis on a yacht others chose to leave the team hotel and spend an afternoon where most the English press corps were staying, Sardinia's Forte Village hotel. Can you imagine that happening now?

Midway through the afternoon after finishing filing all the follow up stories from the Holland game I was walking back to my room when I came across a little drinking club that had just started to get into the swing of things. It was Bryan Robson, Terry Butcher, Chris Waddle, Steve Curry (then of the Daily Express) and Colin Gibson (Daily Telegraph). I was invited to join the team. Robson's ankle was heavily strapped and within a few days it emerged his World Cup ... for the second time ... would be over and he flew home which thanks to the help of the late great Joe Melling (then of the Mail on Sunday) and Alex Montgomery (Sun) was a story I didn't miss and eventually was the one who managed to sit on the plane next to Robson and get his interview.

A few tales came out over that gentle session. What didn't emerge for some years was one of the reasons Robson's Achilles was so bad was that during some 'high jinks' at the team hotel, Gascoigne had lifted then dropped the edge of the bed on his captain's ankle. Yet all the players around that table were at odds to stress that despite some of his manic foibles the positive impact Gascoigne was having on the team was immense.

Which begged the question: Where was he? Almost on cue a drenched Gascoigne, in England shorts and polo shirt, turned up on a bicycle. soaking because, for a bet, he'd opted to leave the yacht party and swim to shore. On a bike because the waiters on the rambling complex used them to deliver room service to the bungalows, Gascoigne had obviously had a few (hadn't we all), but insisted he was going to return back to the team hotel on the borrowed bike. Before the others, waiting for a mini bus to take them back, could stop him, Gascoigne was off.

Well after the tournament was over it transpired that Gascoigne had been missing for some time. Apparently he had cycled out of the complex taken the wrong turn and got lost. Robson had to sent out a search party to find him that returned with their quarry dishevelled but unscathed.

Had the story come to light who knows what pressure Robson may have been under to have sent Gascoigne home? But it didn't. The combination of Gascoigne's brilliance and Gary Lineker's goals led England excruciatingly close to the World Cup final. The dramatic, gut wrenching manner of the semi-final defeat to West Germany on penalties, watched by well behaved travelling fans in front one of this country's biggest ever TV audiences proved a pivotal moment for football in the country.

Gascoigne's tears at the end struck a chord with the nation. He had been an inspiration again but of course would not have played in the final had England won, having lost control and picked up a second booking of the tournament for a petulant tackle. No matter it seemed. Gascoigne was cast as a national hero. He was now Gazza to everyone, not just his mates. And 'Gazzamania', which was to follow, marked a sea change. Football was back on the front pages for something other than violence. Football became part of celebrity culture. It didn't take long for Rupert Murdoch to click that the best way to make his struggling satellite channel succeed was to plug into the new rock and roll. The Premier League was born and the revolution began.

Gascoigne would not really play his part in it. By the time the Premier League started in 1992 Gascoigne had moved on to Italy with Lazio but would never be the player he was or could have been because of that fateful, knee injury he suffered in the 1991 FA Cup final. There still were moments of genius on the way ... notably THAT goal against Scotland in Euro 96 ... and eventually cameos in the Premier League at Middlesbrough and Everton. But his return to English football in 1998 after a successful stint in Scotland tainted by the manner of his marriage break up was also marked by his ignominious axing from England's World Cup squad by Glenn Hoddle that summer.

Gascoigne never really recovered from that blow but Hoddle can't be blamed for that. Until then I'd had my fair share of interviews with Gascoigne on his roller coaster journey. It helped that he felt I hadn't 'turned him over' previously, especially that afternoon in the snooker hall.

The stories were generally good copy. But after that blow of being dropped he started to turn on many of those who tried to see his side of any given story.

Approaching Italia 90, Gascoigne was able to change course when approaching a crossroads and take the right path. Approaching the summer of 2008 such was Gascoigne's pathetic descent into becoming a psychotic alcoholic that he had to be sectioned under the mental heath act. Gascoigne had become more ghost than a shadow of his former self. Yet I and many others will still always remember a player who did so much to bring English football back from the dead.

Rob Shepherd has been football editor at News of the World since 2007, previously with Daily Express, Daily Mail, Today and Hayters Sports Reporting Agency.

__Favourite player:__ Billy Bonds. Growing up watching West Ham in the Seventies, Bobby Moore was naturally my boyhood hero, but Bonds was the player I loved watching. A combination of guts and guile he always sought to inspire the team when it was good or bid. Bonzo played across the back, in midfield and for a while upfront. The best player never to play for England.

__Most memorable match:__ As a fan – West Ham beating Eintracht Frankfurt 3-1 in the 1976 Cup winners Cup semi-final. A magical floodlight Upton Park night in the mud. As a reporter – Manchester United 2 Bayern Munich 1, Nou Camp, 1999 Champions League final. Extraordinary to watch, exhilarating to report.

BY PRECEPT AND EXAMPLE

The FWA have made few mistakes with the Footballer of the Year

By Dennis Signy

MY ASSOCIATION with the Football Writers' Association over the past 40 years as secretary, chairman, committee member and now, with my wife Pat, Honorary Life Member, has led to lasting friendships with some of the true legends of the game.

From Stanley Matthews and Tom Finney to Joe Mercer, Billy Wright, Nat Lofthouse and Danny Blanchflower to Bobby Moore, Bobby Charlton, George Best and Dave Mackay to Gordon Banks, Pat Jennings and Kenny Dalglish to Gary Lineker and Alan Shearer to the welcome 'foreign invaders' Jurgen Klinsmann, Dennis Bergkamp and Gianfranco Zola.

All Footballers of the Year since the original award in 1948. Look down the list and I think that the football writers in England have more often than not got it right.

I remember clashing with Brian Clough the first time I was chairman when he suggested otherwise. I rattled off name after name at the annual dinner, adding each time: "We got it right that time, Brian".

Managers such as Don Revie and Clough used to canvass support for their players to win the prestigious award and sometimes voting might have suggested a London-Manchester divide. Sixty years on, though, managers and players agree that the Footballer of the Year dinner is one of his major events in soccer's social calendar.

It all began on 22 September 1947, when a group of journalists travelling home by boat from an international match in Brussels decided to form an association. They had seen Stanley Matthews – the Wizard of Dribble – lay on all five goals for Tommy Lawton (2), Stan Mortensen (two) and Tom Finney in a 5-2 win against Belgium.

Charles Buchan, of Sunderland, Arsenal and England fame, was one of the founder members – the others were Roy Peskett, John Thompson and Clifford Webb – in those pre-jet-setters days when football writers took advantage of a leisurely trip home to form the FWA.

It was writer-publisher Buchan, whose Football Monthly was a must-read in the post-war years, who later proposed the election of an annual Footballer of the Year. The original minute book, which I housed for many years, records that Buchan suggested an award to "the professional player who by precept and example is considered by a ballot of members to be the Footballer of the Year". It was agreed to award a statuette to be kept by the winner.

So the Footballer of the Year was born. In my time successive chairmen and committees tried to hammer home the "precept and example" theme. Note the word "the" in the original minute. Over the past 60 years this has become, in my mind, the most prestigious individual award in soccer.

Others have followed suit with similar awards but this is THE Footballer of the Year. The FWA has always concentrated on the one award – who remembers who was second last year? The roll of honour contains some of the great names of the game.

The original entrance fee and annual subscription was five guineas, from November 1947 to May 1948, with a subsequent annual subscription of two guineas. Today it is £20 and membership is still at the discretion of the committee.

There were 42 members when Matthews – later Sir Stanley – was voted the first Footballer of the Year. Today there are more than 400, embracing radio and television journalists and ... women.

Julie Welch was the first female member of the FWA but she declined to attend the annual dinner alongside some 700 male members and their guests.

My wife Pat, who became executive secretary when I became chairman for the first time, organised the dinner for years – in her early days she would get the all-male guests sat down to dinner and then go off for a meal on her own in the hotel and watch the presentation from a viewing point on the balcony.

Estimates for the first trophy were £45 for silver and £20 for bronze. Matthews received bronze, but he told me many years later that the original had pride of place in his den at home. He won his second award, by the way, at the age of 46. Today each of the coveted statuettes costs £800.

The venue for the first-ever Footballer of the Year dinner, now traditionally held two days before the FA Cup final, was the Hungaria Restaurant in London, although members also discussed using the restaurant at Waterloo Station.

For more than 20 years the Café Royal, with its plush chandeliered surroundings, was a popular venue, but so great was the demand that a switch was made and today 700-plus sell-outs are held at the Royal Lancaster Hotel.

I can assure you that renowned ticket tout Stan Flashman, famed for getting tickets for all the top sporting events, couldn't get one to sell on for the Footballer of the Year dinner.

The original members set down that not more than six leading personalities be invited. Today there is a top table of 30-plus VIPs and, if there is a good response from former Footballers of the Year, there is a double-tier top table.

Pele has flown in to attend the dinner and Franz Beckenbauer has come from Germany. The FWA award is truly international.

When Joe Mercer died his widow phoned on the evening of the dinner to ask for Joe to be remembered – he said it was the night of the year for him. Bill Slater has been attending every year since he won the award in 1960. Over the years votes for the award were sent to the Signy household in NW London and Pat and I totted them up before I contacted the winner to break the news to him.

In 2008 Cristiano Ronaldo became the seventh double winner, following Matthews, Finney, Dalglish, John Barnes and Gary Lineker. Thierry Henry set a new mark ... a hat-trick of wins during his time at Arsenal.

There was one historic tie when Dave Mackay and Tony Book each collected an award. The votes always came in sealed envelopes at my home, due by first post of an announced date. The exception came when Maurice Smith became chairman and the committee decided that the votes stayed sealed and should be opened at Maurice's office at the People for an official count. Mackay and Book finished all-square after a recount and we rang both players and their clubs and then announced the result. When Pat and I returned to NW London we found two envelopes lying in the hall ... two votes, both for one of the contenders.

So who was the 1969 winner? The record books show a tie. Pat and I have never told a soul what might have been the result if the postman had arrived earlier that day ... we never will.

There was no nail-biting or heartache the year that Billy Bremner won the award – he polled an amazing 95 per of the votes and was the most emphatic runaway winner in the history of the award until Ronaldo's near clean-sweep in 2008.

Only three times has the winner not been present to collect his award. Danny Blanchflower was abroad the first time, playing for London in Barcelona in the old Fairs Cup. He sent a tape eloquently expressing his apologies and grateful acceptance. Robert Pires was in France following a knee operation – he appeared on film accepting his award.

The year Terry McDermott was due to collect his award I received a message at lunch-time saying that he was unable to attend and that he was asking a team-mate to collect the trophy for him. Hours of fruitless phoning failed to locate McDermott. I even had him 'paged' at Chester Races (on information received) but there was no response.

I asked Trevor Brooking, the runner-up, to accept the award on McDermott's behalf but he was not attending the dinner due to a prior engagement. An hour before the dinner Bob Paisley, then the Liverpool manager, agreed to accept the award on behalf of his missing player – and was suitably apologetic. I later met McDermott at a Downing Street reception; he then explained that his sister-in-law had been unwell.

Bert Trautmann was the first player born overseas to win the award ... these days with foreign players dominating the Premier League we look in vain most seasons for a successor to the Matthews, the Finneys and Charltons.

With hindsight you could say there are great players who have never won the award ...Denis Law, Jimmy Greaves, Johnny Haynes and John Charles spring to mind. One fact is indisputable. The 42 members who took part in that first vote in favour of Matthews certainly got it right.

And Charles Buchan and Co sowed the seeds for Sixty Glorious Years.

Awarded an OBE for community and charity work in 1983, Dennis Signy started his football writing career with the London Evening News in the 1940s; was a reporter and later a director in three spells with the Reg Hayter sports agency; 17 years a by-lined writer with the News of the World; five with the Times and several more with the Mail on Sunday and Sunday Express. PR consultant to the Football League for 12 years.

__Favourite player:__ Tom Finney, a one-club man who shone in a golden era of English football for his skills, sportsmanship and goalscoring technique.

__Most memorable match:__ The 1966 World Cup Final. I bought my wife a season ticket for Wembley to celebrate our marriage that year. I forgave Alf Ramsey after extra-time for leaving Jimmy Greaves out of the side.

GINOLA WAS WORTH IT

David was magnifique on and off the pitch

By Neil Silver

DAVID GINOLA was one of the most controversial winners in the long and illustrious history of the coveted FWA Footballer of the Year award ... but then David and controversy have never been far from each other.

After all, David is the man who was accused by Gerard Houllier of "murdering" the France national team when they missed out on qualification for the 1994 World Cup finals – an outrageously ridiculous claim, as anyone who has seen the incident will know. In a qualifier against Bulgaria, one of the flamboyant winger's crosses went unchallenged by his team-mates, and the opposition put together a move which led to their winning goal.

It is not uncommon for someone who is rich, charismatic, talented and devilishly good looking to attract criticism, more often than not borne out of jealousy, so take it from me when I say that David deserved his FWA Footballer of the Year and PFA Player of the Year double in 1999 because, to coin a certain catchphrase ... he was worth it. I became close to the Gallic genius when I was ghost-writing his autobiography, Le Magnifique, in 2000, and saw first hand that, on and off the field, he lived up to the title.

I have so many stories, serious and funny, about my friend David that I could easily fill a few chapters of this book. Let me share a couple of them with you, and then you can make up your own mind.

Princess Diana is probably an impossible act to follow. Few people can walk in her footsteps. But David Ginola proved the perfect choice when he was asked in 1998 by the Red Cross to succeed her as their ambassador for the Anti-landmines campaign.

The most moving chapter for me by far in David's autobiography is the time we spent in Cambodia, when he went to see a village being de-mined in the hope of raising awareness of the problem around the world.

One of our first stops was to a hospital for people who have had limbs blown off by landmines. In my opinion, it takes a special person to deal with those amputees, to put a smile on their face and make them forget their situation for a few minutes. Diana was, of course, one of those special people, and so was David. He has mesmerising eyes, and the way he looked into their eyes as he spoke to them, or gently touched them on the shoulder, or held their hand, you could tell that they felt they were in the presence of someone special – and that, in turn, made them feel special. I could also see that David was touched deeply by the experience ... he wasn't there on some publicity jaunt, he really cared.

We then went to a nearby village where there was a football pitch marked out in a dirt field, and David played football with two teams of amputees, men of all ages who had lost an arm, a leg or an eye thanks to a landmine.

It was amazing to see these men as they tried to stand on their real leg and kick the ball with their prosthesis. Nine times out of ten they fell flat on their face but, instead of feeling sorry for themselves, they picked themselves up and roared with laughter. You couldn't help but laugh too, not in a mocking way or out of pity, but because you could see how much they were loving every second of being on the same football field as an international soccer star. David loved it too, taking it seriously enough to work up a sweat and score a couple of special goals.

I think David's verdict on the whole trip sums it up nicely. He said: "Every single moment was a sad moment, but you have to put on a brave face all the time, smiling for them, looking into their eyes and showing them that you understand their problems. It is important that you show them no feelings of shame, or embarrassment. You must bring them a smile and if they smile too then it is good. Playing football for a while gave them so much pleasure."

At the end of that trip, I saw another side of David, which showed me just how genuine he is. I have seen football players break the hearts of wide-eyed youngsters who worship their every move by refusing to sign an autograph, but in all the time I spent with David, I never saw him refuse one request – he would regard that as a lack of respect not only to the fan, but also to himself.

He often went above and beyond the call of duty, and this was highlighted when we were at Bangkok airport waiting for our connecting flight back to London following the trip to Cambodia.

It was late and we were tired when a smart businessman came up and asked for David's autograph for his son, insisting he was a massive fan. Rather than just sign his name, David told the man to ring home on his mobile telephone and get his boy on the line. Can you imagine the look on that child's face when his dad handed his mobile over to David, who then spent a couple of minutes talking to the boy on the other end as if he was an old friend?

David never tired of telling me that, as a professional footballer, you must respect the fans. That is David, he has an amazing effect on people, women AND men. I still chuckle when I recall the time he swept on to my front drive in his gleaming silver Mercedes and bounced out of the car, arriving at my house after training one afternoon to do a session on the book.

As a jogger passed by he clearly recognised the famous athletic figure standing in my front garden, and as he continued to stare sideways at David Ginola he ran straight into a lamppost. Priceless.

There are FWA members (and a certain Scottish manager) who to this day deride the fact that David picked up our coveted award. It was the season that Manchester United won the treble, but the votes for United players were split, so that no single player polled more than David. All I can say is that David's fellow professionals named him as their Player of the Year too that season, and they are not bad judges, are they? He was honoured to receive our award and he told me afterwards: "It was an amazing feeling. I was on a platform looking down at more than 700 journalists and guests from the football world and I knew this was an audience of people who were really into football. I looked along the top table and could see people like Sir Bobby Charlton, one of the former winners of the trophy, and again I felt proud to be in such distinguished company. It was a huge event for me, and I cannot really put into words how I felt inside."

I voted for David not just because he had a marvellous season, but also because he was a joy for us journalists to deal with, and that is all part of the package as far as I am concerned.

So what about David Ginola the football player? I'd have him in my team every day of the week. People complain that he doesn't defend ... SO WHAT!? Get someone else to do his defending because the damage he will do for you at the other end – isn't that worth it? I know that won't always work because Gerry Francis, the man who signed David for Spurs, explained to me that some players get jealous of the "star man" but David really was loved by his team-mates, and when they didn't want the ball they knew they could give it to him and have a breather.

When I watch football I want to be entertained – I grew up watching Glenn Hoddle every week – and David is a born entertainer and his talent shouldn't be stifled. Does Manchester United manager Sir Alex Ferguson tell Cristiano Ronaldo to work on his defending? I doubt it.

You want to go away from football matches talking about special pieces of skill you have witnessed, or special goals, and, like Ronaldo today, David Ginola gave us those talking points.

Allow me to highlight two of his most memorable goals. One was an outstanding volley for Newcastle in the UEFA Cup against Ferencvaros, and the other was that dribble for Tottenham against Barnsley in the FA Cup. This is how David describes moments like those.

"Sometimes when I score a special goal, I have an 'out-of-body experience.' It is as if time freezes for a couple of seconds and I step out of my body and watch myself scoring the goal. I knew I was going to score that goal against Ferencvaros before I controlled the ball. When it came towards me it was as though there was a voice in my head saying: 'Don't worry, because this is going in the back of the net,' although I couldn't actually hear the voice. I knew what was going to happen a second before it did. Everything around me stopped, the ball came across, I controlled it on my thigh, brought it inside and volleyed it into the goal. When the ball hit the back of the net there was silence, and slow motion, and then it was as if someone clapped their hands to re-start time and I heard the tremendous roar of the crowd.

"People still ask me about the goal I scored at Barnsley when I cut in from the left flank, beat a trail of defenders and tucked the ball home. But I remember only the moment I struck the ball past the goalkeeper, I don't remember the first touch, or the dribble – it was like I was stepping aside and watching myself doing it. I can only remember the end of the action and can't tell you how I started it."

Before Spurs played Aston Villa in October 2007, they celebrated their 125th anniversary with a parade of legends on the White Hart Lane pitch. The heroes included Dave Mackay, Cliff Jones, Pat Jennings and Martin Peters, but who got the biggest ovation in the stadium? David Ginola. He was adored not just by the fans but everybody at the club. He knew the names of all the stewards and even the laundry women and always stopped to chat to them all.

Magnifique.

Neil Silver is a sports journalist on the People. *Previous newspapers were the Jewish* Chronicle, Hornsey Journal, Daily Mirror *and* Sunday Mirror *plus the Press Association. Apart from David Ginola's autobiography,* Le Magnifique, *he also wrote* The Biggs Time, *with Michael Biggs, son of Great Train Robber Ronnie.*

Favourite player: *Pat Jennings. I used to watch in awe the outstanding saves this giant goalkeeper would make week in, week out for Tottenham.*

Most memorable match: *The 1991 FA Cup semi-final when, against the odds, Spurs beat arch-enemy Arsenal 2-1 at Wembley. Gazza was a genius and that match he proved it.*

MY ONE CAUTION IS FRAMED

Refs never change their mind so why bother arguing?

By Alan Smith

THE RED HALF of Wembley couldn't believe it. Was that Smudger getting booked down there? The man who had never been cautioned in his entire career? Surely shome mistake, as Sean Connery might say.

But no, there wasn't any mistake. On 29 May 1993, I picked up my one and only booking in my career – in the FA Cup Final. Arsenal's win over Sheffield Wednesday in a Thursday night replay wouldn't go down as a classic, but for me it ended up proving unique in one sense.

Not that I was too upset at entering the little black book. On the contrary, it was all a bit of a laugh, not to say a relief. After all, nobody wants to be known as a goody two shoes. That's why the referee's report still hangs proudly in my study, recording the details of that yellow card.

So Keren Barratt from Coventry, hold your head in shame for charging Arsenal's number nine with "ungentlemanly conduct" after he had "blatantly and most deliberately knocked the ball away with his hand after a free-kick had been awarded to the opposing team in an attempt to delay the taking of the free kick."

Shocking stuff, I think you'll agree. The kind of ugly offence the beautiful game could well do without.

In all seriousness, though, I suppose it is too easy to hold up my record as an example to today's errant players. Six hundred games and only one caution: if I can do it, why can't everyone else? In an era when respect to officials has been sadly eroded, why can't today's stars show the same kind of restraint rather than losing their heads in a fit of pique, or diving in dangerously without any thought?

Well, let me say right away it isn't quite so straightforward. For a start, I didn't go in for much tackling. Interceptions, yes, and plenty of closing down, but not much in the way of the full-on stuff. To be fair, it wasn't strictly necessary for someone in my position. Still isn't. A striker can get away with staying on his feet.

The crucial difference now is that referees seem to punish the slightest misjudgement, someone arriving on the scene a fraction too late, or get conned by shameless playacting worthy of an Oscar. Under those circumstances, my spotless copybook would never have lasted so long.

With the game so much faster now as well, innocent attempts to win the ball can look 10 times worse when the player in possession crashes to the ground. And you can't always blame the ref for that. In my view, their job has become significantly harder over the last 15 years. Consider how much scrutiny Premier League refs are under when every contentious incident is examined endlessly on television from several different camera angles.

That didn't happen in my day and, as a result, the officials, I reckon, didn't feel under so much pressure. Not only that, you could have a good chat without it ending in tears.

Gary Lineker, my old strike partner at Leicester, used to tell a funny story about the time a referee threatened to book me at Filbert Street. In his best Brummie accent, Gary would recite what he claimed I said in defence.

"You can't book me ref. Don't you know my disciplinary record?"

Gary, understandably, thought this hilarious, though I have always maintained he embellished the facts.

He could talk anyway. Going one better than me, the England striker managed to sail through his whole career without getting booked once. Together, we must have seemed like a right pair of do-gooders.

But going back to my old mate's anecdote, it must have been one of the few times that I got involved with a whistle blower. Normally, I wouldn't even bother since it tended to spoil my concentration. Anyway, I always took the view that the man in black wouldn't change his mind so what was the point of wasting energy? And if an opponent kept kicking me instead of the ball, I took it as a compliment, just as long as the ref provided some protection.

Mind you, it seems like a miracle now that my only booking took so long to arrive, especially when you consider that for 11 years I'd been clashing with beefy centre-halves, arms and legs tangling in an honest fight for the ball. Again, you couldn't get away with a lot of it now, not when a flailing forearm, however innocuous, leads to strict censure more often than not.

Blimey, the number of times that interpretation of the laws would have affected me. Using my arms for leverage in jumping for the ball, defenders often felt a sharp elbow inadvertently connect with their mush.

I wasn't the only one, either, who jumped in this way. Why else do you think centre-halves were uglier back then? Broken noses and scar tissue told the tale well enough of a physical battle taken in good heart.

Usually anyway. One night at Kenilworth Road, I managed to upset Luton's Steve Foster, he of the trademark headband covering a litany of war wounds. A big lad was Steve, who didn't back down easily but, after I accidentally caught him in an aerial duel, he was forced to go off and have a few stitches in a nasty gash just above his eye.

Once back on the pitch, he angrily pointed the finger, accusing me of deliberately setting out to "do him." I was an Arsenal player by this time, and perhaps I should have used that old Leicester line on Steve. My disciplinary record still lay unblemished.

Unfortunately, it wasn't quite the same story for George Graham's team as a whole. Remember that 20-man brawl at Old Trafford in 1990? A few of our lads landed some hefty, blood-spilling punches that afternoon. It turned into a proper fight, with the ref helpless to separate two warring factions.

It just goes to show that today's rucks aren't anything new. More importantly, they aren't nearly as bad as some people make out. Usually, a bit of pushing and shoving with a few insults thrown in is as bad as it gets in the modern game.

Mind you, that's not to say there isn't a problem. The lack of respect shown to officials is a valid concern, especially when kids copy their heroes at grass roots level. There's nothing worse than seeing an 11 year-old moan at the ref or hit the deck as if he's been shot, then roll around pretending to be hurt.

What hope is there if these kind of habits are being ingrained so young? Officials don't stand a chance. More worryingly, fewer and fewer will be prepared to keep tolerating the abuse, not just on the pitch but also from the sidelines where the actions of some parents are an absolute disgrace.

As always, the first steps towards improvement must begin at the top where, along with many others, I would like to see the rugby rule applied to the round ball game whereby only the captain can speak to the ref. When a foul is awarded, only the man with the armband can get involved. Anyone defying that dictum, however civilised their objections might seem, is immediately booked, no questions asked.

As an experiment at first, it would be fascinating to see how this worked out, how the players adapted, knowing that certain punishment awaited the slightest show of dissent. Managers, without doubt, would start making sure their players stayed in line, given that costly suspensions would soon be on the way. You wouldn't get the situation, therefore, where players are actively encouraged to hunt the ref in packs, managers working on the theory that he can't book them all. Safety in numbers: it might seem a sensible idea but only ends up looking in practice like a nasty case of bullying.

Yet so much depends on individual temperaments. Whatever you try, some players will lose it in the heat of the moment to test the patience of Job, never mind the ref.

Personally speaking, I don't have much of a temper, which certainly helped on the pitch on the discipline front but deprived my overall game of the aggressive streak that arguably goes into the make-up of the very best players.

Still, you are what you are. Nothing changes that. Not even a booking for ungentlemanly conduct.

Alan Smith began writing for the Daily Telegraph in 1996, shortly after his career was cut short by injury. After five years at Leicester, he enjoyed considerable success with Arsenal, winning two league titles, the FA Cup, League Cup, European Cup Winners' Cup and 13 England caps. In addition to his writing, Alan is a regular co-commentator for Sky Sports.

***Favourite player:** Diego Maradona. For five minutes, I was on the same pitch. What an experience. He could do things with the ball never seen before.*

***Most memorable match:** 26 May 1989. My Arsenal side clinched the title in the last seconds at Liverpool. Nothing ever came close to the feeling that night.*

JUST LIKE COVERING THE BEATLES

Following France was more enjoyable than England

By Steve Stammers

THERE WAS a feeling a trepidation when, back in August 1998, my sports editor at the Evening Standard, Simon Greenberg, asked me in for a quiet chat in his office. Even more worryingly, he then asked me to close the door. 'Not a good sign,' I thought. In fact he was opening a door to a fantastic adventure.

After their triumph in the World Cup some six weeks before, he thought it would be an idea to have someone from the paper travel with the French team because of the strong London connection within the squad.

There was Patrick Vieira and Emmanuel Petit from Arsenal and their club-mate Nicolas Anelka would certainly be called up after he had helped Arsenal to the Premier League and FA Cup double. They were joined in the capital that summer by Marcel Desailly at Chelsea. In the years to come, of course, the likes of Robert Pires, Thierry Henry, Didier Deschamps, Sylvain Wiltord and William Gallas would all play in London.

But back to that pre-season of 1998/99. After Simon had outlined what he wanted, he asked if I would be up for the job. It was certainly a challenge but that has never unnerved me. Call it Belfast meets East London in the genes and, anyway, if you can get home in one piece from school by walking the length of Harold Hill council estate at the age of 10, covering France was not going to be the most daunting task I had ever faced. And it was great.

At first, naturally, I was greeted with suspicion. That was not unexpected. For some reason the French don't like the English .... something to do with a place called Agincourt I think.

The majority of French journalists are Paris-based. I had lived in Paris for six months when I was 17, so I anticipated it would be difficult. I mean, the Parisians believe they are superior to the rest of the French and the rest of the French are hardly Anglophiles, so I prepared myself for the worst.

In fact, I couldn't have been more wrong. The French papers began sending journalists to England and to the club they re-named "France-enal" in particular and several remain close friends to this day.

Writers like Vincent Duluq, Joel Domenghetti, Bernard Lions, Jerome Le Fauconnier, Regis Testalain and, especially, a giant of man called Pierre Menes – all from the highly-respected newspaper L'Equipe.

To be fair to Simon Greenberg, he supported me all the way even after the early excursions produced little in the way of copy. I was getting to know people, knowing when was the right time to ask questions in a press conference ... and the etiquette involved when I wanted to speak in English. These were, after all, French affairs. Yes, I had a smattering of conversational French but many of the questions were in football jargon and a job washing dishes in a bistro off the Rue du Bac some 25 years earlier was hardly great preparation.

But I got by, and I got to know Pierre and the rest of the French journalists. I would travel with them on official trips to some weird and wonderful places as diverse as Armenia and Chile. Great experiences.

I also covered Les Bleus in the European Championships of 2000 and 2004 as well as the World Cup of 2002. I managed to get a sprinkling of decent tales to repay the faith that had been put in me. It was a privilege to follow the superb French team that won Euro 2000.

The difference between covering France and England? Easy question. You get to know the players. The interviews are more intimate and the players actually know who they are talking to most of the time. Fabien Barthez, for instance, still owes me at least 100 Rothmans, although they are no good to me now because I packed up smoking three years ago.

After the Euro win in Holland and Belgium in 2000, it became, in their terms, more hectic. The French love a strike as I discovered on several occasions when I arrived at the Gare du Nord and that tendency spreads to sport. During the 2000 championship, the players refused to come to conferences because of what they perceived to be a negative press. And they were winning.

Didier Deschamps in particular refused to talk and he was captain. So the journalists boycotted the next briefing from the coach Roger Lemerre in protest. Next day Lemerre in turn refused to speak to journalists.

"Welcome to the world of covering the Beatles," said Joel Domenghetti. In truth, it was never as predictable as covering England – and a lot more enjoyable. What I learned very quickly was that you have to stand your ground and that you earn more respect if you do that.

I recall one coach journey to a game at Euro 2004 when I was surrounded by 15 French journos. One – let's call him Jerome – kept on about France's opening win over England. "Big game today for England against Switzerland," he said. "You have to win."

"Yes," I replied. "But every game is a big game for England."

Then he started humming, to the tune of Mammy, "Scotland, oh oh oh Scotland."

I smiled.

He did it twice more and I couldn't let that go. "First time, Jerome, funny. Second time, not funny. Third time, boring. The French don't do humour and you should stick to what the French do best. "

"What is that?" he said.

"Making cheese, having lunch and every 30 years or so asking for help because the Germans are back." To my relief, the others laughed along.

But Pierre Menes, now he has humour. He was driving me back to central Paris after a pre-Euro 2004 match and he was talking at a million miles an hour to a mate on his hands-free. I didn't understand a word – except for "rosbif", the affectionate name the French have for us.

When he finished, I said: "You couldn't have enough rosbifs 60 years ago, could you? Don't forget, all your menus would have been in German now but for the rosbifs."

Pierre – whose English is immaculate – laughed and retorted. "I wish you hadn't have bothered," he said. "If you had stayed at home, I would have won three World Cups by now."

Not so funny was South Korea and Japan two years earlier. France were in disarray and it showed in both their play and their results. Thierry Henry was speaking to no-one and even a majestic figure like Patrick Vieira was losing confidence as the tournament lurched from one disaster to another.

The travel plans were chaotic to say the least. England had a British Airways jet at their disposal. The French squad travelled on internal flights with the general public and after they had drawn 0-0 with Uruguay, they arrived at check in at the same time as a Brazilian drummer and his samba band. And when muscular athletes like Vieira, Lilian Thuram, Petit and company then have to sit with an unsympathetic general public in a coffee shop, suffer more drumming from our Brazilian friend and then squeeze into an economy size seat, there was more than a suspicion this was all going to end in tears. It did.

But the good far outweighs the bad, no question. And if there was one game I have to pick as an outstanding memory from my time with France, it would be the Euro 2000 quarter-final against Spain in Bruges. It was phenomenal for the quality of football and intensity. It was the match that had the lot ... drama, controversy and superb football. It had everything.

And if there was one casual but poignant conversation that stands out it was with the luckless Lemerre at Charles de Gaulle airport at 2.30 am.

France had won 1-0 in Barcelona against Andorra – and that courtesy of a penalty two minutes from time by Frank Leboeuf. He had, as they say in journalese-speak, been given pelters by the press. "I cannot understand," he said. "We won. Is it the same with England when you win?"

I told him it was worse and I daresay Steve McClaren would agree. But the coach's job does have benefits. Jacques Santini invited me over to Paris on 23 April 2004 for an interview. He told me he wanted the Tottenham job. Good story, good headline and good pay day for Jacques.

One enduring and treasured friendship with a player from those years remains. It is with Patrick Vieira. I was honoured and proud to be asked to be the English director of his Instituit DIAMBARS in his native Senegal. It gives the under-privileged children of that impoverished country both a sporting and academic education. It is a truly magnificent project.

Steve Stammers worked on the now defunct London Evening News before joining the Daily Star in 1978. He then moved to the Evening Standard until May 2006 when he joined the Sunday Mirror.

Favourite player: It has to be Denis Law. There was an expectation every time he went near the ball, a kind of electricity. Brave as a lion with lightening reactions.

Most memorable match: The 1966 World Cup final. The benefits of being 60 are not immense but one is to be of an age to remember every kick of that game. I just wish I had kept the programme.

DRINKING GUINNESS FROM A THIMBLE WITH BIG JACK

The toast was Arthur Scargill and John Wayne

By Tony Stenson

I'VE BEEN lucky to meet many top sportsmen and women over the years, but few have made my back stiffen when they've walked into a room.

Pele, Ali, Moore, Best and Woods are a few who have made me put down my wine and simply gaze. Jack Charlton is another.

Charlton, gruff and ready Geordie, might be a strange choice, but there's something about the man who commands attention. Jack Charlton? You sure? You must mean his more famous brother, Bobby?

Take more water with it, Stenson.

His rumpled clothes, seemingly bought from Oxfam? Flat, creased cap? Gangling height? Fag constantly in his hand? Or simply he had that that something, the intangible whiff of presence.

Here was a footballer, an England World Cup winner, successful manager at club level and for the Republic of Ireland. Glamour, glitz, strut and well oiled bank account and go-faster car? All the trimmings today's successful, well coiffeured football idols? No, he was just ... Jack.

Footballers like Charlton were the foot soldiers of soccer, the beetle crushers, the poor bloody infantry. They might not be glamorous but, by God, they were useful for doing the hard work. He was a defender who ran uphill into the wind trying to keep his side alive, keeping things quiet while the more skilful recovered breath and took over once more.

The likes of Charlton are not exotic creatures. They tend to be large, phlegmatic men with the look of artisans rather than craftsmen. Charlton was in his pomp when bones squealed to his tackles and rivals like the late Peter Osgood tried to kick him into row Z. Former Leeds manager Don Revie, who built one of the most controversial sides ever, wrote he could not have achieved his success without Charlton. This was a side that not only had bone collectors, but skilful players also.

By the time Jack hung his boots up after more than 20 years at the club he had made 629 league appearances, still a club record. One of the last, truly great one-club players. I was part of a group of English journalists who got to know him well during his years as Irish manager. It started in 1987 and finished on a sad night in Liverpool almost a decade later when Ireland lost to Holland in a European Championship play-off. Charlton quit/was sacked a few days later. An era, coated in adventure, laughter, Guinness and total enjoyment ended.

Jack was dour, fun, cantankerous, tight with money, free with warmth if you crossed into his circle. Never dull. On our first meeting I introduced my self as from the Daily Mirror. "Bloody, Mirror! You a socialist paper and yet you've turned your back on Arthur Scargill. Appalling," he said storming away.

Then 24 hours later I was walking pass him on a plane – he was naturally in seat No 1. He shouted to me as I trudged down the aisle. "Got your paper?" he asked.

"Thought you didn't like it," I replied.

"Don't like its turn-coat politics, but I do like the quiz word," he said. Quiz word. That was Jack. Readable as newsprint inside papier mache.

To unravel Jack, first you have to unravel the bloodlines. For as long as there has been soccer played for money the Charltons or Milburns have drawn a wage from the game. Well over a century onwards, Jack was the last in the line to indulge in the family madness. Prosperity has driven the clan away from the playing pitches.

Jack and Bobby Charlton, brothers and fourth generation footballers, took the family as far as it could travel when they both won World Cup winner's medals on a fabled day at Wembley in 1966. Bobby makes his living in boardrooms and business halls. Jack was the last to wear studs and trampled onto grass.

Ashington of his childhood was a gaunt working town whose male provided fodder to the mines or recruits for the footballing empires of Newcastle and Sunderland. Jack spent one day down a mine and realised working in darkness wasn't for him and quit. Football was his dream and that was it. Places have change. Not Jack. A year spent in the Horse Guards, guarding the Queen at Windsor only fired his appetite for soccer. Jack told us of just once having a quick glance at the Queen, but having a close encounter with Prince Phillip.

He recalled: "Part of our duties was to walk the polo grounds in Windsor Great Park the day after a game, flattening the ground replacing divots. On one occasion a mate and me decided to nip into woods for a smoke.

"Neither of us had matches, so we went out to the path and hailed a man walking past: 'Excuse me mate, got a light?' Who turns round? Prince Phillip. Tell you something, my mate and I scarpered fast away."

In the army Jack learnt to smoke, something he still does today, although he has a comical way of trying to hide a fag in his palm so kids can't see him do it.

Through his soccer days, Jack always spent his leisure time hunting and shooting and has exclusive bits on riverbanks for his use only, one in Ireland, given to him by a priest for answering his thanks that Ireland would one day have a decent soccer team. During those wonderful years, Jack supplied a legion of stories, telling us his other hero apart from Scargill was cowboy actor John Wayne and that pride of place in his house goes to a painteding of the man on a wall.

In Orlando at USA 94 he invited a group of English journalists who covered Ireland to his room and we enjoyed drinks from a barrel of Guinness supplied by the makers wherever he went. As he offered us a drink he discovered he didn't have enough glasses to go round. So we drank from his tooth-brush cup and one even from a thimble.

Colleague Christopher Davies has written a book on his sporting life called Behind The Back Page. Christopher covered Ireland for almost 20 years and recalled many anecdotes in the book: Of how Charlton was the same old Jack despite his wealth he wrote: "The miner's son became a multi-millionaire, but he claimed his life had not really changed. He told me: 'You might think my life is different from the way I grew up, but really it's basically the same. I've never been hungry in my life. It's just we live in a better house, have a few spare ones and eat different stuff. When I was a lad you'd buy a loaf of bread, rip it in six and share it with your pals. Now you get them round and eat salmon you caught yourself and drink decent wine. But it's the same thing.'"

Once, when Ireland played Romania, Charlton kept calling them Bulgaria, even to a totally baffled Romanian press.

Charlton is also famous for getting people's names wrong, not just Paul McGrath's. For while Paul McGrath was always John, so was QPR midfielder Gary Waddock. More worryingly, Arsenal's Liam Brady would be Ian.

And when asked by a Swedish journalist which Sweden player could cause Ireland most problems, Charlton said it was "the blonde feller."

Life with the big feller Jack was never dull.

Tony Stenson spent 28 years at the Daily Mirror, covering World Cups, major tennis, golf and snooker tournaments. Now works freelance, mainly for Daily Star Sunday, who allow him to indulge in his love of soccer.

Most memorable match: Liverpool 0, Wimbledon 1: 1988 FA Cup Final, Wembley. Even now I weep at the memory. The REAL Wimbledon of old finished a long, amazing journey from non-league to Cup winners in 12 years. The team I called 'the Crazy Gang' launched several forgotten nights. Sadly, they were to split. Greedy men took money and life was never the same again.

Favourite player: Dave Mackay. The rock hard Scot caught my eye when he rolled his sleeves and pulled his shorts to thigh high on a bitterly cold day. Now this was a man. Defensive mainstay of Spurs in the Sixties and inspiration behind Derby's revival - despite breaking his leg twice.

FAN OF THE DECADE

All things Brighton beautiful
thanks to Paul

By Nick Szczepanik

ON 2 March 2008, a chartered accountant named Paul Samrah stepped onto a stage at the Football League Awards ceremony to collect an award as fan of the year. It should have been fan of the decade.

Samrah has spent over 10 years following his club – and leading his fellow supporters – through a series of trials that few sets of fans have ever had to bear. His is the story of every supporter of Brighton & Hove Albion, only more so.

Brighton played their last game at the Goldstone Ground in April 1997 after their home of 95 years was sold by a previous board of directors. Since then, a club that routinely drew crowds of 20,000 has been effectively homeless, and haemorrhaging money while playing games in quaint but cramped temporary accommodation at Withdean Stadium.

For most of that period, Samrah has been at the forefront of the fight to secure a new stadium at Falmer, on the outskirts of the city, in the teeth of opposition from the neighbouring Lewes District council. Two public inquiries were held, which meant endless writing of letters, planning of demonstrations and organising of petitions, among a number of more colourful stunts.

The fight was won when planning permission was finally granted in 2007 but as the leader of the Falmer For All campaign, Samrah has spent more hours than he cares to remember keeping the club's cause before the decision makers, co-ordinating schemes such as the mass delivery of flowers to John Prescott, then the deputy Prime Minister and final arbiter, on Valentine's Day.

"We were fighting for our survival," he said. "There was a battling instinct, a trench mentality that came to the fore. People contributed their skills and helped in any way they could – printing posters, making pop records, coming up with ideas, whatever.

"The Falmer For All campaign harnessed the best of our abilities. We were always making progress. We never actually hit a brick wall where we thought: 'Now what?' We thought we were doing everything right, we believed in what we were doing and if you are doing all that, it should all work out.

"We had support from the wider football community, and we were lucky that we had the internet, and football phone-ins. We're not sophisticated, but we were streets ahead of our opposition. The longer the campaign went on, the more Nimby-ish they looked."

At every home game, Samrah assumes an additional role as stadium announcer, sharing the PA hut with John Baine, aka Attila the Stockbroker, another of the prime movers in the supporters' campaigns.

"One of the most successful and uplifting aspects of our battle to save the Albion," said Baine. "The way that people from all backgrounds and walks of life, who had nothing in common except our love of our club, joined together in a united front against the bastards who were destroying it – typified by the fact that the co-founders of Brighton Independent Supporters' Association, now PA announcers at the club, are a City accountant and a punk rock poet."

"We are an odd couple, but we work together well," said Samrah. "He has ideas that sound off-the-wall, but actually are bloody good. He suggested forming a political party about six years ago. The time wasn't right to my mind, but our final throw of the dice was the forming of the Seagulls Party in June 2006.

"It fought local council seats in Lewes and ousted four anti-Falmer councillors. And the record he made [We Want Falmer by Seagulls Ska] was fantastic. It went straight into the charts at no 17, getting airplay on Radio 1. It was that eclectic mix of people that made our campaign the unique thing it was – non-aggressive, very serious, but with a lot of humour thrown in as well."

When time allows, Samrah also occupies a seat in what passes for a main stand at Withdean, although "occupies" may not be the word. Utterly absorbed in the game, he kicks and heads every ball, and is usually half out of his seat in anticipation, despair, frustration and occasionally joy – every fan's typical gamut of emotions, in fact.

"There's nothing better than watching a game," he said. "It's a tremendous, cathartic experience. It's brilliant. You do switch off from all the pressures and tensions to watch the football. I've got a season ticket, and if the club tells me next week that they've found a professional stadium announcer, I'll say, 'Fine, okay.' I've been doing the PA for 10 years, which, now I think of it, is bizarre – absolutely ludicrous. But supporting Brighton is a passion, and when you have passion, anything is possible."

Withdean may not be anybody's idea of an intimidating arena, but Brighton have been promoted three times during their stay, and relegated twice. It was a matter of frustration that promotion campaigns at the Goldstone would have drawn full houses approaching 30,000, but fewer than 8,000 were able to cram into Withdean.

"Going to the play-off final and playing at the Millennium Stadium was lucky – we only went through after a goal in the last seconds of the semi-final – and it enabled us to ratchet up the campaign, because we had 30,000 people going to Cardiff. We organised 60 huge banners to display at the match, we gave away postcards to send to John Prescott to everyone buying a ticket. Probably 14,000 of 16,000 were sent off. So what happened on the field has helped us off the field."

It also helped that Brighton regularly hosts the big three party conferences, and thousands of fans converged on Labour's events in both 2004 and 2005, including Steve Coppell, one of a number of successful managers who had left the club citing the lack of a stadium as a barrier to their progress.

"I bumped into Tony & Cherie Blair during the 2004 Conference in reception at the Royal Albion Hotel, of all places, spoke to them and gave them our postcards," said Samrah.

"Luck was with us so often. If we had gone out of the league [in the final game of the 1996/97 season] at Hereford, we would have been hard pushed to drag people to take action. We had good weather for all our demonstrations. We were lucky that we were playing away to Hull City, only a few miles from John Prescott's constituency office, on Valentine's Day.

"We were lucky that we had supporters like Des Lynam – you couldn't wish for a better ambassador; Norman Cook [alias Fatboy Slim], who appealed to a different generation, and was prepared to muck in and do his bit – as well as putting money into the club; and we had supporters working for the national press like Paul Hayward [of the Daily Telegraph and later the Daily Mail] and yourself."

Like this writer, Samrah contributed to the Gull's Eye fanzine that was the earliest focus for dissent against the regime that sold the Goldstone. "We refused to accept what we were being told by the club. They said the club was solvent, but they were appearing at the High Court [to fight winding-up orders]. As an accountant, I was able to see that the accounts told a completely different story from the one we were being told. That's where it all started."

Is he looking forward to being an ordinary fan again? "I don't think we will ever get back to being 'ordinary' football fans, because we aren't, really. We're more united than we have ever been, we know the problems that clubs face better than we have ever done, and we trust the board, who are fans and know what we have been through. We are consulted in a way we would never have been before."

Samrah recently fronted the club's unveiling of its revised plans for the stadium for which he fought so long and hard. But, sharing the stage with the chairman and chief executive, is there a danger that he is now part of the establishment of the club? Has he crossed the line between 'us' and 'them'?

"There is no line between 'us' and 'them' now. We are all singing from the same hymn sheet. There is a mutual respect. And we know that without them, there would be no club."

Ten years in the future, where will he be?

"This week we were looking back 25 years to the FA Cup final. I wonder if we'll be looking back 25 years from now as we sit at Falmer saying 'Do you remember the stadium campaign? It was good, wasn't it?' There's nothing better than seeing a lot of smiling faces united behind a plan of action."

And the club, with Brighton the largest city in the south-east outside London, and Crystal Palace, the nearest competition, 40 miles away? "We should model ourselves on Ipswich, a credible Championship-level club with a solid fan base. We have the ambition and the potential to be that, but our biggest challenge, once the stadium is built, is to rebuild that fan base. The previous board didn't just sell our ground, they lost us something like 10,000 fans and two generations of supporters.

"We have to secure the next generation, and that will be difficult. It needs success on the pitch, but also reasonable prices, which is a Catch-22. Whether Falmer For All can metamorphose into some other campaigning 'Let's Get Behind The Club' group and start driving it, we'll see."

Nick Szczepanik has been the Paul Madeley of the Times sports desk for around 10 years – happy to be selected, whether it be reporting Arsenal or Aldershot. He previously contributed to the Guardian, FourFourTwo, Total Football and BBC Radio Five.

***Favourite player:** Brian Horton (Brighton & Hove Albion). Peter Ward grabbed all the headlines as Brighton rose through the divisions in the late 70s, but Horton, an inspirational captain, was the brains and the heart of the team.*

***Most memorable match:** England 1 Poland 1, 1973, World Cup qualifying competition. Talk about divided loyalties but it was a gripping, edge-of-your-seat occasion, and Poland made the most of the luck they enjoyed by putting on a great show in the finals the following summer.*

PAISLEY'S SLIPPERS THE DEFINING IMAGE OF LIVERPOOL'S SUCCESS

No footballer exerted more influence over the other 21 players than Souness

By Clive Tyldesley

I T IS THE image that best captures the spirit of Liverpool's greatest years. Not the swaying, swaggering Koppites. Not the 'This Is Anfield' sign above the players' entrance. Not the European Cup in the hands of Emlyn Hughes or Graeme Souness. Not Bill Shankly, not Ian Rush, not Steven Gerrard. No, the defining image of the Liverpool trophy-winning era is that of Bob Paisley attending a European Cup-winning banquet in his carpet slippers.

Paisley did not allow a drop of alcohol to pass his lips that night at the Holiday Inn, Swiss Cottage in May 1978. When asked "why?" he said it was because he wanted to remember every single moment. He was probably the only party-goer that remembered *any* of it. While his players and their guests danced the night and their recollections away, the mastermind of the triumph sat quietly in his cardigan and slippers and committed it all to memory.

Open up the memory vault of a 50-year old Liverpool fan and you will find many of the greatest events in modern-day English club football, and two of the most tragic. It is not only the country's most successful club, but also the most vocal and theatrical. And yet behind the deafening din of the choral, comical Kop with its poetic pronouncements and embroidered flags were some of the quietest, most unassuming heroes that football has ever produced. It is a model that will never be *re*produced.

Paisley was Shankly's sponge man – a down-to-earth, wizened Geordie who went about his business in the shadow of the evangelical orator that shaped the outgoing, outspoken personality of Liverpool FC. Paisley was as bad at communication as Shankly was good. But when the unlikeliest handover of power occurred in 1974, Paisley's vision for the next stage of Liverpool's progression was conveyed not in vivid, inspiring words, but in vivid, inspiring football. The players got the message.

When the busy, bustling, running, jumping Kevin Keegan moved on, he was replaced by the clever, cunning, passing, prompting Kenny Dalglish. For a decade or more, the team never had to go through 'a transition period' because the changes were foreseen and controlled.

Evolution at Anfield was achieved almost without anyone noticing. The basic methods and homely routines never altered and yet brutal decisions were being taken on an annual basis – taken by the brains trust of Paisley, Joe Fagan, Ronnie Moran, Tom Saunders and Roy Evans over a pot of tea in a cramped boot room with saucy calendars on the wall.

When the best players in Europe finished their daily preparations at the club's Mellwood training ground, they all piled into two spluttering old motor coaches to be ferried the three miles back to Anfield to shower and change. When they finished an away game, they climbed aboard an ever so slightly more modern team bus that made for the nearest fish and chip shop so that these wealthy young athletes could eat their Saturday night dinner out of the same newspapers that heralded their achievements. It was a form of sports psychology.

Everything was done to keep their feet nailed to the floor. I once travelled with the official Liverpool party to a European Cup first round match near the Arctic Circle in Finland. Oulun Palloseura, a team of part-timers, were subsequently beaten 10-1 at Anfield. But on the eve of the away leg, I visited their stadium to find a track and field meeting in full swing on the pitch. Shots and javelins were being thrown onto the sodden playing surface, and when I returned to the team hotel I happened to tell Ray Clemence and Phil Neal.

As soon as the players retired to their rooms, the wily old coach Ronnie Moran came over and promptly tore several strips off me.

"Don't tell the players it's a bad pitch. Don't give them any excuses," he yelled at me. Even against the humblest of opposition, Liverpool's own simple humility remained a founding principle. New signings at Anfield were constantly amazed at how little specific instruction they were given. They were encouraged to find their own place within the culture of the club and the dressing-room. Their personalities had to develop with their talents.

It was an era when the 'senior pros' still exerted as much influence as the manager or his staff. It is no accident that so many Liverpool players of that era have found careers in management or broadcasting.

Their personal characters were vetted as closely as their playing abilities before that most revered of football administrators, Peter Robinson, moved stealthily to complete a transfer deal. Just as negotiations with Dalglish were being finalised, he took the local journalists into his confidence but asked them to first float a story about Peter Sayer of Cardiff by way of a smokescreen. Liverpool were always one step ahead of their time.

The first European Cup in 1977 was won without Dalglish, Souness or Alan Hansen, but the three Scots emerged as the dominant figures in the era of unparalleled accomplishments that followed. Dalglish transcends all other modern Kop heroes because of his success both as a player and manager. Indeed, he clinched the club's first League and FA Cup double as player-manager. When Liverpool was plunged into a very real crisis by the Hillsborough tragedy, Dalglish somehow knew exactly what to do and say on behalf of everyone involved. The Glaswegian possessed that stubborn, single-minded, passionate conviction that is the epitome of Merseyside.

Souness had all that too, but almost to a fault. He was ruthlessly demanding of himself and all around him. Craig Johnston once said that playing next to him was like having your big brother alongside you. Whenever anything needed 'sorting out' Souness would do it without needing to be asked. I can't recall seeing a footballer exert so much influence over the other 21 players on the field. His exacting standards were perhaps his undoing as a manager. He couldn't understand or tolerate anyone lacking his ravenous appetite for success.

Hansen could occasionally appear casual and slack compared to the bravehearts among his predecessors like Ron Yeats, Tommy Smith and Phil Thompson. But he emerged as a prototype for a new breed of defender who could contribute as richly with the ball as without it. Quite apart from his elegance and style, Hansen was the keeper of the dressing-room sense of humour – invariably the architect of each stunt and prank. His piece de resistance was an address to all his team-mates during which he introduced himself as their next manager, complete with a new hard-line code of conduct. Everyone fell for it.

The scouting, recruitment and deployment of these and many other extraordinary players was the 'magic' of Liverpool's period of dominance. Not every signing was a success story as Frank McGarvey, Wayne Harrison and others can testify, but the club's eye for a player and its magnetic attraction helped maintain a consistent level of performance that only human tragedy finally interrupted. The Heysel Stadium disaster in 1985 cost Liverpool their annual involvement in European football, and some of their pulling power. Their recovery was then hit by Hillsborough, with all of its many repercussions.

The Liverpool Ex-Players Association is one of the most vibrant and active of its kind in English football. Every game at Anfield is attended by a host of former stars. There is a strong sense of communion between the men that have shared in the club's successes. Many of them were achieved before the English game became truly cosmopolitan and old teams were scattered far and wide by retirement. Ironically, the 1986 Liverpool side that completed the double in the FA Cup final at Wembley did not include a single Englishmen, but most of them still live on Merseyside. Their children have scouse accents, at least.

It was Shankly who identified and fostered the link between the team and the community. He empowered the fans by calling them his "12th man" and making them feel important. Robinson never liked the idea of private boxes at Anfield for fear of alienating the ordinary fan.

The recital of 'You'll Never Walk Alone' on a big European night remains one of the great staged productions of English sport. But just as the individual members of the Kop choir left their dreams behind on the Anfield terraces at the end of the game, the powers behind the Liverpool successes of the Seventies and Eighties somehow gave the impression they were doing much the same.

I was a bit taken aback when I got that rollicking from Ronnie Moran in Finland until I spoke to Ray Clemence the next day. "Don't worry," he said. "Every year we win the Championship we return to the dressing-room and Ronnie says 'this won't count for anything *next* season, you know.'"

Ronnie probably wasn't happy until he got home and put his carpet slippers on.

Clive Tyldesley worked for the Merseyside local radio station, Radio City, between 1977 and 1989. He is now ITV's senior football commentator and a regular contributor to the Daily Telegraph.

__Favourite player:__ George Best – simply my boyhood hero and the best dribbler, passer, header and tackler in my boyhood team. Everything I have subsequently seen of him on film has only confirmed in my head what I knew in my heart back then.

__Most memorable match:__ The 2005 Champions League final – both professionally and personally, it simply left me exhausted. To try to describe and account for the events of that night in Istanbul, to an audience of many millions, was a near impossibility. Which is just what my job SHOULD be.

THE KIDS AREN'T ALRIGHT

Academy system not doing enough to help next generation

By Sam Wallace

IT IS EVERY football fan's secret dream. Your son shows an interest in football from the day he first gets a ball at his toes. He's in the garden dribbling around the rotary drier every time you open the back door. What's more, he seems to have some talent. When he plays with his mates he stands out. A few of the parents at the school gate mention it too. They say you might have a potential professional on your hands.

So where do you go from here? The development of young footballers in this country is one of the biggest issues in modern football; for some of us it is the most important issue. Just 38 per cent of the players who started games in the Premier League in the 2006/07 season were English. The England team catastrophically failed to qualify for Euro 2008, the first major international tournament they have missed in 14 years. The English footballer is becoming like some endangered species – overtaken and killed off by its fitter, stronger, more accomplished rivals. There are few issues more important than how English football develops its next generation of players.

If your son is a good player, the chances are he will be identified and spotted quickly. There are 50 million people in England. Our electoral register is in disarray; local authorities scarcely know how many people they serve, but strangely when it comes to football it is easier to dodge your television license than keep a good young player a secret. If your boy plays football in the remotest part of Devon or Cumbria or the Isle of Sheppey and looks like a prospect then the scouts will come knocking. Football is like that. There is a huge market for young talent and word gets around. Every club has a network dedicated to finding the next Wayne Rooney or Steven Gerrard.

What age do clubs start looking at players? As young as possible. English clubs sign boys at the age of eight so they have to make decisions based upon children who are nowhere near a mature development age. The big clubs pour resources into finding them and they do not like to cut out a player they think has a chance. And with good reason – no-one wants to be the man in popular mythology who rejected a schoolboy Alan Shearer. Or the scout who told Michael Owen he was too small to play the game. Most English boys are in a Sunday team by the age of eight, and the scouts are watching.

It seems like an extraordinary age to make a decision about a player's potential but it is set down in the rules and the clubs have little choice in the matter. In 1998, most of the Premier League clubs – and some who are now in the Championship and beyond – agreed upon the academy programme to develop youth players. It was the Howard Wilkinson blueprint to revolutionise player development and govern the way in which clubs bought and sold these youngsters. The academy generation is now just starting to come of age in the first teams of major clubs.

If your son is good enough, aged eight, to earn a place at one of the 41 clubs in English football with an academy then that institution will define his football career. Under the academy rules, clubs take on boys at the age of eight, with the same cut-off as the traditional school year that starts in September. Academy rules dictate those boys must live within an hour of their club's academy; aged 14 or more they can live within 90 minutes of the club's academy. If parents want to move house and move their child from one club's academy to another then they must prove to administrators that the move has been undertaken for "non-football reasons."

And that is the first, and perhaps biggest change, imposed by the academy system. The academy rules reduced, at a stroke, the pool within which the big clubs were fishing. A modern-day Sir Bobby Charlton or David Beckham would be unable to sign for Manchester United's academy because both grew up a good three to four hours drive from Old Trafford. Instead Sir Alex Ferguson and his academy staff have to battle it out in the north-west with Liverpool, Everton, Manchester City, Blackburn Rovers and Bolton, to name but a few, for the best players in a relatively small area. If you live in Newcastle or Cornwall or London and your child is good enough to spend his school holidays training with United's youth coaches, as Beckham once did, then bad luck. He is not allowed.

The rule was brought in for a good reason, to give smaller clubs the chance to develop local talent. It was also intended to encourage them to improve their coaching facilities and give them the benefit of selling these players at a profit – think Scott Parker and Charlton – when they developed as professionals. It is a laudable aim and the academy system has undoubtedly improved the standard of facilities and coaching – all coaches must have a UEFA Level 3 license as a minimum. But there are serious questions being asked about whether it is the right approach to developing the elite footballers who might one day win England a World Cup.

In France the system is very different. Clairefontaine is the famous academy about 20 miles outside Paris where players like Thierry Henry and William Gallas were developed; it is run by France's equivalent of our FA and is one of a string of academies across the country which take the best boys in every region. Every centre is a hothouse for the best local talent. Regardless of what club they are affiliated to, the best in France go to their regional centre and train. They play with their clubs less frequently.

What works better? At Manchester United and Liverpool and Chelsea there are plenty of good young players who will help the very best in every generation to develop. But imagine if you put all the best players together – as they do in France. The exponential improvement of every player would be far greater playing with their most talented peers. Unfortunately for English football, the best young players of each generation are left in their club academies, often playing and training with players who do not challenge them sufficiently.

Would English clubs really agree to release their best young footballers to train at regional centres? I put the question to Brian McClair, the former Manchester United striker who now runs the club's academy.

"If you had all the best players in the north-west at one academy you do not have, for example, Liverpool's best player training with the next best 12 players they can find," he said. "It's going to be the 16 best boys training together and playing against the other nine academies. It would be an elite thing. It's the right system if you want to improve English players."

And there are other problems with the academies. Because of the competition to sign young footballers, any player who shows real promise aged eight tends to get taken on. If not by a top Premier League club's academy in their locality then possibly by another of the 41 academies or those clubs lower down the divisions who have centres of excellence – a lower status academy. Once those players have joined another academy – and the trend is that parents prefer their boys to be in another academy if they are rejected by their first choice – then they are out of reach of even the very biggest clubs.

If a player tries to leave one academy for another then the destination club will have to pay compensation set by tribunal – which tends to be so high that even the wealthiest clubs are put off. These are not fees for the faint-hearted – Chelsea paid between £600,000 and £1m for Sheffield United's teenager Jacob Mellis.

As a result, the best young boys stay at the academies they join at the age of eight. If, for example, Arsenal reject a boy at that age, the chances are that they will not be able to revise their opinion in two years' time because he will be at another academy and off limits. There are huge decisions being made on players at a very raw age and they have a potentially long-term effect on English football.

When the boys reach 16, they either leave the club or are offered a 'scholarship' for two years, the latest incarnation of what was previously a "YTS place" and before that an old-fashioned apprenticeship. At 16, any boy in the European Community is free to move. However, there are still punitive transfer fees to be paid on boys who move within England. Those who come from European clubs to English academies have their fees set by FIFA – which tend to be cheaper. The result? English academies are filling their scholarship programme with boys from abroad.

Cesc Fabregas at Arsenal and Gerard Pique who was at Manchester United are two such examples. The French teenager Gael Kakuta is one of many young foreign players in Chelsea's academy. It means that the best young players in Europe are coming to England which is not necessarily the best news for young English footballers. Even those who have trained and improved with their clubs from eight and earned a scholarship are finding their way blocked in their late teens by imports poached from the youth teams of clubs like Barcelona and Parma.

Elite-level football has always been the preserve of the few. There is only one Cristiano Ronaldo in every generation. There are many talented young footballers who never make it at a professional level because of injury or plain bad luck. But, as never before, young English footballers have to be immensely talented to make it at the biggest Premier League clubs. And they could be entitled to ask whether the Premier League academy system that has provided them with such wonderful facilities is giving them an equally wonderful chance of making the grade.

Sam Wallace has been the Independent's chief football writer since 2004. Before then he was the north-west football reporter for the Daily Telegraph.

Favourite player: Bryan Robson was the prototype for the modern midfielder. He is remembered too often for his injuries, rather than the times he carried Manchester United and England on his own.

Most memorable match: The 1985 FA Cup final: Manchester United 1, Everton 0. A great game in a raw, brutal decade for English football. Triumph in adversity for the underdogs – the vital ingredient for any classic.

A LOST CAUSE THE ULTIMATE CHALLENGE TO GLADIATOR GERRARD

The Liverpool captain unleashes Hell

By Henry Winter

O F THE many "good luck" texts Steven Gerrard received on the eve of Liverpool's 2005 Champions League final against AC Milan one message stood out, highlighting the respect he stirs amongst his playing peers. It was from John Terry, captain of the Chelsea side overcome by Gerrard to reach Istanbul.

Terry could have been jealous, could have refused to acknowledge the fact that the final was even taking place. Certain of his bitter Chelsea team-mates behaved that petty way. Terry fought valiantly against Liverpool but the Blues had fallen to a controversial Luis Garcia goal. Yet no frustration polluted Terry's view of Gerrard walking out in Istanbul. He just told the Liverpool captain to go and bring the trophy back to England.

Even afterwards, as Terry watched Gerrard collect the European Cup amidst a snowstorm of red glitter, the Chelsea man reached for his mobile and despatched another text to the banks of the Bosphorus. "I'm buzzing for you," wrote Terry.

Fast forward two years, and a similar "good luck" text leapt out of Thierry Henry's phone to Gerrard, as Liverpool encountered Milan again in the 2007 European Cup final. The high regard Gerrard is held by fellow-professionals was also reflected in his being voted the Professional Footballers' Association Players' Player of the Year.

Gerrard's popularity in the nation's dressing-rooms is not difficult to understand. Every player would love to have such a driving force alongside them, raiding forward to score the type of match-rescuing goals that Gerrard seems to specialise in. Supporters of Olympiacos and West Ham, amongst others, have their sleep stalked by the image of Gerrard unleashing from range, the ball flying into the roof of the net.

Admiration for Gerrard arose particularly because of extraordinary events in Istanbul. For those of us present, it seemed a straightforward tale to relate at half-time. The laptop filled with paragraph upon paragraph about Milan's supremacy, about how Liverpool were embarrassed time and again by Kaka, Hernan Crespo and Andrei Shevchenko.

The Italians led 3-0 at the break, and the presses were ready to roll on English heartache. Some Liverpool fans wandered into the press box – Liverpool fans seems to possess Access All Area tickets at major events – to lament the first 45 minutes. Others even left the ground and headed back to the bar area of Taksim Square.

The widely held view was that Liverpool were out. No one scores three times in 45 minutes against a well-drilled Italian defence who would rather sell their grandmother than concede a goal. One man continued to believe. Gerrard was angered by what he perceived to be gloating by Milan's pug-dog midfielder, Gennaro Gattuso. The Smirk, Gerrard called him.

So Liverpool's captain stormed into the dressing-room and launched into a tirade about how Milan thought they had won. He was quick to emerge from the tunnel for the second half, determined to show Milan Liverpool still meant business.

So unfolded a six-minute period that shook the world, stretching credibility as well as the stitching in the Milan net. Gerrard scored the first, with a leaping header, before Vladimir Smicer and Xabi Alonso made it 3-3. Gerrard was everywhere, driving Liverpool on, organising the rearguard resistance movement when Milan sought to hit back.

In extra time, with cramp filling his legs, Gerrard went to right-back to deal with Serginho, the pacey Milan sub who threatened to run riot. After the triumphant penalty shoot-out, Gerrard was so drained he almost fainted while being interviewed. No wonder. He had just delivered one of the great individual European Cup final displays.

Running on emotion, Gerrard kept embracing the European Cup, later receiving the wry admonishment from his partner Alex that "you gave the Cup more kisses than you gave me". Gerrard even took the trophy back to his room, propping it up at the end of the bed. Less romantically, Gerrard promptly fell fast asleep.

Gerrard's ability to transform games, cutting opponents to pieces, has made him the hero of the Kop, where they have a banner of him as Russell Crowe's Gladiator saying "at my command, unleash Hell". Even when all seems lost, such as when Liverpool trailed to West Ham in the 2006 FA Cup final in Cardiff, Gerrard dug deep to find an answer, in this case a 30-yarder that arrowed into the net.

Nature and street-football nurture explain his determination. He grew up having kickabouts on glass-strewn Merseyside streets, dreaming of performing on the big stage. He played against his brother's mates, older than him, and unwilling to make allowances for a smaller player. Those impromptu games toughened Gerrard up. So when all seems lost, the fighter in Gerrard from his schoolboy days comes to the fore, and he unleashes Hell.

Others have performed similar marvels yet not earned the respect granted Gerrard. Where individuals like Terry and Henry think particularly highly of Gerrard is that he has no airs or graces off the field. A touch of humility characterises him. No Bling. No flash cars. No designer clothes.

His home has changed, from a terraced council house in Huyton, to a beautiful abode in a far leafier area, but Gerrard has remained true to his roots. He resisted moves to Chelsea in 2004 and 2005 because the city of Liverpool is so much part of him. He is a child of the Kop, although Everton fans delighted in the day when they found pictures of Liverpool's captain wearing an Everton kit as a kid (an uncle had bought it for him).

Where some footballers stand still, not developing their game, Gerrard continues to work on aspects of his formidable trade. His left foot has improved markedly, and he has gained a greater intelligence on how to channel his prodigious energy for the good of the team.

Rather than haring everywhere, as earlier in his career, Gerrard acquires a greater tactical discipline, although Rafa Benitez clearly harbours some reservations. Deploying Gerrard behind Fernando Torres has proved a master-stroke by Liverpool's manager, allowing Gerrard to bomb on, secure in the knowledge that he has defensive midfield cover behind him in Javier Mascherano and Alonso. The arrival of Robbie Keane will also help Gerrard.

Sometimes in the past, when collecting the ball off his back-four, Gerrard would attempt a Hollywood pass, a 50-yarder to a forward and it could get picked off. By pushing his No 8 further upfield, Benitez ensured there was less gambling in possession and when Gerrard did attempt a risky pass, it was in the opposing danger zone.

Flaws can still be detected in his game. Fortunately, Gerrard has cut out the reckless tackles that put opponents on the deck and him in the stands, suspended and remorse-filled. A decent five-a-side unit could be formed out of the players Gerrard clattered early in his career.

George Boateng, Patrick Vieira and Graeme Le Saux were all crunched by Gerrard. The Merseyside derby often set his fuse burning, and he flew into Kevin Campbell and Gary Naysmith. Fate taught him a lesson after both incidents against Everton.

Needing a pee at a city-centre night-club, Gerrard dashed to the urinals to discover the person standing next to him was Campbell. He apologised for the challenge, and escaped quickly. After the Naysmith foul, which sliced open part of the defender's leg, Gerrard boarded a plane to Faro and as he settled in his seat, he realised he knew the passenger sitting next to him. It was Naysmith, accompanied by his wife. They never mentioned the tackle, although Gerrard detected a certain frostiness from Mrs Naysmith.

If the bad tackles have been erased from the debit column of the Gerrard ledger, they have been replaced by an occasional tendency to fling himself down to win penalties. He dived early on in his career at Villa Park, and the Holte End has neither forgotten nor forgiven. Gerrard also threw himself to the ground when the Hungarian full-back, Csaba Feher, came hurtling in during an international friendly at Old Trafford.

Gerrard calls it diving for cover, fearing another broken metatarsal. Ever since the list of English broken-foot patients and being forced to miss the 2002 World Cup, Gerrard has been mindful of the risk of damaging his metatarsal again. He has dived more recently, the one stain on his reputation.

Otherwise, there is no English footballer who garners more respect. Ask John Terry. Ask Thierry Henry.

Henry Winter is football correspondent, Daily Telegraph.

Favourite player: *Marco van Basten. Grace, touch, vision, all-round class on and off the field.*

Most memorable match: *Liverpool 3 AC Milan 3, Champions League final 2005. A magnificent example of never giving up.*

"CUE BRIAN" AND LET THE ROWS BEGIN

Keegan tried to get Hold The Back Page taken off air

By Brian Woolnough

IT BEGAN with a row and we have been arguing ever since. It's what we do. In bars, hotels, restaurants or on television … always about football.

Journalists are no different to you fans. We love the game and get passionate about it. I think I'm right and the next man thinks he is.

It was a row, no let's call it a fierce exchange of views, between Steve Curry, then of the Daily Express, and me, that began The Sunday Supplement, or Hold The Back Page as it was known then.

We were in Shepherd's Restaurant, London and a fascinated onlooker was Vic Wakeling, Sky Television's Head of Sport. It was Sky's annual pre-season lunch for daily football correspondents and Steve and I were in full flow.

Vic thought if he could transfer the row to a television studio it would make a good programme and the rest, as they say, is history.

It has been a programme that has become a cult in football with managers, players, officials and, of course, supporters. It has been my privilege to be the regular presenter, apart from the first programme back in August 1994.

We began the adventure on the first Saturday evening of the 1994/95 season, the day German legend Jurgen Klinsmann made his debut for Spurs and marked a goal with his infamous dive celebration.

The panel that night was Neil Harman, then football correspondent of the Daily Mail, the late Chris Lander, cricket correspondent of the Daily Mirror (in those early days we introduced other sports and, luckily Devon Malcolm had taken nine wickets against South Africa at the Oval) myself and the presenter was freelance journalist Pat Butcher. The first show was an hour and a half.

On the Monday morning producer Andy Hornett rang to ask if I was prepared to have a go at presenting as they wanted to experiment. Saturday brought nerves, a new adrenalin, wearing an earpiece and the first time I experienced the instruction of "cue Brian".

It is a strange experience. You are surrounded by people and yet completely alone. You have the producer and director talking in your ear, yet realise that it's you in control if something goes wrong. An airline pilot once told me flying a plane is easy until a problem occurs. That is like presenting a show on television. Make a mistake and you can't claw the moment back. I have always liked an open feed back in my ear, where you can hear every instruction from director and producer to cameramen and control room staff.

Once, re-introducing the guests at the top of part three, I knew I had completely forgotten the name of the third gust as I went around the table. The fact it was Paul Hayward, one of the top writers in the country, then of the Daily Telegraph and now of the Daily Mail, didn't help. I had blanked. What I should have said was say: "My next guest needs no introduction" and moved on. I didn't, somehow bluffed it, and it was a moment I was happy to forget. Certainly a lesson learned.

In the early years Sky introduced a Hold the Back Page Writer of the Year trophy, voted for by everyone that appeared on the show throughout the season. Hayward won it every year apart from one and it was a fitting tribute from his colleagues.

A feature of the Saturday night show was the first editions of the Sunday newspapers hurried into the studio at the top of part four. Hugh McIlvanney, the Sunday Times legend was a regular guest and once was so intent on reading his column in the ST he didn't look up from the paper throughout the last part. What do you think Hugh … . silence … ok then!

Those moments are what the programme is about. It's live, raw and honest. Journalists are not afraid to speak their minds, they tell it how it is.

Christmas Specials were introduced and once the panel were taken out to lunch before a pre-record. Curry, Nigel Clarke, then of the Daily Mirror and now the Daily Express, the late Joe Melling and I were entertained by the producer. Halfway through the show Clarke fell asleep and was only woken by Curry raising his voice over a controversial subject. "Steve would say that, wouldn't he?" said Nigel without having a clue what he was talking about. Brilliant.

But it became a programme that began to annoy certain managers. What were journalists doing passing comment about the game? That became their grievance. Kenny Dalglish listened to every word, so too George Graham. He told the story of how once when as Leeds manager he was slumped asleep in his armchair and had a nightmare involving Clarke and Rob Shepherd, then of Today. He woke to see the journalists shouting on his TV screen. "Thought I was going mad," said George.

It has been a programme that has given sports journalists a platform they never had before. It has snowballed into far more comment and forthright views in today's newspapers.

After a couple of years Sky switched Hold The Back Page to Friday nights and it took on a different meaning. Instead of reacting to Saturday matches we started to preview the weekend and look back over the footballing week. More predictions were made and more controversy caused.

This climaxed on Friday in October 2000, the night before England's last game at old Wembley, the World Cup qualifying defeat to Germany. We broke the team that night, with Gareth Southgate playing in midfield, and I asked Henry Winter, football correspondent of the Daily Telegraph, what would happen to manager Kevin Keegan if England lost?

"Simple," said Henry. "Keegan would have to go."

The watching England manager was so incensed by the remark and the debate he stormed over to David Davies, then the FA's executive director and demanded he rang Sky and order them to take the programme off air. Davies was shocked (why wasn't he concentrating on beating Germany instead of worrying about Hold the Back Page?). "It's only a television programme," he told Keegan.

But it isn't, of course. Not to me or the regular guests who have made this such a success. It has become the show the game listens to.

Another change came a year later, in the summer of 2001, when Wakeling rang and asked what I felt about the show being switched to Sunday morning? We are changing the format, too, he said with Jimmy Hill as your fellow presenter. The title also changed, from Hold The Back Page to The Sunday Supplement. My first reaction was Sunday mornings would be difficult for daily correspondents and, of course, how Jimmy would fit into a round table debate with journalists? Once again Vic had struck upon a winning idea.

Jimmy and I met a few times before the first Sunday morning show to discuss ideas. He is a legend of the game having been player, manager, chairman, owner, introduced three points for a win, all-seat stadiums and the man who helped smash the minimum wage. The game owes him a lot and he has always been grateful to Sky and Wakeling for giving him a platform so late in his career. Jimmy's enthusiasm was incredible, even if he did almost come to blows with his regular line of "Can we really believe that story?"

Yes Jim, the bloke on your left wrote it.

When he felt strongly about something he didn't let go. Turning former players into referees was his biggest campaign (the only thing I have failed to introduce in my career, he said), England's lack of a big number nine, how he wouldn't mind marking David Beckham and not enough English players in the Premier League. These were stated on a weekly basis and we loved him for them.

The setting was his kitchen and after a few early teething problems it settled down. At first it was Jimmy's responsibilities to go to each break with a small comment but after he told the watching public we would be back in a minute while he went to baste his meat, it was taken from him.

Jimmy's commitment was confirmed by one extraordinary story. One Sunday he hadn't arrived and producer, Mike Curry, took a phone call from his wife, Bryony, who said Jimmy was held in a huge traffic jam on the M25. When it got to nine o'clock, one hour before the show started, Bryony rang again to say Jimmy had a plan.

He was going to leave his car on the hard shoulder of the motorway and run to the next junction where Sky could send a car for him. How far is the next junction, Curry asked Bryony? About three miles, she said. The show went out without him and it was the only one he missed. The image of him sprinting along the hard shoulder is still with me.

Now Jimmy has retired The Supplement is back to its original format, with three top journalists and myself around the kitchen table arguing, predicting and hopefully making sense. Yes, the croissants are eaten and orange juice consumed.

The guests are rotated with one or two new faces introduced each season. We use around 25. They all get on, well almost, but finger pointing and disagreement makes good television. Every Supplement apart from the odd "special" is live.

So, after 14 years we were still going strong at the end of 2007/08. As I said before, it has been a privilege to present Hold The Back Page and The Sunday Supplement and has been a huge, enjoyable part of my career in journalism. Every Sunday I still get the buzz and adrenalin rush when director Ian Brush says "cue Brian".

I'm sure Vic Wakeling would not have thought his idea would still be running after so long. He would have known, of course, that we would still be rowing.

Brian Woolnough was with the Sun for 27 years as football correspondent and associate sports editor, before joining the Daily Star as chief sports writer in 2001. He has presented Sky TV's Hold The Back Page and Sunday Supplement since 1994.

Favourite player: George Best. A player who changed the image of football, on and off the pitch, and whose skills in an era of no protection from referees and terrible pitches, was simply magnificent. There are not enough videos of Best to do him justice. Worth £50 million and £150,000 a week in today's market.

Most memorable match: How do you choose, there have been hundreds? It would be easy to say the 1966 World Cup Final, which I watched with my father, or the 1999 Champions League Cup Final when United completed the Treble, but for me the game that had everything was England against Argentina at the 1998 World Cup Finals. Michael Owen's stunning goal, David Beckham sent off, Sol Campbell's disallowed goal, England so unlucky and then the penalty shoot out. Hope, happiness, drama and heartbreak.

LET US ENTERTAIN YOU

Newcastle may let the fans down but they will have a day to remember

By Colin Young

WHEN KEVIN KEEGAN talks, the people of Newcastle listen. And when, amid the delirium of the 2008 derby win over Sunderland, he claimed that St James' Park is unlike any stadium in the world, not surprisingly no-one contradicted him.

"You can travel twice round the globe," he said from his seat on the stage which hosts the manager's press conferences deep in the bowels of the main stand. "You won't find an atmosphere like that. I have played in many great stadiums, the Maracana, the Nep, Boca Juniors, Liverpool and it's nothing like that."

It was only when he'd finished his chilled glass of water and departed that those of us present who have experienced European nights at Anfield, Old Trafford, San Siro, Nou Camp started to questioned his judgement. We all recognise exaggeration when we hear it. And of course it wouldn't be the first or last time the former England manager got a little carried away.

But he had a point about St James' that day. The ground was throbbing with noise from the moment the Geordies finally took Michael Owen to their hearts as he headed a fourth minute opening goal. He claimed legendary status when his penalty squirmed under Craig Gordon's chest for the second. And that's what it means.

Try telling the 52,000 in the stadium, and the thousands in bars and living rooms across the region, and beyond, that North East bragging rights mean nothing. Yes, the winners were guaranteed safety, but more importantly, pride was at stake. That, and the right of their supporters to be the first to send abusive text messages. It's the law, after all.

The much-maligned former chairman Freddy Shepherd may have made mistakes along the way, and earned a tidy buck, but he put his wallet where his mouth was and backed all his managers, even if their appointments and the timings of their departures were questionable.

Kenny Dalglish and Ruud Gullit took Newcastle to the FA Cup Final, both failed miserably on the big day as the Toon Army invaded Wembley with its unique panache. Their team may let them down time after time, but they'll have a day to remember all the same. Sir Bobby Robson came closest to matching the dizzy days of the Keegan era. The wily old County Durham lad took the club on memorable Champions League adventures. He taught Alan Shearer how to score again, built a team with pace around The Number Nine, but both men failed to deliver the one thing they, the club and its desperate supporters crave.

It doesn't help Newcastle managers and players that in the 40 years since Bobby Moncur lifted the Fairs Cup, Sunderland, and to a lesser extent Middlesbrough, have enjoyed and deserved their open top bus tours. Newcastle once took to the streets to 'celebrate' losing the Cup final. What does that tell you?

Every August brings renewed optimism that the current captain will be the one to replace the black and white images of Moncur clutching the beast that is the UEFA Cup to his shoulder back in 1969.

But even when reality kicks in – after two minutes, two games or two months – they will always expect to win at home and win well. In the mid-Nineties Keegan created The Entertainers, but they played with full-blooded commitment too. And no-one lets his successors, and their players, forget it.

The new Keegan revolution is in its infancy and he inherited players from Sam Allardyce who are bruised by years of under-achievement since Keegan quit in 1997. And they have not been alone. Every one of Newcastle's most recent managers has acknowledged the inability of even the most gifted footballers to cope with the expectation that comes with inflating your bank account by playing football on Tyneside.

The eventual spring rejuvenation, topped by that derby demolition had Keegan's players talking about Europe and trophies again. That's more like it. It is that ever-lasting optimism which makes Newcastle such an attractive soap opera. They will do it one day surely, and we all want to be there to witness it.

Terry McDerrmott, Keegan's trusted number two from both reigns, turned to him as the cruel mocking of their Mackem visitors overwhelmed the players and benches. "He said it's the like old times, gaffer," Keegan remarked.

Keegan once created unforgettable vibes around his team which everyone plugged into. Geordies were euphoric. Their team was finally competing for the English title and Champions League places, playing football which was the envy of the whole country. Ultimately of course, Keegan and his team blew it. His extraordinary outburst towards the climax of the 1995/96 league title race as

Newcastle let slip a seemingly unassailable lead, directed at Sir Alex Ferguson as he fell victim to his infamous mind games on live television, was blamed, and repeatedly replayed when he was named as new owner Mike Ashley's surprise choice to replace Allardyce in Jan 2008. But Newcastle just lost their nerve and the big matches and Manchester United, who won crucially at St James', were too good not to capitalise.

Allardyce was the sixth man to attempt and fail to erase the ghost of Keegan. Ashley may be new to the business of football, having created Britain's biggest sportswear chain, Sportsworld, to become no. 25 in the Sunday Times's 2007 Rich List, but he knows an astute appointment when he makes one, and Keegan could prove to be a masterstroke. He is probably the only man who could replace himself.

As Keegan talked in his press conference, Roy Keane's forlorn Sunderland players assembled in the reception area, Sir Bobby's impressive and deserved bronze statue regarding their misery, no doubt with a wry smile. To add to the gloom, it would be another hour before their departure. Not a Sunderland fan in the world would say it was the least Keane's £40 million-plus squad deserved for their pitiful surrender on black and white turf.

Keane needs aeons to catch up on Newcastle alone, but he is determined to get there, creating a refreshing mentality which is alien to the club and those who cover it, but long overdue, nonetheless. It helps having a few quid to spend, mind you.

Such extravagance, funded by admirable chairman Niall Quinn's Irish backers, is new to Sunderland supporters. Previous managers Peter Reid and Mick McCarthy grew accustomed to managing in the Premier League on a shoestring and were too hastily relieved of their duties when loyalty was required.

Reid, whose two top seven finishes are now distant but still unappreciated memories, strived throughout his reign to get the funds from former chairman Bob Murray. But while he was quite happy to pay for bargain signings like Kevin Phillips and Niall Quinn, who helped transform the club, Reid wanted and needed bigger names. A month before his departure, having failed to land Robbie Keane, he signed Tore Andre Flo and Marcus Stewart . . .

After the Howard Wilkinson fiasco, Reid, who won eight of Sunderland's 19 points in eight games that season, was eventually replaced by McCarthy, but the former Republic of Ireland manager was unable to halt relegation.

He stopped the slide in emphatic fashion two seasons late, masterminding promotion against the odds, relying on hidden gems from the Football League to gain his first shot at its superior brother. When Murray tightened the purse strings again, McCarthy could only land Kelvin Davis and Jon Stead. Yet he didn't survive beyond March.

Like Reid and McCarthy, even Keane has found luring players to the North East a tricky business. Few of his first summer targets were prepared to contemplate a move to the club. But with him at the helm, attracting publicity beyond anyone's wildest dreams, and having established that all-important second season, that could all change.

After three years writing Dean Windass back pages for the Hull Daily Mail, Colin Young joined the Sun in 1996 to cover the fortunes of north-east football. He moved on a free transfer to the Daily Mail in 2001.

Favourite player: As a Glasgow-born York City junior red who supports Liverpool, it has to be Kenny Dalglish. No player handled a ball, or the media quite like him.

Most memorable match: Standing to the right of the goal at Bootham Crescent when Keith Houchen slotted home the penalty to knock Arsenal out of the fourth round of the FA Cup still takes some beating.